The Eternal Flapper

The Many Lives of Edna Wallace Hopper

James Alessio

The Eternal Flapper: The Many Lives of Edna Wallace Hopper

Published by Page Bloom Publishers: June 2025

Suite 337 7950 NW, 53rd St. Miami, Florida 33166 USA
www.pagebloompublishers.com (800) 419-3014

Printed in the United States of America. This book is printed on acid-free paper.

INTRODUCTION 2023

Now looking back on 2009, I objectively see the whole picture of the many lives of Edna Wallace Hopper. Decades of amazing, tragic, historic, and unique events unfold along with the dark secrets she never expressed to the public. I realize now that Edna Wallace Hopper knew by 1953 of the importance of having her life remain eternal through a book and a musical film. The test of passing time would prove so.

Somehow Edna Wallace Hopper did indeed know this was to happen in the 21st Century.

Through the years of digging and investigating the hidden truths Edna carefully guarded, I began to realize why they were kept under lock and key. These hidden truths were not only her secrets but those of the famous people who surrounded her life, such as her mother Josephine, a divorce who lived out of wedlock with one of the richest men in the world. Josephine lived out fantasies as a ghost writer for a then-famous risqué romance writer. Edna's secret love affair with a theater mogul who may have murdered his diva opera wife in the heat of his love madness for Edna. There is a secret letter from 1886 that refers to a dark secret held in the Royal House of Windsor. The truth about Edna's wealthy stepfather, Alexander Dunsmuir's, infidelity and addictions reveals one of the deepest dark secrets, which became part of the famous trial Hopper VS Dunsmuir. My investigation leads to an even deeper secret regarding her encounter with Dunsmuir.

Included in this book is how Edna's obsession with remaining youthful and beautiful changed her life, and her marketing genius for her own products. Reinventing her image for Broadway, as well as her key trader expertise on Wall Street, made her a first achiever for women. Taking women into achievements such as sports, men's suits, pants, short hair, and careers that only a man could do before her, and risking new "technology" such as plastic surgery, makeup, and yoga. This makes Edna Wallace Hopper one of the most successful and diverse women of the 20th Century.

Her secret world of spiritual projection, esoterica, numerology, astrology, the Skull & Bones Society, the Illuminati, ancient scriptures and life beyond our dimension, as well as mysticism and eastern religion, I believe, somehow projected into my psyche and consciousness. This was at a time when I was performing deep meditation in Hatha Yoga after reading a book published in the 1930s by a Yogi.

My dreams, which led to reality upon finding the painting she posed for in 1907, done by artist/ photographer Burr McIntosh, which had survived a fire. Years later, I met a man who, in 1953, had met Edna at a dinner party. Edna asked him to be the Messenger and, with confidence, asked him to give me a message in January 1989 to do this book and to start a musical film project on her life and her secrets to be revealed. Without a doubt, Miss Hopper did, in fact, know of a way to foresee, if not lead the way for events to happen to fulfill her desires of Eternal life here with us. Too many coincidences for it to be otherwise.

My passion for seeking the truth had opened risky paths of intrigue, mystery, and danger with the MI5, the Royal House of Windsor, with a secret informant, and the Illuminati. A Skull & Bones Society member threatened me for exposing guarded information, along with my suspicions of who was behind the 9/11 events. The events mentioned in this book are those that occurred in the 120 Broadway building, which housed the Federal Reserve, Enron, and Skull & Bones members. The intrigue and the world of espionage pumped heavily in my blood. I wanted you, the reader, to experience the same excitement as I had. You are about to follow the decades of her many lives, along with the mysterious journey of finding the secrets, with an occasional opening of Pandora's Box along the way.

This journey takes you through her dark secrets, her music, her comedy, and tragedy, both on and off stage. Exposed are the addictions of those famous people who surrounded her life with their lives entwined into hers. The birth of the silent film era, Broadway, and Vaudeville will be part of this journey. Edna's interest in the Wall Street trading chapter includes how Edna convinced Edison to hook up the first light bulbs of Wall Street over to Broadway to replace the gas lamps and dirt roads that existed in her early years.

Infidelity, rape, and murder, sex, an obsessed stalker named Mad Max, sports like boxing and horse racing that only men did, were now for her to enjoy. Singing, acrobatic dancing, nudity, and stock trading are all parts of this 10-decade life.

The investigative journey I made in the decades of my life led me to open Pandora's Box many times. I encountered espionage moments with a secret informant who knew of the contents of the Letter written in 1886, with instructions to be opened in the year 2000. The MI5 and the secret of the Royal House of Windsor, the Skull & Bones, and the Illuminati member from a famous family had made a threat to me after reading my published book in 2009, in reference to the 120 Broadway: The Dark Shadow of Wall Street chapter.

I actually found a passion and the courage to publish a revised version, including more of this underworld knowledge, as part of this revised book in 2023.

Enjoy the journey. Jim Alessio

A quote from Edna Wallace Hopper: My Message to the Whole World - Keep the spirit young -

Table of Contents

THE MESSENGER MEETS THE ASSIGNED INVESTIGATIVE WRITER 1989

In 1989, I met a man who met Edna Wallace Hopper in 1953 at an after-theater dinner party at the home of one of the Barrymores in New York. That year, he was an actor on Broadway in a hit musical. "You will meet a man in January of 1989". Tell him to write a book on my life, and to find and include the secrets I have never told. Edna then asked him if he would be the Messenger, as it was charted through her spiritual esoteric helper (s). "You are to be called The Messenger".

Six years later, Edna died in 1959. As he learned of her passing, the man placed the large scrapbooks containing Edna's large original photos, newspaper articles, magazine stories, and interviews into the Metropolitan Opera Archives vault in New York (The Lincoln Center Archives).

Larry Johnson, creator and producer of the *Today* show on NBC, shown on the studio floor while Julia Child was on the air. Johnson, who also gave Barbara Walters her start, later connected the author to Edna Wallace Hopper's story, leading to the creation of *The Eternal Flapper*.

My Cape Cod friend Larry Johnson, an original producer for an NBC radio daily news broadcasting show, was one of the pioneers who transitioned his show over to television in January 1952, called The Today Show, one of the first television shows aired. In 1952, while other producers thought he was nuts, saying things like, "Television is just a fad. You are making a mistake, Larry", producer Johnson proved them wrong.

In the blistery winter of 1989, Larry asked me to close up my antique quilt shop in Brewster, MA, and spend time in New York for the winter. Larry had a place on Cape Cod and his terraced apartment in the Bronx.

With encouragement, Larry suggested, "I have season tickets for the Opera at the Met. You can ship your quilts to New York and sell them in Manhattan. We can go to Broadway shows and shop and dine."

I said, "OK, it's all dead here and depressing in the winter. Say, Larry, have you ever heard of an operetta singer and actress named Edna Wallace Hopper? I've had dreams of her posing for a painting in a clown suit. The day after the last dream of her posing for the painting, I was actually in shock seeing the painting, by accident, at the New Haven antiques show! I told Larry, "There is something strange about the whole thing. A dream of someone who was real! There is a reason for this, a connection for some purpose."

Larry replied, "I don't know much about operettas or her. Most of the operettas are lost. When I get to New York, I will check at the MET Opera library."

When Larry arrived at The Lincoln Center, he asked this man, whom I call the Messenger, for info on Miss Hopper. He gasped, looked at his calendar, and said," Is this for you?"

Larry answered, "No, for a friend on Cape Cod."

The messenger said, "It's the end of the month! Get him here tomorrow! I will pay for his air ticket. He needs to be here tomorrow. I have something important to tell him. I met her, and I have a message for him, from her."

Larry telephoned me and said, "I have a ticket for you at Logan. You are to come to New York, and I will pick you up. There is a man at the Lincoln Center who has information about Edna Wallace Hopper for you! He won't tell me and insists on seeing you here tomorrow. I bought your ticket, and he offered to pay for it."

After flying through a terrible snowstorm, Logan Airport closed and I arrived safely.

The next day, we arrived at the Metropolitan Archives building. I signed in a login book, we requested the leather-bound books, three of them, and we were escorted into a room with a large table. We wore special white gloves, and the man who was present watched every move and listened to every sound we made.

The archives assistant grabbed my arm with this gloved hand and said, "I met her, and I have a message from her." With his gloved finger, he said, "You must find the whole story of her life; there are things to reveal."

With surprise, I said, "Oh, YOU are the man who met her! I didn't know, Larry, you didn't tell me this is the man! Sir, I am not a writer. I was just curious about this actress/songstress because she came to me in sequential dreams, posing for a painting, and then I actually saw the painting at an antique show in New Haven!"

I explained, "This is all so interesting, but I am not a writer, so why do you think I am the one to do this?

The Messenger brought the login book over to Larry and me and pointed to my signature and the date. Then, he points his index finger to the prior request date and signature on the manifest. It was his signature and a date in December 1959.

The Messenger then explained, "She said I would meet the writer in January of 1989. This is the last day of January 1989, and here you are. No one else had requested to view these books since I placed them in the vault, just as Edna requested, at a time after her death in 1959."

I asked the Messenger if she ever mentioned anything about spiritual projection. He paused and said, "Wait, yes".

He went on to say that when the men who surrounded her asked her how she knew of the secrets to eternal youth, Edna replied, "I am no longer interested in my physical appearance being youthful. The only way to remain eternal is through the minds and imaginations of the living. Books, recordings, photos, and storytelling are ways to remain among the living for eternity."

With a stern look, the Messenger advised, "You have plenty of work ahead of you, so you'd best get going on it, find the truth, and solve the mysteries. Do a book and a musical of her life."

Larry looked wide-eyed at me and me at him while my heart pounded.

It was years later that I began to piece together this story.

Chapter One

The Coal Rush in Scotland 1847 - 1850

Twenty-two-year-old Robert Dunsmuir was a hardworking, small-boned man with petite facial features and large eyes. Coal mining was part of his heritage, as his father and his grandfather before him were all miners of coal in the region of Kilmarnock, Scotland. He met and married a pretty hazel-eyed nineteen-year-old girl with a square jaw and thin lips that gave her the appearance of strength, determination, and power. Joan White, as time has told, was indeed all that and more, and although Robert appeared to be meek, he would have Joan give him the strength to add to his inherited sense of working with fortitude, to take them from a bleak and humble reality to an unimaginable fairy tale world of existence.

Robert's father had mined Hurford coal, acquired several coal leases, and trained his two sons to manage his mines. Furnaces were using Hurford coal throughout Glasgow, putting the Dunsmuir family in a lucrative position.

Then at one time, cholera struck out amongst the family, killing off Robert's mother, father, grandmother, and sisters. This brought much hardship to him as a boy at the age of four. He survived and remained in the coal business.

On December 19, 1850, Robert was offered a position from Scotland with the Hudson Bay Company on Vancouver Island off the northwest coast of North America. The Hudson Bay Company was mining coal that was discovered off the northeast coast, and wanted to branch out and start mining the northwest. Trade was being done with the native Indians, who sold it for two shillings a ton. Then things began to become unsettling. The coal miners were being threatened by the native Indian villagers to move out. They were upset because they were earning less than they had been promised.

Robert Dunsmuir had twenty-four hours to make a decision on whether he wanted to take the position; he and Joan decided to do it. "Joan, I promise to someday build you a castle," he said as she accepted his decision to go with feelings of hesitation. They boarded the ship, the Pekin, along with another family of acquaintances. Joan was pregnant with her firstborn daughter. The Pekin took to the rough waters for a one hundred ninety-one-day journey to Fort Vancouver. This would be the beginning of a long and difficult road from hardships to success.

Scottish-born coal miner Robert Dunsmuir, known as the Coal King, became the richest man in British Columbia and one of the richest in North America. Behind every great man lies a great woman. His wife, Joan, became the master mind behind his greatness. Photo courtesy of The Craigdarroch Castle Archives Collection, Victoria, BC

As Good as Gold:

Dunsmuir Coal, British Columbia, 1851

On June 29, 1851, the ship named the Pekin and its weary passengers arrived on the shores of British Columbia. The hopeful Scottish settlers had found things to be of much disappointment at Fort Vancouver. Scurvy ran amongst the newcomers; incontinence and low wages made most of the coal mining company members desert their posts to join the forces that headed for the California gold fields. The word of the gold rush created havoc in the unrest already played upon by the conflict with the native Indians. Added to this was the unpleasantness of dirt, dust, and mud surrounding their single-room cottage, furnished with simple benches, stools, a coarse pine table, and bunk beds.

Robert stuck with it as others came and went. Eventually, he had made it into a management position.

By 1858, the word was out that gold had been found in the northern region of North America. The early summer of that year was the time of the great migration to Victoria, British Columbia, for the second gold rush.

As the word in California got around about the newly discovered gold region of the Fraser's River and its surroundings, the excitement created a mass movement of workers, especially miners, from southern California by way of steamers. Additional steamers went into operation to accommodate the traffic between San Francisco and Vancouver Island. For thirty dollars a head, the disappointed California miners from the 1849 Gold Rush and the early settlers from the Yuba and American rivers could try their luck for a second time at the gold rush up north. Many who could not afford the fare would hang on the sides of the boat and were called hangers-on.

The June 5, 1858, Alta California, San Francisco newspaper read: At the present time, the boats from the interior come down every night, loaded with miners and others all bound for Fraser's river. The hotels in this city are fairly crammed with people, waiting for an opportunity to leave…Throughout the entire length and breadth of the state, the "Fraser

River fever" seems to have hold of the people, and threatens to break up, or at least seriously disarrange for the time being, the entire mining business of the state (California).

While this was going on, the word in Scotland was that coal mines were being found as well as gold in the Fraser River region.

Robert had a bit of a drinking problem and would enjoy taking to his spirits after a hard day of work. One day in October 1869, while fishing, Robert came across a ridge of rock that was an untapped coalfield. "I've found coal!" he told Joan with glee that evening. As others were preoccupied with gold, Robert stayed with coal mining. His decision to stay would eventually prove wise, and his determination to succeed was unending. Robert Dunsmuir became the most experienced coalmine manager on the island.

There was a story once told that Robert, at one of his many times while being drunk, had passed out on someone else's property en route to his home. Throughout the evening, as he slept, his foot had scraped the mossy ground underneath him. Lo and behold, he had found coal. He went to the owner's daughter and asked her if her father might want to sell his land to him. The owner, who was another disappointed poor miner, was eager to sell off his land to Dunsmuir, not knowing what he was sitting on. He went through ups and downs and eventually learned how to own and manage the coal business of the region. Most of his opportunities were the misfortunes of someone else. He became a partner with Wadlam Nestor Diggle. Dunsmuir was responsible for selling coal to Diggle, who had his major business sales in San Francisco. San Francisco was the most important coal market on the West Coast.
By 1879, Dunsmuir's Wellington Colliery was worth at least $1,200,000.

By 1883, Robert Dunsmuir became one of the richest men on the Pacific Coast. He was as rich as the "Big Four", the four wealthiest men of San Francisco who built their wealth on the construction of the Central Pacific Railroad and had built their famed mansions up on Nob Hill. Dunsmuir had made a partnership with the "Big Four" and signed a contract with the Canadian government, which now made him one of the richest men in the world. Whenever Robert Dunsmuir would arrive in San

Francisco, the word on the streets was that the "Big Five" was in town.

Robert and Joan gave birth to two sons, Alexander, the oldest, and James. They also had eight daughters. They built a comfortable home, and as business got better, so did the homes they lived in. Robert looked to Joan for advice on his business affairs. By the time Alexander and James were young men, Robert trained his two sons to run the business, eventually, where they did it all. As he found Alexander to think more like himself than James, he decided that James should take matters into his own hands with the mines in British Columbia while Alexander was representing him in San Francisco with the sales end of things.

Craigdarroch Castle (Dunsmuir Castle), Victoria, British Columbia

Wellington Colliery San Francisco

Castaways from Society, San Francisco 1878

By 1878, Dunsmuir's coal business was booming while the other smaller collieries were struggling to stay in business. Now, the Wellington Colliery was the largest producer of coal in the Northwest. Not only was his company the largest producer, but his sales also exceeded all the others. This was due to his aggressive sales approach, cutting his rates and giving a fast turnaround time. In that same year, he took over the South Wellington Colliery, making him known as "the coal king". At this time in history, coal was the main heating source in homes and industries. Robert Dunsmuir was now in a position to buy valuable land. Being one of the richest men in North America, he was now working on becoming one of the richest men in the world. He needed his two sons to manage the coal business so that he could now concentrate on expanding his enterprise.

Robert Dunsmuir sends his son, Alexander, down to San Francisco to work with his partner, Wadham Diggle, at the sales office of his business, The Wellington Collieries. San Francisco was where the major coal business was taking place for Dunsmuir. Robert found Alex to have more of a business sense than James and found Alex to think more like his father as well. He kept James at hand with the Wellington Collieries for matters of managing the mines in British Columbia, while Alex was to become his right-hand man with Dunsmuir, Diggle & Company, the sales office, and marine operations in San Francisco.

Alex was a tall, handsome, and charming twenty-six-year-old man with a quick, sharp mind. His only drawback was that he possessed a negative trait of his father's as well - he liked his liquor.

As part of his daily routine, Alex would go into the office of Dunsmuir, Diggle & Company on East Street in the morning, and then eventually he would end up at the Merchant's Exchange, where the San Franciscan businessmen would make business deals, gossip, and drink somewhat heavily. After this, he would take the afternoon at leisure in one of the gentlemen's clubs where he would play cards while making more deals, all the while drinking more brandy and wine. This was the lifestyle of the rich and powerful businessmen of San Francisco. San Francisco, at this time, was growing by leaps and bounds. The banking business, the railroad, the gold rush, and the import business created a city of opulence and grandness unlike any other city in America, and much like the style of the great old cities of Europe. It must have been a fascinating place to be for a young and wealthy man like Alexander. Alex could handle his liquor well and could manage his business affairs without being affected by his habit.

One of the more popular places for Alex to be in the early evening was down by the docks, where he would continue drinking. There at the docks, he developed a close friendship with William Harrison, an Irish immigrant who worked as a marine insurance salesman. They would meet frequently at the Merchant's Exchange, where the "drinking.

Buddies would end up drinking by the docks. William was renting a room at the home of Waller and Josephine Wallace on Eddy Street.

Alexander frequently visited the theatrical circles in such places as the Bella Union, Alhambra at Bush Street, and the Old California Theater. At The Old California Theater, he met a young man named Wally Wallace, who worked there in the evenings as a head usher. They quickly developed from a mere acquaintance to a buddy friendship.

Alexander Dunsmuir
Photo courtesy of Craigdarroch Castle Archives, Victoria, British
Columbia

Joan Dunsmuir, the Matriarch of the Dunsmuir family Image
A-01256 courtesy of Royal British Columbia Museum, BC Archives

Alexander Dunsmuir, stepfather of Edna Wallace Hopper. Photo taken in San Francisco by Dore Gallery, circa 1880, prior to his marriage to Josephine Dunsmuir, Edna's mother. Image courtesy of Craigdarroch Historical Museum Society

Waller Wallace not only worked as an usher for the old California Theater by night but also as a clerk for a law office of W. H. L. Barnes by day. His time at home was brief for dinner and sleep. In his spare time, he was an avid baseball fan who kept score for his favorite team as well as playing ball himself.

To make ends meet, he and Josephine rented a room in their house to William Harrison. His wife, Josephine, was a tiny thirty-four-year-old woman of outstanding beauty with deep brown eyes, pure velvet peach skin, and raven-colored lustrous hair. Josephine

Wallace, born in New York of French parentage, was said to have the most attractive figure of any woman in San Francisco. She had all the characteristics of her Gallic ancestors, particularly concerning her beauty, its cultivation, and above all, its preservation. Josephine was a most charming woman with sweetness, vitality, and a wonderful sense of humor that made both men and women adore her. The Wallaces had two children, a boy named Willie and a charming, tiny girl named Edna. Edna looked as if she were only nine or ten years old, but was actually fifteen. Her brother Willie, a simple boy who grew to become an even simpler man, was younger than Edna. Edna had similar traits of charm, optimism, and the vim and vigor for life that her mother had. In many ways, Edna was a carbon copy of her mother, except for her brilliant blue eyes and auburn hair.

Edna spoke of her childhood years, "I was born a tom-boy, much preferring boyish amusements to those ordinarily enjoyed by little girls. This was fortunate, as it encouraged me to get much outdoor life and exercise."

At another time, she wrote, "I started life as a rather plain girl whom few young girls would envy. I seemed to have no great advantages. My hair was scanty, my complexion poor. It was that fact which urged me to gain the beauty I so much desired." It was clear that Edna felt as if she was not born into this world properly.

At Pratt's Hall, an old-time exhibition building at the corner of Montgomery and Bush Streets, there was a six-day marathon-walking match going on, starring Mme. La Chapelle, the favorite pedestrienne of the day. Waller, being a sports lover, wanted his wife, Josephine, to see part of it. As Waller could not take Josephine since he had to work and since this was not the kind of event a Victorian woman would attend without an escort, he asked William Harrison if he could escort his wife to the event. William told Mr. Wallace that he didn't mind doing so, but he was not able to stay there all day with her, so he would have to ask a friend to escort her home.

There at Pratt's Hall, dozens of contestants paraded around the floor laden with sawdust. Walking matches were quite popular at this time. They were marathons based on endurance instead of speed, sometimes lasting for several days and nights. While Josephine and Mr. Harrison were watching the match, there amongst the spectators was Alexander Dunsmuir, who happened to see William. William introduced Alexander to Mrs. Wallace. From the moment that Alex met Wally's wife, Josephine, he was mesmerized by her charm and beauty.

Their eyes met, and something sparked between them. William asked Alexander if he would kindly remain with Mrs. Dunsmuir and afterward escort her home.

Alex had found her vivacious, bright, and so cheerful. Alex later stated, "She has the finest figure of any woman in San Francisco." Unaware of their instantaneous attraction to each other, Harrison had left the couple.

As Wally was constantly busy working night and day, he was glad to know that his wife was amused and had her entertainment paid for by the wealthy coal business owner's family member. Before long, he was in fact welcomed into occupancy in the Wallace Family home on Eddy Street.

Harrison had to leave for a business trip to England for a few months, and upon his return to the Wallace home, he met Josephine at the door. She regretfully told him that his room was no longer available as someone else now occupied it. Harrison later found out that the "someone else" new occupant, surprisingly, was his drinking buddy, Alexander Dunsmuir. There was some speculation that Alex had actually paid Wally a considerable sum of money to live with his Josephine.

Little did Waller know that the favor he had asked of William would come to this. Waller had taken both children and moved in with his mother. Edna wrote of her grandmother, "My Grandmother, on my father's side, was a particularly unattractive, homely, old lady. There was no love lost between us. She thoroughly disliked me because I had been inconsiderate of her wishes in being born a girl, and she constantly reminded me of that fact, insisting upon calling me "Eddie"- having named me prematurely.

Sensing her hostility and disliking her sour disposition, I had a horror of ever resembling her in the least, and no punishment was as effective as the threat that if I were disobedient, I would surely grow ugly like my Grandmother. But to be told that if I were a good girl, I would be beautiful like my mother was always an incentive to good behavior. My childish dream was ever to resemble her." Here, at such an early age, did Edna acquire such a strong role model of her mother and develop distinctive goals to be as beautiful as her mother. By the same token, at such an early age, she developed a fear of becoming ugly and old. Formulating old and ugly as being evil while youth and beauty are of goodness is something that stayed with her throughout the next 80 years.

On December 15, 1880, Waller and Josephine were divorced. Josephine and Alexander were now in love and living together, renting. a portion of a private home on Jones Street. Edna was sent to live with her mother and Alexander, while Willie remained with his father.

Separating from her father's "ugly" side of the family and being part of her beautiful mother's and her rich and famous stepfather's world at first would seem to one as a fairy tale fantasy. Instead, Edna's change of father figures would turn out to be more like a living nightmare.

Edna Wallace as a child

17

Sausalito, California, 1880

During the summer of 1880, Alexander had taken Josephine, Edna, and her little dog to stay at a fashionable seaside resort in Sausalito called the El Monte. This was becoming the place for the well-to-dos of San Francisco to enjoy the days of summertime. Originally, planners attempted to lure the wealthy San Franciscans to buy lots and build summer homes in Sausalito. This was not happening too quickly, so instead, a number of resort hotels were built so that people would come to "try it out" with the hopes of the investors that they would eventually want to build there. The El Monte had been a hotel since 1878, catering to the wealthy class with accommodations for servants in adjoining small rooms. The suits were elegantly designed for lengthy periods of stay. The El Monte was a gathering place for the political and social groups of nearby San Francisco. Amongst the residents were many British merchants and their wives who set the high social style of Sausalito. The British Benevolent Society (the first of many such ethnic organizations) was formed in San Francisco, and by this time, Sausalito was well represented in the Society. The Americans and the British mingled in a friendly way, but the English set the tone "informal and natural, but when there was a formal party, it was properly conducted", quotes from a long-time resident of Sausalito.

Josephine was registered in the hotel as "Mrs. Josephine Wallace". It was whispered that Mrs. Wallace was the widow of a "sporting gentleman". Gossip stirred around the tea tables. "Was she a widow or a divorcee?" Word had it that Mr. Wallace was merely an usher, so how could she afford to stay at such a luxurious resort and wear such high fashions? Was she being kept? And what about her dainty daughter and that awful dog? Josephine was clad in a neat black dress, always buxom and tightly laced, with the curves of her figure outlined by costly materials that fell in folds impossible to weave with a cheap price. And little Edna was the despair and envy of all the other little girls on account of her stylish gowns and multitude of hats. Then one day, Alexander arrived, and all knew just who he was. Here was this young, handsome millionaire with the beauty of blonde, ruddy coloring and a fine physique with this widow, his senior by several years, fifteen to be exact. They were seen roaming the hills together, enjoying their existence apart from the other guests at the hotel. Josephine seemed absolutely oblivious to the side glances and whispers.

One morning, seated on the veranda of the hotel, little Edna Wallace was eating an orange and threw the peelings on the walk-in front of the hotel. As Mrs. Wallace and Mr. Dunsmuir walked by, Mr. Dunsmuir noticed   Edna littering and sharply ordered, "Pick that up!".

"Pick them up yourself," she cried. "I'm no scavenger!"

As stillness fell upon the scene, Josephine broke up the silence by ordering her daughter to go inside and go to bed. Perhaps this was the beginning of a rebellious attitude that Edna would have for her stepfather, planting the seed for a desire to break away from his rule over her.

Alexander and Josephine decided it was best to send Edna away to boarding school. Alexander told her that she was to go away to school and that he would take care of her as well as her mother. "I was to be his little girl, and (he) told me about my school, and what I should do, and what I should have, and so forth." Edna went off to a private school in San Mateo for about a year. "I was placed in a girl's school in the country, where I would have a great deal of outdoor life, play with other girls, and, in that pleasant environment, develop both mentally and physically. I was an adept in the gymnasium, I delighted in tennis and handball, and no fish had anything on me as a swimmer". Although she speaks pleasantly of her early school days, she also expressed a dark memory of it all. The following year, she was sent to another school in Bernicia. "My ambition to be an emotional actress was not forgotten during my days at school, and I staged "Uncle Tom's Cabin", casting myself as Little Eva. If any of my schoolmates did not weep and wail to my entire satisfaction in the "Going to Heaven" scene, she was not invited to any future performance of my play. As Little Eva, I was a "knock-out", in my own opinion at least, and whether they wanted it or not, they always got the same program." She added, "My will was so strong that I dominated the entire school and did what I wanted, and made them like it." It appears that it was here that Edna first realized she had the power to create an audience of fans and that she had the power to control them.

After about a year in Bernicia, Edna was moved again to another school. Edna had a nickname for Alexander; she called him "Snobs". Edna never spoke of "Snobs" to outsiders, as she was not allowed to. She spoke of "Snobs" in a loving way, "very kind and affectionate in every way, generous; and (he) amused me and played with me when I came home on my vacations; I had my regular full hour with him every night; it was his custom to come home at eight o'clock, it was understood that he would come home and play with me every evening;

I had my games with him. He was generous and affectionate in every possible way, and kind."

"On one occasion at San Mateo, they brought me some beautiful presents and candy, and he came up to see me in Bernicia. He used to write letters to me occasionally; on the holidays, he would write to me and ask me what I wanted for Christmas, and tell me to write my letters to Santa Claus and send them to him, and he would post them. I remember that. I remember other letters that he has written to me, encouraging me in my studies, and my good marks in school; asking me to bring home (report) cards that we got, and he would get me something nice if I brought home some good ones. Edna believed his attitude towards her was that of an indulgent parent.

The next school she attended was in Oakland in 1885. "I left school very suddenly at Oakland; my mother came there early in the afternoon, and took me away on the same day, packed up my things herself, and took me away." "I remember that the girls at school would not play with me and would shun me at times, and hurt my feelings, and I felt bad about that, and I talked about that (with Alexander and Josephine). After I left there, I spoke about that, and I said I was rather glad to get away. I said that the girls would not play with me anymore, and said they knew something about me, and shunned me, and he (Alexander) said to me, never to mind what the girls did, not to pay any attention to it."

"They said they knew my mother and father were divorced and that it was a disgrace; and I asked him if it was, and he said it was not; and that I must not say anything to them about it.

Alexander got another place for Josephine and Edna to live with him. It was a little house on Post Street where Edna could attend day school at the Van Ness Seminary in San Francisco and live at home with them after school hours. It was here, living with Alexander on Post Street in 1886, that Edna first began to notice his drinking habit. "I have a distinct recollection of every Saturday and Sunday it being a custom of his to stay in bed and drink." During the week, he would come home at night as a rule. "But he would come home at night at one o'clock, two, three, or four, as the case might be, and he would come to my room—my room was first and his was second, my room was nearer the front door. He would come in and wake me up, whatever mood he would happen to be in. If he was in a playful mood, he would wake me up and bring me into his room to play." It was expressed that he came in under the influence of liquor. It was during the time on Post Street that Alexander first became serious.

I'll and had delirium tremens. "I remember that we were very much worried because he did not show up for—did not come home for about four or five days, and we were very much alarmed, did not know where he was, and finally Mr. Crocker called, and said that he was at the Pacific Union Club." Alex was brought home by Mr. Russel Wilson in a very bad condition and was put to bed. Dr. Marshall examined him at 7 am. Alex was having hallucinations, seeing things on the wall coming toward him and from the corners of the room. He would see the pictures on the wall moving. Edna would pretend to put the imaginary object in the closet and shut the closet door, which would seem to satisfy him somewhat. "He wanted his coal mines brought down and put on his bed. And he was afraid someone was going to take those mines away from him." Alexander remained in this state for a week or longer. Alexander would have had delirium tremens many more times. Somehow, he would make a point of getting to the office in a sober state in the morning.

It was during the years on Post Street that Edna was sent away from the Van Ness Seminary and sent home with a letter to give to her mother. Josephine was crying when Alexander wanted to know what it read. "I told him that I could not go back to school anymore, and he wanted to know why, and I said, It is all your fault. Alex told her not to say that. "Mama says it is because she is known under the name of Mrs. Wallace and not by the name of Mrs. Dunsmuir, and I don't think it is quite fair. Alex told her not to worry. "Don't feel bad about that; that cannot be helped now, and you must have patience. You must both have patience," he said as he looked at Josephine and Edna. Josephine told Edna that she must have patience because she also had to, and not to feel bad about it. The only thing Edna knew was that it had something to do with his family. "She said that much; that I must not ask any questions, I was too young to understand it; and I must be satisfied with that." What Edna did not know was that Alexander could not marry her mother for fear that his parents, Robert and Joan, would cut off his inheritance and his position in the business. The thought of marrying a divorcee, especially a woman without money, was morally against their ways. The companionship of Josephine and Alexander was to remain a secret from the Dunsmuir family and the socials of San Francisco. Only those who worked closely with Alex and a few friends knew of their living together. Once again, they had moved, this time to a house on Ellis Street.

By now, a certain effect was produced upon Edna by the actions of her stepfather. Her anxieties due to the social slights and due to the physical treatment she received had made her ill; she had nervous prostration. "I went to New York for my health." Her doctor had told Alex that he must not get Edna out of bed at night like that. Edna and Josephine stayed in New York for eight months while Alexander went off to Europe. He stayed with them in New York for two weeks prior to leaving for Europe.

It was during this time that Edna must have had a dream of being an actress in New York. She and Josephine returned to San Francisco to live in a house on Turk Street. Most of the time on Turk Street, Edna watched her drunken stepfather wearing nightshirts, going in and out of bed to get another drink. It was during this time that Edna had had enough of his drinking and needed to get away.

Edna had taken an interest in theater. Her fantasy had become true when, at a reception in San Francisco, she met and charmed the light comedian Roland Reed into issuing her an invitation to join his company. Impressed with her vivacity, he laughingly offered her a position in his company, and she accepted quickly. Either Josephine or Alexander did not approve of the plan. Still, she did it. It was the way for Edna to escape from the control, the troubles, and the drunken abuse of Alexander.

In May of 1891, six months after returning to San Francisco, Edna returned to New York. "I told him (Alexander) I could not stand the present circumstances any longer and that as long as they existed and my mother was not acknowledged before the world as his wife, I should have to leave and do something for myself, and earn my own living. He begged me not to do it, offered me anything, and said I could have anything under the sun I wanted if I would only stay with him".

"I said no, that I felt that I ought to go, and I had quite made up my mind to do so; and if he would not help me, I would do the best I could."

Alexander said he would not help her and would do everything he could to prevent her from going. "I will stop your allowance and not give you any more money. As long as you stay in the house, I will keep you. I will hold you down."

Edna waited for him to leave and then went to New York. She now knew she had to support herself, and her dreams of becoming a dramatic actress were now the solution to her needs.

Josephine seemed to have lived locked away socially, as the high society friends of Alex's and their wives didn't seem to receive Josephine's presence in their company well. Few friends ever came to the house.

Socially, as Josephine would walk past those on the streets, she could hear the vicious muttering and sometimes snide remarks spoken behind her back. The victimized Josephine somehow gave the appearance   that she was totally unaware of it.

Josephine Wallace was a woman who was in love with one of the wealthiest men of the West and could not convince him, nor wanted him, to give up his wealth in exchange for their marriage vows. Her years of devotion to him were spent taking care of his illness and addiction. It was during the year 1886 that Alexander was falling apart. His drinking was getting out of control, perhaps partly because of the pressures and frustration of having to live his life in such secrecy from the rest of his family and acquaintances, and partially because of an addiction. There is another reason, unknown to

Josephine or Edna, why Alexander seemed to have fallen apart in 1886. This secret of Alexander's, I will tell you later on in the story. There is also another secret that Edna had taken with her to New York and kept silent for many years to come. This too will be revealed. And as for Josephine, I had found yet another secret that was hers. This, too, will be revealed later in this book. For now, remember them as the secrets of 1886.

Young Edna Wallace by Falk, New York, c. 1886

Chapter Two

The Ingénue & the Soubrette Boston and New York
1891–1893

Tobacco card illustration of soubrette Edna Wallace, 1892

1891

Edna journeyed east in the summer, and in August, Roland Reed decided to have Edna Wallace debut in the musical comedy The Club Friend, first appearing in Boston for two weeks at the controversial Boston Museum. Edna Wallace took the insignificant part as Mabel Douglas. Located near Scollay Square on Tremont Street, the so-called Boston Museum was actually one of Boston's earliest theaters, its name nodding to Puritan distaste for the depravity as well as the Brahmin distaste for the vulgarity of such pursuits as musical comedies. Even the main stage was euphemistically called "Lecture Hall". To go to such a performance was a bit taboo yet tempting. Needless to say, to be one of the performers was so much more so.

Comparably seen by the general public in the same light as the rock and roll performers of the early 1960s. The origins of musical comedy, or comedic operetta as it was called, started as some of the serious dramatic operas, particularly the German ones, were so overly dramatic and so overly serious that young viewers would snicker at them. A new breed of playwrights, such as David Belasco, would make the experience of theater a more lighthearted event, bringing tears of laughter as well as tears of sorrow to the audience. Many operagoers had seen this as a disgraceful defecation of opera. Edna had found herself in musical comedy, or perhaps, musical comedy had found itself in Edna Wallace.

Two weeks later, the show was moved to the Star Theater in New York City.

Six weeks later, on November 9th, 1891, after six playing Mabel Douglas in The Club Friend, Edna was advanced to the position of leading ingénue, in a supporting role next to Roland Reed, in Lend Me Your Wife. She was perfectly designed for ingénue work, delicately beautiful, vivacious, and so petite, weighing only eighty-five pounds and standing less than five feet tall. She would probably have stayed in this line of characters if fate had not gotten in the way by putting her on a different track.

One night while performing as the leading ingénue in Lend Me Your Wife, she caught the eye of the famous and most successful producer of the time, Charles Frohman. He was so smitten by her that he made her a member of his own famous stock company.

In Charles Frohman's company, Edna performed as a lovely little soubrette named Lucy Morton in Jane, then as Mrs. Patterby in Chums, and then in 1892, as Margery Knox in Men and Women.

Early Broadway in the 1890s by day… and by night

1892

While on tour with the Frohman Stock Company, she performed back home in San Francisco in February 1892. Edna had stayed for two weeks with her mother and Alexander at their home on Turk Street. At that time, Alex stayed in the house, drinking nearly the whole time and staying in bed. He was unable to go to the opening of her show on account of his condition. For the next three nights, he was so drunk that he could not see her performance as well. Finally, on the fourth night, he was able to see her show.

Upon Edna's return to New York, her life was about to change.

Charles Frohman and David Belasco were about to make her a star.

1893

Charles Frohman was so impressed with her portrayals of soubrettes in his shows Jane, Chums, and Men and Women that he convinced the great playwright-producer David Belasco to create a comedic vehicle especially for her. Frohman believed implicitly that "a play really requires a star artist, man or woman-woman for choice". He would usually select his star actress or actor, and then would have a show made to showcase them or cast about looking for something in which to show them off. In

In this instance, Frohman wanted the great Belasco, called "the bishop of Broadway", to create a show to spotlight Edna Wallace.

Charles Frohman, the Ohio-born theatrical manager and producer, started his career as a box-office clerk in Brooklyn, NY. He became a successful producer with Bronson Howard's Shenandoah (1889), a historical pageant play complete with an actor playing General Sheridan atop a live horse. He was soon to become the largest owner of theaters in America as well as abroad and the manager of the top stars of the stage. Charles Frohman was the first to import and export top shows between Broadway in New York, London, and Paris, which is still done to this day. He appeared as a painfully shy man, resembling a frog in a starched collar, who would dart down a side street to avoid meeting one of his resplendent actors in public. He could not bear the strain of opening nights and almost never appeared at them. Instead, he would stay at a nearby hotel and have someone bring him the word of the audience's reaction. He and David Belasco would become dear friends as well as business partners for quite some time. Years later, they would have a falling out of sorts, but would still think highly of each other and would acknowledge each other at holidays and such.

Belasco had built and owned the opulent Empire Theater on Broadway and 40th Street in New York. Charles Frohman was the manager of the theater. It was said to be the grandest of all theaters of Broadway, in the richness and grandeur of the theaters of London and Paris. For the grand inauguration opening of the theater, Belasco had written and directed The Girl I Left Behind Me, a thrilling red-blooded melodrama musical that was the original "western" as we know it today, as well as being the respectable antecedent of the "horse opera". Insurgent Indians and punitive military expeditions were timely subject matter for the theater of 1893. The exploits of the late Sitting Bull and General Miles' campaign against the Sioux were vivid memories that lent a thrilling reality to this melodrama of a besieged army post in the Blackfoot wilderness of Montana. The title refers to a regimental ballad popular during the Civil War, and a painting with the same title was done by Eastman Johnson, who had witnessed the battle of Manassas in 1862 and later made a painting of a lonely, windblown woman looking out towards the distant landscape filled with the smoke of cannon and rifle fire. This must have inspired Belasco to envision his version of The Girl I Left Behind Me.

The story is of an intelligent Indian chief, educated by the white man, who returns to his people to inculcate new refinements in barbarity. The suspense and excitement are elevated with the ambush

and the massacre of the army, which was led by a cowardly army officer. A hero makes a desperate dash to secure the relief and rescue of a garrison by mounted cavalry, just as the general is about to take the life of his beloved daughter to spare her a fate worse than death.

The night of January 25, 1893, was the opening night of the Empire Theater and the premiere of The Girl I Left Behind Me. Edna had skipped out onto the stage as a comical country lass in the part of Wilber's Ann, when a burr had stuck to her stocking and upset a pail of strawberries. Her performance was delightful, as she had stolen the hearts of the audience. They instantly fell in love with the ingénue.

The play was a smashing success. It was the prototype for many western frontier musicals that followed due to the popularity and demand for more of its kind. The press gave it plenty of praise, including the Herald saying that it was one of the best, if not the best, of the dramas yet produced by American playwrights. The Tribune wrote, "an excellent piece of romantic melodrama," but added, "Mr. Belasco tends much to childishness and overlays all his work with frippery, such as he supposes will please a desultory audience… it is incredible that anybody can be so foolish with a pen in his hand." The Times referred to Belasco's preoccupation with petticoats. The reference was to the underclothing of the ladies, which was torn up to make bandages for wounds and used as towels by the gentlemen. Mrs. Carter, an actress in the show, recalled that Belasco grasped her by the arm, as they stood in the wings, and shouted in her ear, "Do you hear that? Do you know what that means? It means that never-never-never again will we have to eat in a Third Avenue restaurant!"

In the audience that evening was the well-established and famous star actor DeWolf Hopper. He was so attracted to Edna's charm and presence that he begged Frohman to arrange for them to meet and also to put them in a show together. At first, Belasco too wanted the hand of Edna, while Frohman, who felt like a father to her, was hesitant to grant DeWolf's request. DeWolf Hopper was the number one comedic opera star of his time. He was a tall and very handsome six-foot-two-inch man with broad shoulders and a deep basso voice. Women found him to be most attractive, and the men found him to be "a man's man".

DeWolf Hopper was the king of the comedic opera stage. By June of that year, Edna had been courted by many rich and famous bachelors, but she made a decision to marry DeWolf.

Newlyweds Edna Wallace and DeWolf Hopper circa 1893

Illustrated poster of DeWolf Hopper as El Capitan

Early image cabinet card of Edna as a new Broadway star, circa 1998, photo by Newsboy, New York, from the private collection of Jim Alessio.

On June 28th, 1893, Edna Wallace married DeWolf Hopper in New Jersey and became Edna Wallace Hopper. She was the third woman to marry DeWolf. Edna was thirty years of age, and DeWolf was thirty-four. Born in New York City as Will Hopper, DeWolf, as he was later called, had been an actor since the age of twenty. He financed his own acting company by the age of twenty-three, using the money he had from his inheritance. DeWolf's original intentions were to perform in grand opera. However, as DeWolf once declared, he was "ticketed for life" as his first professional role was comic in a light opera. His reputation for the rest of his life was as an eccentric comedian with a fine bass voice. In 1890, he became a star in Castles in the Air. By the next year, he had produced the musical comedy that made him famous, Wang. It was in Wang that he set forth in song the plight of a man with an elephant on his hands. He was now most adored by the American and London theater audiences. Wang celebrated its 100th performance on August 14, 1891, at the Broadway Theater, and many more performances would follow, including a revival in 1895 with his new wife. Later on in his career, DeWolf would recite Mighty Casey at the Bat, something that

would forever after be his biggest claim to fame.

DeWolf once said of himself, "I was much more obviously equipped by nature for the heroic than for buffoonery, and it was by chance that

I have sported the motley of a clown rather than worn the dark cloak of tragedy on the American stage."

"I had the first two physical essentials of the classics, stature and voice; not a singing voice, but speaking voice, that deep-chested volume and resonance of such speech demanded by the heroic roles of blank verse. My stature is not so uncommon, but such chest tones are, and suggest the classics at once".

Being well over 6 feet two inches tall, having a bass rumble, and proper enunciation are essential to tragedy. Will's early experience in the theater was in drama.

He, as well as Edna, had somehow been pre-destined to be labeled as a singing comedian. Once an actor is cast into a role and the audience loves it, then there is no turning back. By circumstance, DeWolf was with Colonel McCaull's Theater Company and had been tried out in the comedy role of Pomeret in "Desiree", John Philip Sousa's first operetta. The opening at the Broad Street Theater in Philadelphia was a big success. "I was cataloged as a singing comedian, and a singing comedian I have remained." Will declared. "There are worse destinies," he added.

On one occasion in Charles Frohman's office, DeWolf and Augustus Thomas came to visit. Thomas had expressed, "Charley, here is your choice to do a big thing for the theater. Hopper's talents are being thrown away in comedy. He has the form and the voice for tragedy. He added with strong emotion, "Here is Wil, a man intended by nature for the heroic, and the stage is using him as a clown. You are the manager to rectify this blunder, to give our stage a tragedian who looks that part".

Frohman listened to Thomas, who spoke with much sincerity and enthusiasm. When Thomas was through speaking, Frohman said, "What you say is substantially true, no doubt, Gus, with the important exception that it can't be done. Will has all the physical attributes of tragedy, and he is a first-rate actor, but his public expects him to be funny and would resent his being anything else. They have labeled him a comic, and a comic he must be. DeWolf never felt that his stature and voice were thrown away in comedy. He said, "Nothing is thrown away in comedy".

In 1893, the DeWolf Hopper theater company was a hot success, and a new musical comedy, Panjandrum, was running with Della Fox as the delightful costar. Della and DeWolf had enjoyed their success together for three years. While DeWolf was playing in Panjandrum, Edna was doing a musical melodrama called The Girl I Left Behind Me. During the season, Edna was also the understudy for all the principal parts in Mr. Frohman's various companies, among others, Miss Maude Adams's in The Masked Ball, Miss Josephine Hall's in Aristocracy, and for three parts in The Lost Paradise.

A few weeks after the Hoppers married, Della Fox, the Paquita in Hopper Company's "Panjandrum", was taken suddenly ill and journeyed off to Europe. Mrs. Hopper jumped into the part and played it successfully until the end of the New York season.

Alex and Josephine had left San Francisco and gone to Mexico for the drying out therapy as the doctor had ordered. They made plans and arranged to spend a year in Europe, where Alex could visit the health spas in Switzerland, Austria, and France to regain his health.

They were bound for New York first to celebrate Christmas with Edna and DeWolf would leave after the holidays for Europe.

For the Hoppers, the hand of fate was soon to turn America's sweetheart couple into America's number one musical comedy team.

na Wallace and husband DeWolf Hopper in the comedic operetta musical Wang
in 1895. Poster from the archival collection of Jim Alessio

'olf Hopper, whose opera company was the most successful in the 1880s and
1890s. Baker Art Gallery, Columbus, OH

Chapter Three

The Hoppers: America's First Sweetheart Couple
1893-1898

In 1893, the DeWolf Hopper theater company was a hot success and a new musical comedy, Panjandrum, was running with Della Fox as the delightful costar. Della and DeWolf had enjoyed their success together for three years. While DeWolf was playing in Panjandrum, Edna was doing The Girl I Left Behind Me. During the season, Edna was also the understudy for all the principal parts in Mr. Frohman's various companies, among others Miss Maude Adams in The Masked Ball, Miss Josephine Hall's in Aristocracy, and for three parts in The Lost Paradise.

Panjandrum had already been underway when the decision was made to have the newlywed Edna Wallace Hopper replace Miss Della Fox as the leading lady, Paquita. It was announced to be merely temporary as Della had health issues. Della Fox, who had been playing the leading soubrette roles with Mr. Hopper for three years, without a vacation, became utterly tired out and insisted upon a rest. Della was most clever and well-loved by the cast and crew. To have her leave the cast was a serious matter for the company. Mr. Stevens had made the expensive production with Della Fox in mind as Paquita. It looked as though the darkest of business troubles was ahead. DeWolf had asked Edna if she would take the part of Paquita in this comic opera. "Well, I did it," she explained, "To this day I wonder where I got the courage, for I doubt if any woman could live and be more painfully nervous at first performances than I am. I cannot explain how I ever got through without disaster. But I did, somehow. Probably the gravity of the occasion to those financially interested gave me strength, wit, and confidence. I will never forget the "dead and alive" feeling I had when it was all over. However, left me like the mist before the sun, when the kind and approving words of those around me sank into my anxious heart." She added. "And this proved the turning point of my career".

It was only a few weeks after the Hoppers married that Della Fox was taken suddenly ill and journeyed off to Europe. Mrs. Hopper jumped into the part and played it successfully until the end of the New York season.

The following comment on Mrs. Hoppers shortly after her first appearance in light opera is quite interesting:

"A winsome little woman recently bounded into the affectionate regard of New York audiences at the Broadway Theater. The severely critical may take occasion to compare her with her predecessor as Paquita in 'Panjandrum', possibly to her disadvantage in some instances, but the fact still remains that the audiences liked her immensely, because she is young, pretty, modest, and because she can act. Edna Wallace Hopper, if not able to sing quite well as some comic opera performers, is a capable actress, and in this respect her advancement has been somewhat remarkable."

Frohman, Belasco, and DeWolf all wanted Edna to pair up on stage with DeWolf as a comedic opera team. Edna recalled, "I was well placed at the time as any aspiring young girl could wish. I was the ingénue in Charles Frohman's Repertory Theater Stock Company. This position, certainly, was one of which any girl might be proud. The management was kind to me, and the critics said I had dramatic talent. Situated as I was then, under the dramatic guidance of the ablest in the profession, it will not be hard to understand that comic opera, even under the most tempting conditions, did not appeal to me very strongly. I had the desire to leave well enough alone." Comedic opera was still a new fad, and in Edna's eyes, to be engaged with the finest in the established dramatic arts and to risk leaving that fortunate opportunity for a new form of art that was not quite as established could be a downfall to her career.

"My husband thought otherwise, so did his manager. They kept at me, for a long time, trying to make me believe that I had special advantages for comic opera. I felt quite sure that I had neither the vocal power nor the musical training for such work. No adroit flattery nor forceful argument could make me feel differently. I was satisfied I should only make a fool of myself, or perhaps a better way to put it would say, I knew I should make a miserable failure, and if that doesn't come near entitling one to a dunce-cap, when the move is made with eyes wide open and heart benumbed with fear, I don't know what will".

Musical comedy and the revue were yet unborn. The opera bouffe, also known as light opera or comic opera, was now in its heyday, when DeWolf had asked Edna to join him. The contrast of their stature and voices would be quite comical as an oddity seen by a loving audience. She really did not feel comfortable doing it, but gave in to her husband's and their managers' request and joined the DeWolf Hopper Stock Company on stage.

One of the New York newspapers said, "Mrs. Hopper makes the most of a very small voice, and her acting is above the style of work required. There is a fund of sentiment in her nature that is a pity to waste on such a production as "Panjandrum", and the lack of vocal power would be an insurmountable obstacle to success in a better opera. Mrs. Hopper's gifts are for comedy, and the public will surely echo the wish that her marriage to Mr. Hopper will not lure her far on the broad road that leadeth to destruction."

In September, De Wolf not only produced a new volume of the popular Panjandrum at the beautiful Broadway Theater, but he also introduced the world to a new musical comedy star, his wife, Edna Wallace Hopper. The show had brought much attention as the public wanted to see the husband and wife musical comedy team. As the name of the show was difficult for many to remember or pronounce, people would line up at the box office and ask for tickets to "the Hoppers' show". "Have you seen the Hopper's show?" was the question of the day.

Panjandrum was a delightful musical comedy written by J. Cheever Goodwin and composed by Woolson Morse in 1893. The synopsis of the play goes like this: The action takes place in Subaya, in the Philippines. The hero, Pedro, played by DeWolf, is a tall, handsome, fine type of modern manhood and picturesque in his physique- a lovely and loving gentleman indeed who meets the heroine, Paquita, played by Edna, a dashing young woman full of accomplishments and with the joyous flush of glorious girlhood in her features, and falls desperately in love with her. One thing falls in the way: her mother.

In the first scene, DeWolf Hopper is a sailor who is going out to sea after his failure as a matador. Alfred Klein, who plays Paco, is transformed into a plump and jolly little seadog. One scene takes place off the coast of Borneo, one in the jungle of Borneo, and the last scene is at the Courtyard of the Palace and Temple of the Sun. Mandolins, guitars, and mandolas are a major part of instrumental music. Spanish ladies, peasants, natives, Aguazils, Narranjeros, Banderilleros, Matador's priests, priestesses, guards, sailors, and picadors are all part of the large cast. New songs were introduced and were repeatedly encored. Hopper kept his audience in a long laughing state with his comicalities. DeWolf, with his tallness and deep basso voice, along Petite Edna, with her soft, chirpy voice, had become the talk of the town and everyone's delight to see.

The placement of Edna as Paquita was only temporary, as Della Fox was to return to the role after a few months ' rest. New projects were immediately being thought out and written as the audiences loved and demanded to see the Hoppers perform together.

While the winter of 1893 had brought much success and happiness to DeWolf and Edna in New York, a different situation was at hand in San Francisco. Alexander's drinking had gone too far as he was in a serious condition, near death. Josephine had contacted his office manager, John Lowe, for help. Mr. Lowe had Dr. Cornelius Buckley come to the hotel. The doctor stated, "He was perfectly delirious, perfectly insane. He was suffering from bad kidney trouble. Upon one occasion, he did not pass water for 48 hours. I did not expect that he could possibly live". Alex was tied to the bed, shaking with convulsions. Several narcotics were administered, but they seemed to have no effect.

Josephine decided to send a telegram to James Dunsmuir asking him to come to San Francisco, as she felt Alex was dying. She identified herself as Alex's landlady, but after spending time with her by his brother's bedside, he realized that this was not the case. Doctor Cornelius finally gave Alex chloroform, and in a week, to his surprise, Alex was in good condition again. The doctor had recommended that once Alex is well enough to travel, he should go to Mexico to dry out in the sun.

James had left San Francisco and gave Alex a note which read: My Dear Alex:

I am sorry to write what I am going to, but I have known it for a long time and never said anything about it; that is the reason I asked you before when you went down this time if it was a woman's troubles that were troubling you. I knew it was, but you said not, so I did not like to come right out with it. I feel awful sorry and would help you all I can to get rid of her. I think you should let me know the whole thing, so that I could help you out of your troubles, if there is any way that it can be done, so far as money matters are concerned, or by advising a way to get you out of it. I am your only brother, and I think it is your place to let me know so that I can help you. Write me all about it, or I will come down before you go to Mexico and talk it over, to see what is best to be done. There are lots of men in the same fix as you, and surely there is a way out of it, and settle down to life in a different way than you have been living for all these years. It is bound to worry you, so I want to help you out of it if I can.

Mother and all of us are well.

Hope that you will be better than ever after your sickness and get rid of the thing that is troubling you.

Your effect, Brother James Dunsmuir

It was from this point on that James had seen Josephine as the reason for his brother's alcohol problem. But in reality, it was not Josephine who caused Alex to be troubled; it was Joan and Robert Dunsmuir, for they would not allow Alex to marry a divorcee with no money. Perhaps Edna's absence was also a reason for Alex to fall apart?

Alex and Josephine had left San Francisco and gone to Mexico for the drying out therapy as the doctor had ordered. Afterwards, they made plans and arranged to spend a year in Europe, where Alex could visit the health spas in Switzerland, Austria, and France to regain his health. They were bound for New York first to celebrate Christmas with Edna and DeWolf, and would leave after the holidays for Europe.

In December 1893, Josephine and Alexander arrived in New York City from their trip to Cuba and Mexico. By this time, the Hoppers had been married for almost a year. This was DeWolf's first time meeting Josephine and Alexander. It was Christmas night, and the Hoppers met Alex and Josephine for dinner at the Imperial Hotel. They had just been seated for Christmas dinner and been introduced to each other when Alex leaned over to DeWolf and Edna to say, "I've been very ill. I nearly died". Alexander had told Edna and DeWolf that his doctor advised him not to drink anymore, or it would kill him. "But you are drinking right now," Edna remarked. "Oh, this little bit won't hurt me," Alex responded. "I told him that a little bit might lead to a great deal more!". His condition was feeble and shaky, a result of his illness. For the first time, Edna noticed a change in his mannerisms, as he was quite impatient and could not understand why it took her so long to get dressed, although she had gotten dressed very quickly. After their stay in New York, Josephine and Alex went off to Switzerland for the rest of the year to have Alexander recover from his illness. DeWolf would later in life remember Alexander as "being the worst case of a drunken man I had ever seen".

Alexander and Josephine stayed for a little over a week at a small apartment house on Broadway between 40th and 39th Streets, where Edna and DeWolf also had an apartment at the time. They then went off to Europe.

1894

Della Fox had resumed her role in Panjandrum while Edna took on a part as Betsy in Poor Girls at the American Theater on January 22, 1894. In the fall, Mrs. Hopper returned to Charles Frohman's management, but she was not long after released from her contract so that she could play the part of Merope Mallow in DeWolf Hopper's production of "Doctor Syntax". This was an attractive part for Edna, in a natural and
an artistic way.

DeWolf and Edna were back on stage together in the new musical comedy Dr. Syntax at the Broadway Theater on September 3, 1894. Edna played the role of Merope Mallow, and DeWolf was Dr. Syntax. The critics loved it and Edna was coined as "the girl with the auburn hair". Her daintiness against his tallness was perfect for visual comedy, while the sound of her soft, high voice against his deep, strong sounds was the sound of comedic opera that made them so famous. This was an attractive part for Edna, in a natural and artistic way. On the road, Edna also assumed Della Fox's old character of Mataya in "Wang".

It was in Lucerne that Josephine realized how fragile Alex's condition was and that if he died, she would be alone and without money. The trip to Europe was not effective in bringing Alex back to Health; instead, he drank even worse there.

On Christmas Day 1894, Josephine and Alexander returned to New York from Europe. Edna noticed that Alexander had been drinking much more than when he had left for Europe a year before. His condition was poor. He had another severe illness while in Lucerne, which had lasted about three months, and he had nearly died. The doctors in Lucerne warned him that he should not drink. Nevertheless, Alex drank while he was in New York. They had stayed in New York for about a week, and then Alexander was put on a train bound for Victoria, BC. Josephine remained in New York with Edna, as she was not welcome to visit the Dunsmuirs in Victoria.

1895

In October or November of 1895, Edna was back in San Francisco with a four-week run of Wang playing there. She lived at the Palace Hotel with DeWolf and daily visited Josephine and Alexander at the Grand Hotel nearby. DeWolf had met with an accident, so Edna had spent much of her free time tending to her husband. Edna recalled that Alexander had been drinking heavily and would remove his "baby" from between his legs. His "baby" was a pillow that he would nurse between his legs and would continue to do so for the rest of his life. Although he wanted to, Alex was no longer strong enough to romp and play rough with Edna as he had in the past. She grabbed the pillow that looked so ridiculous between his legs, away from him. "I saw this pillow lying there, it looked so silly, and I pulled it away from him; and he made a fuss about it and told me not to be so rough with him, that he was not so strong as he used to be."

Both James and Alexander Dunsmuir were in their forties, and none of the money that was coming into the Dunsmuir family business was theirs. All of the profits produced by the companies they had managed went directly to their mother, Joan. Joan Dunsmuir, the powerful family dictator, had intentions of expanding the business, but instead was concerned with using her millions to acquire husbands for her eight daughters. In January, Alexander went back to Victoria to speak to James. He explained that Josephine had been his mistress for 15 years. He asked James if he would approach their mother, Joan, to know if she would give her consent for him to marry Josephine. James went to the family castle in Craigdarroch. Not only did Joan Dunsmuir show anger and disapproval for Alex's request to marry Josephine, but she also warned James that if he even mentioned "that woman's name" in her presence again, his inheritance as well as his brother Alexander's would be cut off.

The Grand Hotel in San Francisco, where Joseph Wallace secretly stayed
with Alex Dunsmuir in adjoining suites. They were lovers who wanted to
marry, but Alex was threatened by his mother, Joan, to be cut off from
the Dunsmuir wealth if he remained with Josephine.

1896-1898 El Capitan

John Philip Sousa, the famous American composer and bandmaster, wrote many kinds of music, including operettas, orchestral suites, songs, waltzes, and a symphonic poem. He was and still today is most noted for his marches, forever to be known as the "March King". Sousa took the rather simple form of the military march and gave it a personal style and a new rhythmic and melodic vitality, the best known of his one hundred thirty six marches include "Semper Fidelis", "Stars and Stripes Forever", "High School Cadets", "Liberty Bell", "Thunderer", "Manhattan Beach", "Hands Across the Sea", and "El Capitan".

Sousa was the son of a Portuguese father and a Bavarian mother. His father was a trombonist in the U. S. Marine Corps Band. His parents could not afford to send him to music school in Europe. Sousa had once said, "I feel I am better off as it is, for I may therefore consider myself a truly American composer". Being born in Washington, DC, during the Civil War. Growing up there and seeing the unending parades of marches after the war was the inspiration for him to compose. At the age of fourteen, he enlisted in the Marine Corps and composed his first march, "Salutation". By age ten, he was a violinist, and by the age of sixteen, he was engaged to conduct a pit orchestra. By seventeen, he was touring with variety shows, playing in orchestras, and in the theater. In 1876, the famous French composer Jacques Offenbach arrived at New York Harbor. Offenbach was invited, for a large fee, to come to the International Exposition in Philadelphia to conduct his waltzes and his famous cancan. Upon his arrival at New York Harbor, there were masses of little boats decked with flags and hung with Venetian lanterns, carrying journalists who had waited since the night before. Offenbach got along fine with the American orchestra. His concertmaster was the young violinist, John Philip Sousa. The event of the rehearsal at the old Madison Square Garden was bigger than any foreign attraction since the advent of Jenny Lind. Outside were hundreds of messenger boys, inside were ten thousand spectators, and the hall was decorated with tropical plants and fountains with silver spray.

Sousa was appointed the leader of the U.S. Marine Band in 1880 and made the band into one of the finest in the world. By 1892, he obtained his discharge and formed his own band. Sousa's Band quickly became famous in America and Europe. He was honored wherever he went. Enjoying his popularity and fame, he decided to compose comic operas.

Both Offenbach and Sousa would be composers for future musicals starring Edna Wallace Hopper.

In 1896, the book, "El Capitan" by Charles Klein, was written as a comic operetta in three acts by John Philip Sousa. The operetta was based on European models and had the characteristic Sousa martial music that was so well-loved.

John Phillip Sousa was interested primarily in creating operettas, and Hopper's Company was who he wanted as performers to blend with his specially worded, worldwide-selected musicians, the very best of the best. His decision to have the Hopper Company as the players was simply because they were the best. He wanted to shower the newlywed couple with a wedding gift, a showcase for the Hoppers named "El Capitan". While "El Capitan" was being produced in Boston in April of 1896, Edna, along with DeWolf and Sousa, created the special part of Estrelda, the hero-worshipping coquette, to showcase the talent and allure of Edna. It was her first original role in opera, as the previous one in "Dr. Syntax" was taken directly from a similar conception in "Cinderella at School".

The setting of the operetta is Peru during the sixteenth-century Spanish possession. Don Medigua has been appointed Viceroy of Peru by the King of Spain. This was engineered by the overbearing, ambitious wife, Princess Marghanza. DeWolf Hopper's role as Medigua is of a self-admitted blundering ditherer, a pacifistic milquetoast with high regard for non-confrontational living, and a person with no leadership aspirations or abilities at all. The movie roles of both the Wizard of Oz and the Cowardly Lion may have been inspired by the well-loved, then unforgotten character El Capitan developed by DeWolf Hopper. He is a loveable, pitiful, and comical coward hiding behind a mask of great power and strength. The great and powerful man hiding behind a meek and incapable man who says' "I have spoken!" and the sissyish whimpering coward hiding behind his bigness seem way too familiar as the two Oz characters.

The debonnaire, gifted, and legendary composer John Phillip Sousa. J.P.. Sousa adored Edna Wallace Hopper and wrote two comedic operettas to showcase her.

Photo of DeWolf Hopper as the comical "El Capitan" from 1897 by Falk Studio. From the archival collection of Jim Alessio

"El Capitan" is the story of Princess Marghanza and her daughter, Isabel, who lament the fact that they only rarely have the opportunity to see Don Errico Medigua. He is the Viceroy of Peru appointed by the king of Spain (and sometimes the recently appointed governor of Guaru, a small island off the coast of Cuba, perhaps the comic opera was updated at some moment in time. He is the Princess's husband, Isabel's father. Don Medigua is in isolation mainly because he detests quarreling and violence. But violence is how he had risen to power. He overthrows his predecessor, Luis Cazarro, who has the support of the local populace. Now there is unrest on the island. Don Medigua takes over Cazarro's ranks by posing as El Capitan, a warrior of legendary accomplishments. Within the political battle, there is a comic romantic subplot involving El Capitan, the disguised cowardly Medigua (DeWolf Hopper), and Estrelda (Edna

Wallace Hopper). This situation angers the Princess. The Spanish army lands and proceeds to tackle the rebels. El Capitan marches the rebels in circles, exhausts them, and gets them drunk. The Spanish proclaim El Capitan as victor, and it ends with a happy ending.

The music consists of flutes, an oboe, clarinets, a bassoon, horns, trumpets, trombone, percussion, harp, strings, three women, eight men, and a chorus. The costume was quite spectacular, elaborate, and costly, and the set designs were great works of art.

Needless to say, El Capitan was a huge success. It premiered in Boston on April 13, 1896, and then opened in New York at the Broadway Theater on April 20, 1896.

DeWolf and Edna sang the duet "Sweeheart", I'm Waiting", and "A Typical Tune of Zanzibar". The show celebrated its 100th performance at the Broadway Theater in July, and then the show went on tour in America from 1896 to 1897. In later years, it would go to London, but not with Edna. El Capitan is the only one of Sousa's operettas with any broad general recognition. Performances of portions of the score appear in modern times with regularity on pops-concert programs. A radio adaptation was broadcast on NBC's The Railroad Hour in 1953, and a concert version was done at Columbia University. Several stage revivals have been attempted in the past thirty years. Given the sustained popularity of Sousa's march music, why have Sousa operettas virtually disappeared? Well, Sousa wrote many of his comic operas for DeWolf Hopper, whose opera company became noted for the Sousa productions. When Hopper retired and when Sousa died, no advocate remained to assure the survival of the theater pieces. In addition, Sousa's publishing company for the operettas was sold twice, and the works were relegated back to the stockroom. The libretti for the fourteen comic operas disappeared under circumstances that are questionable as to whether it is coincidental. Add to this fact that Broadway had changed, and the thought of preserving its forerunners was not considered.

A costume illustration of Edna Wallace Hopper as Estrelda in "El Capitan" in 1897. From the archival collection of Jim Alessio

On September 28, 1896, El Capitan opened the New Academy of Music in Baltimore. De Wolf Hopper Opera Company's most successful production, El Capitan, Messrs. Al Hayman, Charles Frohman, Klaw, and Erlanger operated the theatrical market of the world, while Charles Frohman had contacts with all of the American and foreign dramatic authors of note for their new plays and musicals for the next ten years. The New Academy of Music in Baltimore was the grand reopening of their newly renovated and beautified temple of music and drama. The entire work of remodeling the Academy of Music was done by the famous Philadelphia architect, John D. Allen, who was said to have done the most beautiful theaters in America, as well as the Philadelphia Base Ball Club's Cantilaver pavilion. Frank Sima, who also had designed the most beautiful playhouses of Philadelphia, designed the frescos and murals. The chandeliers, the draperies, the furniture, and the electric wiring were all of the latest and the greatest.

The Concert Hall had been completely overhauled, re-lighted with the latest improved incandescent system, and beautified throughout to conform with the new age of theater.

A robin's egg blue crimped crepe-bound souvenir program was given to the ladies and gentlemen who attended this gala event. In it was a suggestion of encouragement to participate in the introduction for the first time of the European custom of those attended the promenade between the acts. As this was first done in New York a week before at the Knickerbocker Theater, this was the second promenade intermission, as no other theater in America was so well adapted to this long-awaited and most needed custom. The lobbies, foyers, and reception rooms were designed as attractively and luxuriously as possible, with promenading in mind. The foyers resembled drawing rooms. Ladies who usually sat through the long waits would now take advantage of the comfort of a stroll through the elegant lobbies, where a bell would ring in ample time for them to resume their seats before the curtains rose. The large restful chairs, wide aisles, and spacious passageways between the rows added to the convenience for the wide gowns worn at the time. In the program book was written, "The Academy in its handsome new dress is well worth an inspection between the acts, and there is no time like the present for the introduction of what should have been in vogue in American theaters long ago".

In London and Paris, as well as the other cities of Europe, it was considered quite the thing to promenade between the acts. In fact, it was the highlight of the evening. It was an opportunity for the fashionable ladies to show off their latest attire, for distinguished men to socialize with other men as well as glimpse at the other ladies, while taking on the appearance of a drawing-room reception.

The audience was almost prodded to participate as the program read, "It is needless to say that such a custom adds considerably to the auditor's enjoyment of an evening's entertainment and the ladies for whose especial benefit it has been provided at the Academy should not be slow to start it going, particularly when so much has been done by the management to make it a successful feature.

Edna Wallace Hopper was not only part of the newest form of entertainment; she was now present to witness the new look of the theater and the new image of the audience.

And the rest is history.

The Lyceum Theater at the Academy had a pre-renovation performance of the marvelous Baldwins running two weeks before, and closed just before the grand opening performance of El Capitan. This husband and wife, called the White Mahatmas, were an unusual new age form of entertainment. A mahatma is a Tibetan priest of high degree. The word literally means "purified soul," technically a master mind among wonder workers. Professor Baldwin spent two years among the recluses of Tibet and was known by them as the White Mahatma, for he really mystified them in his developments of their own mysticism. Mrs. Baldwin was a clairvoyant. People would come to see them as skeptics and then would walk away most convinced of their special sense.

A Note from the author: Could it be possible that these two people had introduced Edna to the world of the powerful sixth sense, a world where the mind takes over matter and thoughts could be projected into the mind of someone else in the future?

The robin's egg blue crimped crepe souvenir from an El Capitan program booklet I had acquired tells me yes, indeed.

1897

Light opera was climbing in popularity and ranking close to drama. Most of the American productions were imports from Austria, Germany, and France, with the exception of Sousa's, along with Gilbert & Sullivan's. Light opera had a distinct European flavor, based solely on romance. In the operetta, the music and the story blend together. In musical comedy, which followed later, the story and the score may ignore each other or send the scenes wildly from one place to another. El Capitan was successfully touring the country. In San Francisco, Edna and DeWolf performed for two weeks. She stayed at the Grand Hotel in adjoining suites with Josephine, Alexander, Mr. and Mrs. Stevens, her manager and his wife, and their little boy. By this time, she had not seen her mother or Alex for two years. Now she noticed that Alex was just as weak as he had been when she had last seen him. The doctor came to see him every day. Edna was impressed that Alex was affected by liquor more quickly now and could not stand as much. His speech was faltering indistinct, and muttering at times.

There was one peculiar incident when the Stevens, the Hoppers, Josephine, and Alex went in carriages for a long drive to show the Stevens the Presidio and the park by the bay. While driving through the Park, Alex told the driver to go to a place called Dicky's Saloon. This was a roadhouse drinking saloon located right by the side of the park. Edna said to him, "Snobs, you don't want to stop there, you would not do such a thing?" He said yes and insisted on stopping there. While in the saloon, he talked in a baby-voiced manner, calling himself "itty boy". He would say, "Itty boy wants a jinky." He continued to baby-talk quite frequently since this moment. Edna was convinced that his drinking had damaged his mind and personality.

Trouble In Paradise

DeWolf was a member of the Lambs Club, an exclusive, distinctive, and successful club for actors, meaning men only. It started on West Forty-fourth Street just around the corner from Broadway; it was named after Charles and Mary Lamb in 1869 and was, as DeWolf put it, "the most successful club in the world, and one of the most distinctive. I say most successful, because no other club is used so intensively by its members, is given such a collegiate loyalty, or is so literally the home, hearth and headquarters of its personnel". By 1895, there were 272 members. Here DeWolf would visit almost daily or nightly, smoking cigars and having brandy, playing cards and singing merrily together; he was a true Man's man. Meanwhile, Edna spent many nights alone or with her own friends, one of whom was a short, handsome, British man named Tod Sloan. Tod Sloan was a racehorse jockey who was quite successful and quite famous as well. Historically, Ted Sloan was the first jockey to change the riding position of a racing jockey, as his slumping forward became the new form to be recognized as a plus.

One afternoon, DeWolf had been in the Lambs Club with his fellow actor friends and decided to ask them if they would be interested in taking a tour of the new and beautiful townhouse he and Edna had recently acquired. They agreed and left immediately. DeWolf took them on the first floor from room to room. Then they walked upstairs, where DeWolf said, "And here is the bedroom." He opened the bedroom door only to find Edna lying naked on the four-poster bed, fast asleep next to Tod Sloan, also naked and asleep. It appeared as if they were both exhausted from a good case of lovemaking. The members of the Lamb's Club looked at each other with horror while they wondered what the tall and strong DeWolf was about to do. DeWolf quietly walked over to the side of the bed, glanced down at the two tiny figures in their delicious state of sleep, and then looked up at the fellow members and whispered, "Aren't they beautiful?" This was an event that the Lambs Club and all the actors of Broadway would never forget.

As every story has two sides, Edna may not have been the first one in her marriage to have an extramarital affair. Nella Bergen was the prima donna of the company, playing the role of Isabel, the daughter of Don Medigua, the Viceroy of Peru. While playing on tour with El Capitan at Manhattan Beach in the summer of 1897, Nella Bergen was responsible for the misunderstanding between DeWolf and Edna. It was apparent that they were having an affair, ironically, Nella was a rather large and unattractive-looking woman in comparison to the dainty beauty that Edna was. For professional reasons, Edna remained cool with her husband's company and the tour until they returned to New York City.

Once she returned to New York City, Mrs. Hopper was in communication with her lawyers and prepared to file for divorce. The professional world expected trouble at any moment. Edna had seen fit to defer her appeal to the courts until March 1898. It seemed that her intention was to save her husband's good name. If she had begun suit in the State of New York, it would have necessitated the naming of a co-respondent. Edna was concerned about sparing her husband's feelings as much as possible. The divorce was finalized in 1898. Edna decided to keep her name as Edna Wallace-Hopper. But from here on, DeWolf's wife number three was referred to as Miss Hopper. DeWolf would go on to marry Nella Bergen and would soon divorce her to marry yet another woman. In fact, DeWolf would end up marrying six times in his life, including the famous Hedda Hopper.

Edna was living at 120 West 47th Street in a luxurious building. Now that Edna was divorced, she was the toast of the town, courted by dukes and millionaires, applauded by the press and an adoring public. She was bait at the end of a hook in a pool of hungry sharks. Her popularity rose to a zenith while every play in which she appeared was a big hit.

Illustration of Edna and DeWolf in El Capitan, as performed in 1897, NY
Journal 1897

Souther Farm San Leandro, California

James and Alexander Dunsmuir purchased the Wellington and Bristol Collieries, along with the tugs Pilot and Lorne, for an amount of $410,000 in addition to the buildings housing Dunsmuir's Victoria office near E & N Store Street Station through negotiations with their lawyers.

These purchases, they asked their mother, Joan, to be in their names, and she finally accepted, now that Joan was in an ill condition and her doctor felt she would not live too much longer.

Now that Joan would soon be dead and Alex had finally owned something and was a wealthy man of his own right, owning E & N, Union Colliery, as well as the future ownership of Wellington Colliery, he could finally plan a marriage to Josephine after twenty years of waiting for this moment.

Alex looked for a perfect hideaway spot just outside of the city of San Francisco, where he could quietly build their dream home, where the social gossip crowd of San Francisco would not know of its existence, and word would not reach Joan. He purchased Southern Farm from Gilbert Tompkins, a horse farmer who needed money for a racetrack investment. Alex paid a mere $80,000 for the three hundred fifty-acre property that was valued for so much more. When Alexander purchased the large estate in the rolling East Bay foothills, the land featured fruit orchards, farms, and vestiges of the Spanish rancho days.

Alex spent $150,000 to tear down the racetrack and build the farm. He spent $20,000 on the construction of a thirty-seven-room mansion and chose architect Eugene Freeman to design it. He could have chosen any architect, but he chose the son of his friend, who helped Josephine often in bad times with his drinking at the Grand Hotel.

The Dunsmuir mansion is an example of Neoclassical Revival architecture popular in the late 1800s. It features a Tiffany-style dome, wood-paneled public rooms, ten fireplaces, and inlaid parquet floors within 16,224 square feet of living space. Servants' quarters in the house are designed to accommodate twelve live-in staff members.

Alex spent an additional $40,000 on luxury features such as mahogany paneling, beamed ceilings, and ornate tiles, inlaid floors and mantelpieces, all of which were at Josephine's request.

The elegant colonial mansion was a wedding gift to Josephine as they now planned a marriage in December 1899. Alexander converted the hill section into a park and decided to keep an actual working farm on the estate, so that they could have a supply of their own meat, fruit, dairy, and vegetables. A chicken coop, a brooding house, a milk barn, a shed, horse stables, an equestrian riding grounds, and a beautiful horse carriage house with wood paneling, fireplace, and tiled interior, along with a grotto and conservatory. A porte-cochere was made at the end of the large veranda where coaches would arrive to collect or drop off guests. Since there was no electricity in San Leandro at the time, Alexander had installed his own electric lighting generator plant to supply the Souther estate with their own electricity and private waterworks to supply it with their own fresh running hot and cold water. Among the delights of the place was an electric waterfall. Rare exotics, including palms and other varieties of semitropical foliage, were utilized, while the rarest flowers bloomed on the broad green sward, and in the nooks and corners of the superb villa home.

The Dunsmuir home, built in 1900, is located in San Leandro, near San Francisco. Originally built by Alexander as a wedding gift to his beloved Josephine. The newlywed Josephine arrived at her new home as a widow, only three weeks after the Dunsmuirs' long-awaited marriage.

Alexander was concerned as to just how much he was now spending on this gift home for her. Edna looked over the original blueprints and suggested that changes be made in the interior and exterior. The original design was for four large two-story high Corinthian columns with cast iron capitals to support the small pediment in front. Edna changed it to a most unusual number of three pillars. When the mansion was constructed, Alexander was furious with the view of the three pillars, complaining that the center one blocked the vision of the doorway. It is possible that Edna wanted three pillars to represent Josephine, Alexander, and herself, as she had seen this long-awaited home as a symbol of their family of three. She also made the choices for the rich tiles used on the fireplace mantels and in the bathrooms. The original design was for a much more elaborate carriage house and horse stable. Edna had seen this as a foolish added expense and designed a more simplified stable and carriage house.

The Souther Farm Estate was ideal for Josephine and Alexander, private from San Francisco yet close enough for Alex to get to for business. He wanted it to be a profitable working farm for Josephine in the event that he died. It would be designed so that she would be able to produce enough profit from fruit and livestock to live comfortably if his existence were no longer.

1899

Alexander had explained to Josephine that this San Leandro estate would be in her name. Edna had invited the San Francisco newspaper press to interview her at Southern Farm. Alex was quite upset with Edna when he saw the reporter from the San Francisco Examiner arrive, as he wanted this new living situation to have no notoriety. He hid in a room away from the reporter the whole time as Edna took him on a grand tour, acting as if it were equally hers as well as her mother's home. The article was featured in the Examiner with the headline "Hatless, She Wanders the Fields. A Summer Day with Edna Wallace Hopper." Edna led the reporter to the kitchen garden, through the orchard, through the mansion, through the farmhouse, the cow barns, and to the stables. At the stables, she introduced the ponies. "Aren't they cute little fellows?"

Then she went over to one pony and said, "Here's Toddy." The reporter was surprised to know that Toddy was named after J. Todd Sloan, the charming and handsome jockey friend who was found naked in bed with Edna by DeWolf and the Lamb's Club members.

Tod was a comrade of Diamond Jim Brady, who made a fortune betting on Sloan. Diamond Jim had married Edna's dear friend and fellow actress, Lillian Russell. The two couples were seen together at many social outings. Women would go crazy over the adorable Tod Sloan, as many women cheered out of control and wooed as he raced around the tracks. Oddly, or maybe not so oddly.

George M. Cohan had written a newspaper story about Sloan, which inspired him to create a new musical about this man who appealed to so many men and women. He cast himself in the role of Little Johnny Jones, a tiny jockey modeled after Tod Sloan. The oddity was that Johnny was to ride the world's greatest horse, which was named Yankee Doodle. Edna's character name was Teddy Twoshoes in her performance of Yankee Doodle Dandy. Edna and Tod were secretly, and in many ways not so secretly, kindred spirits. I had found a photo of the two walking proudly and gallantly into the entrance of a racetrack with Edna's arm over Tod's shoulder and Tod's arm over Edna's waist. It appeared that the diminutive

Edna towered almost a foot over the even tinier Sloan.

To the reporter, Edna claimed that Southern Farm belonged to her. She also had mentioned financial details, which Alex did not want to be made public. The San Francisco daily paper printed gossip that Mrs. Hopper was rumored to marry Tod Sloan under the heading: Would Edna marry Tod? Alex Dunsmuir said "N!"

Alexander was furious when he read the paper. Josephine had spent part of the day writing a will and had presented it to Alex to examine. Alex, upset from Edna's display with the press and fear of her and Willie taking the farm and more, threw the will into the fireplace. He told Josephine that he didn't want either to have a cent of his money. Alex wanted it deeded back in the case of Josephine's death.

The Gender Bender Knows - Sex Sells

George Lederer, Gus Kerker, and Hugh Morton wrote and produced a new musical comedy, Yankee Doodle Dandy, and had Miss Edna Wallace Hopper star in it, playing the male roles of Teddy Twoshoes and Willie Wildwave. Her hair was cut quite short, the likes of which was not seen in any woman in 1898. Her unusual look of bobbed hair off stage was admired by women and fascinated men, who would make it a vogue much later, after 1910. In addition to her boyish look, her stage costume was most controversial. At the Casino Theater opening night on July 4, 1898, Edna walked out onto the stage in a costume which consisted of a lieutenant's cap, a sleeveless, scanty, tight coat reaching to a point just short of where her legs joined her trunk, a pair of long gloves, a pair of transparent blue tights, and a pair of slippers. It was quite evident from her demeanor that she was going to shock the audience immeasurably. Miss Hopper dashed up to actress Miss Lessing, who was already on stage, turned her back to the audience, and giggled in a restrained fashion, while the murmur of astonishment merged into a mild round of applause. A July 27, 1898 newspaper called the Telegraph wrote, "It must be said in the first place that Miss Hopper's forecast of the effect of her appearance did not fall short of what really happened, and in the second instance it must be admitted that she has every reason for a sense of satisfaction at the liberality with which nature has gifted her in the matter of legs "from the ground up"- a long way further up, in fact, than anyone had expected to view in public. It went on to say, "If the future of 'Yankee Doodle Dandy' has been in doubt for any reason whatsoever, I freely believe that Edna's densely blue tights would have favorably settled the matter." Today, one can imagine how taboo this was when you consider that the journalist who merely wrote this article was fired for being too graphically vulgar in his description of Edna. Chicot's article began with him saying, "I held off as long as I could, but man is only human after all, and so on Friday I went down to the Casino to see Edna Wallace Hopper's legs and incidentally take in 'Yankee Doodle Dandy.'"

"She wore Pants!" was the claim that started a lawsuit against the gender bender Edna.

Miss Hopper as the young man Chris Wagstaff in John Phillip Sousa's
Chris and the Wonderful Lamp.

Edna as Teddy Twoshoes in the musical Yankee Doodle Dandy. Her
controversial scanty attire caused quite a commotion in 1898 and nearly shut
down the show for good. Ticket sales soared as lustful men and, yes, admiring
and astonished women rushed to see her in her daring attire.

Edna as Teddy Two Shoes in Yankee Doodle Dandy, Morrison Studio, Chicago, 1898 rotograph series 625

In June 1898, during an intermission in the rehearsal at the Casino, Edna looked out the dressing room window on the south side of the theater to get some fresh air. She caught a glimpse of DeWolf Hopper, who was also getting some fresh air from his dressing room fire escape during intermission. DeWolf shouted out to her, "Hey, Edna, did you see 'Divorcons' at the Fifth Avenue?" Edna shook her cunning little head by way of an invitation to the speaker. "You ought to see it the first time you get a chance," he resumed. "For the way the husband and wife arrange their little difficulty in the piece would have been right in our line. We ought to have done exactly as they did". Then both DeWolf and Edna smiled heartily and branched off into other phases of pleasantry. Those who doubt that there was any more sincerity than the law allows in their brisk exchange of amenities, at the same time, they both showed the thoroughbred qualities and demonstrated that they were above such small matters as expressions of skittishness. For those few who had the opportunity of witnessing this private spectacle, it was a cheerful experience.

- Telegraph July 1, 1898.

I have found that a similar reunion had occurred with Edna and DeWolf in 1924, as described in the only paragraph mentioning Edna Wallace Hopper in DeWolf's autobiography, "Reminiscences of DeWolf Hopper - Once a Clown always a Clown".

DeWolf remembers: "I saw her in Philadelphia when we both chanced to be playing that city last summer and she looked as young and charming as the night we opened in 'El Captain' at the Tremont Theater, Boston, May 13, 1896."

I had read somewhere else about this sentimental reunion that occurred while they were both cooling themselves off by the fire escape stairs at the back of theaters, coincidentally across the way. In this report, I read that someone had witnessed DeWolf telling Edna that she had not changed since they last met like this. She, in turn, looked surprised to see him and said, "Oh my, how you have changed so!"

While touring with Yankee Doodle Dandy in Philadelphia in November 1898, it was announced that the angry damsel Edna would quit next Saturday and that Louise Beaudet would take her place. It was reported that Walter Jones had given Edna the wrong cue. She shouted at him in a loud tone, and he, in turn, said, "Edna, it's a mistake, and I am very, very sorry." She replied, "That's a lie. You do the same thing all the time." Mr. Jones responded, "No, Edna, I do not. The occurrence was a mistake and I am very sorry." Her next reply was in her shrillest treble, "You gave me the wrong one intentionally. Yes, you do! Yes, you do! Yes, you do! And don't dare contradict me."

At that, Mr. Jones burst out with, "Who are you anyhow?"

"I'll show you who I am," she retorted, "I'm EDNA WALLACE HOPPER!"

"Oh, go to the devil", he said and walked away. Then Edna said some severe things. Edna reported that not only was Mr. Jones not a gentleman, but he was a cad, a dog, and an idiot. She then told the manager that she would not appear with the company again unless Mr. Jones apologized.

"I'll be damned if I will," said the stagehand, Mr. Jones. The rest of the matinee was not to the liking of the stage manager.

Edna's side of the story and how she will do one more performance at the Boston Museum, and then bow out of the show. She did, however, express her fondness and respect for Mr. Lederer.

From a New York newspaper printed in March 1899, an article titled, "The Undressing of Edna Wallace Hopper," reads, "She did not rely upon any particular dressing or undressing to bring her into prominence. Then came "Yankee Doodle Dandy". Mrs. Hopper had a prominent part and startled the town by coming out on the opening night in tights that showed the lines of her figure in such an essentially open-faced manner as to win the admiring plaudits of every man in the house. It will be remembered that the front page of the September number of the Broadway Magazine was a reproduction of Mrs. Hopper as she appeared in "Yankee Doodle Dandy". It was a big hit."

That same year, Offenbach wanted a piece of the Edna Wallace Hopper allure. He cast her in his American revival of "La Belle Helene". Edna played a young boy named Orestes in ancient Greece. Offenbach's lighthearted opera is based on the story of Helene of Troy. "La belle Helene" mercilessly satirizes the social mores of the declining Parisian upper class under the Second Empire, highlighting their preoccupation with sex and their moral laxity. Lillian Russell, known as the "Queen of Comic Opera", was also appearing in "La Belle Helene" in April 1899. This was to be the Queen's step off the throne, as it was her last appearance in opera. It was also the beginning of a lasting good friendship between the two actresses/singers.

Once again, Edna made a "controversial splash" by coming out in a scanty outfit this time in flesh-colored tights, bare arms, a tight-fitted short garment, and had an excuse as the public and press hounded her. "I'm supposed to be a young boy in ancient Greece- that is how they appeared". She and everyone else knew that her reason for playing the role was to appear in this sensual, gender bender garb. Again, the audiences flocked not to hear the great sounds by Offenbach, or the great performance of the legendary Lillian Russell. They came to see Edna's controversial "get away with it" appearance.

On June 28, 1899, an article appeared in the newspapers titled,

"Quick and The Dead Have Verbal War". It went to describe a catfight that broke out in public between Edna Wallace Hopper and Nella Bergen. The co-header read, "THEY SAID REAL MEAN THINGS." The Former wife of the tall comedian and the expectant bride unfortunately met in New York. On a Monday evening, before the morning when Nella Bergen was to board the St. Paul ship for London to debut in a new show, and with secret plans to marry DeWolf Hopper. Edna, unfortunately, met Nella Bergen, the prima donna of the Hopper Company, and the lady who was wearing the matrimonial shackles from which the law recently freed Edna. During the last act of "The Man in the Moon", the auditorium was crowded, but the promenade deluxe was quite deserted. Suddenly, a dazzling quartet stepped out of the elevator, consisting of one glimmering Edna, wearing a white laced Parisian designed gown, glittering with gems adorned around her throat and throughout the curls of her uncovered head, and her three cavaliers, Counselor Abe Hummel, Edward Crowninshield, son of a statesman, and a celebrated young millionaire equally known in politics, theatrical circles and in the "400 Club". A messenger was dispatched in search of Mr. Lederer, with whom Ms. Hopper wished to discuss a business arrangement. Just then, two ladies, none other than Nella and her friend Alice Judson, entered and seated themselves at a table next to the one adorned by the dazzling Edna and her attractive escorts. Immediately, a glacial chill was visibly apparent. Crowninshield's teeth shattered like castanets while Mr. Hummel had the shivers.

"My professional and personal understudies," snorted the gorgeous Edna while glowering at the chandelier.

"Speaking of rhinestones, did you ever see anybody who looked like such a showcase?" murmured Nella, while casting her eyes upon the ceiling. "Bareheaded too", she cooed.

"I'd rather be bareheaded than bare-faced", retorted Edna suavely. More words passed back and forth while the gentlemen sat there in agony. Edna's remarks were not consistent with the pure white elegance of her array. "Anything but a big woman in a last year's sailor hat, and readymade shirt waist," she said with anger. Included were remarks thrown out about Nella's private personal history. The atmosphere went from icy to hot and steamy. Edna's escorts persuaded her to retire from this scene, leaving the shirtwaists and sailor hats in undisputed possession of the scene. An eyewitness said that had it lasted one minute longer, there would have been physical blows.

Nella Bergen and DeWolf Hopper sailed for London on June 29th, 1899, where both parties appeared in "El Capitan". DeWolf had married Nella Bergen on October 2nd in London, although it was rumored that they were secretly married before they arrived in London. Within the year's time, DeWolf had eyes for yet another woman, Alice Judson. He and Nella were married less than a year when she filed for divorce. DeWolf would later go on to marry several other women in his life, including the famous Hedda Hopper. Hedda, who was actually named Helda, had changed her name to Hedda as suggested by Edna because their names were so similar that many people had them confused as to who was who.

1899 British Columbia

Seventy-one-year-old Joan Dunsmuir was ill, spending her time in her second-floor sitting room and bedroom. Once again, James, now Premier of British Columbia, tried to convince her to hand over Wellington Collieries, and once again, she said no. If she did not find a buyer before her death, then James and Alex would own it. However, the girls would have established trust funds. Joan offered the Wellington to James for $500,000, and he argued that it was too much.

When James returned to Victoria, he called his attorney, James Pooley, and notified him of his brother Alex's marriage to Josephine. He gave Pooley the newly signed will for safekeeping. He had received word that his mother, Joan, had gotten wind of the marriage of her son to Josephine Wallace and was furious for being kept in the dark.

Hesitantly, he made an effort to visit his mother in the castle. He approached her as she was in her sitting room.

"Well, James, you've gone against my wishes and helped Alex marry THAT woman. I suppose this is why you and your brother were so anxious to buy me out of the firm! Well, it'll do you no good nor him either. With THAT HARLOT by his side, he'll drink himself to death in a very short time!" She then tapped her stick on the floor and said with anger, "I told you no good would come of this plan, but you and Laura would not listen to me, and now you'll see that I was right and that whore will spend every dollar Alex has."

"But mother, Alex made a will deed all his interests back to our family, and if anything happens to him, I'll only have to give Josephine enough to live on, and she, too, is a sick woman, so the doctors tell me."

A stern Joan then tapped her stick on the floor once again and said, "No good will come of it, Jim, you will see. As sure as I sit here, THAT WOMAN will ruin Alex and spend every last cent he has. I cannot believe that you and Laura can be friends with her, and if you're going on in this way, I don't want anything to do with you or him either."

Joan then received a letter of notice that James was in the process of dismantling the mine without her consent. She was outraged and confronted him. "Don't listen to tittle tattle, just sign the papers," he said to his mother. A sick Joan ordered the doctor into the room. The doctor asked James to leave the room. James yelled at the doctor to stay out of their affairs and threatened to throw him out of the window. At this, Joan commanded, "Leave my house at once!" This is the last time that James and Joan would see each other.

James and Alex were determined to purchase Wellington from their mother. Negotiations continued through their lawyers, and in October 1899, Joan had agreed to drop her price to $410,000, and James accepted this final price.

Now Alex had told Josephine that they could set a date for their marriage.

On December 22, 1899, in East Oakland at a small old country hotel, the wedding ceremony took place in the sitting room. From Victoria, James is present to witness the marriage. Josephine claimed to be 38 years old, although she was 54, and Alex was 46 years old. Josephine's only known friend, Emily Agnew, was present. James Taylor, a coal dealer and friend of Alex and John Lowe, office manager of the San Francisco office, was present as a witness to his marriage, and the will would be drawn immediately afterward. In California law, any will made between a man and woman before marriage becomes null and void at the time of marriage. The atmosphere during and after the ceremony was rather melancholy. Just after the ceremony, Alex took the new will out of his pocket and signed it in front of the witnesses. The wedding feast that followed was at the Agnew's modest home in East Oakland.

On the 23rd, the newlywed Dunsmuirs took the train to New York for their honeymoon and visit to Edna. The porter recalled that Alex was hammered upon his arrival at the train. He had to put him in his bed, and then Alex had asked him for more whiskey as he was suffering from withdrawal symptoms while on the railway. This was given to him to prevent his delirium tremens.

On Christmas morning, the train arrived in Chicago, where Alex had to be carried to the transfer train bound for New York. They arrived in New York and stayed at the Imperial Hotel. Edna had just returned from

Boston and arrived in New York on the last day of December to open a new show. She had wished that her newlywed parents would arrive there for the opening night. When she arrived at the Imperial Hotel, she found Alex lying on a couch in the lounge. She noticed that Alex appeared to be in one of his typical drunken sprees, with his head wrapped in a kerchief and a pillow between his knees.

Josephine pulled Edna aside and told her of the horrific journey they had across the continent. "Oh, Mama Dear, I am so sad that this trip, which could have been such a happy one, should be turning out in this tragic fashion. What can we do to get Snobs better and back on his feet again? The play opens on January 1st, and I do want you both to be there on that night."

"Well, I'm afraid Doctor Dumond considers we should summon outside opinions because your stepfather appears to be getting worse. He doesn't seem to know what is happening. He recommended a certain Doctor Janeway to be very competent in these cases."

Edna replied, "Well, he doesn't even recognize me. We should do everything we can because you and Snobs are married now, and Snobs has given you such a lovely place out at the Coast, a new and carefree life should be awaiting you on your return. I want you to be happy at last, Mother".

Alex remained for the next few weeks in his hotel room in a dazed condition. On many occasions, he hallucinated and showed fear while exclaiming that there were pink monkeys flying around the room.

Chapter Four

New Day in a New Century

On New Year's Day, January 1, 1900, Edna starred as Chris in the debut of "Chris and the Wonderful Lamp", starring in her 2nd musical comedy written by the March King, John Phillip Sousa, who had made this his very brightest composition.

Josephine and Edna took great care to see to it that Alex could attend the opening by giving him a small allowance of whiskey in order to make the effort of getting to the theater. Assisted by Mr. and Mrs. Stevens, Josephine and Alex occupied one of the stage boxes.

The musical extravaganza by the famous, ever-productive, and versatile composer Sousa was based on the story of the Arabian Nights romance of Aladdin and the lamp, and on this, he erected a comical conception that brims with quips. The libretto he wrote was actually based on the book by Glen MacDonough, "Chris and the Wonderful Lamp", which took the old story of Aladdin and rekindled the lamp in the nineteenth century. McDonough collaborated with Sousa on this wonderful adaptation, which is colorful to both the eyes and the ears. The piece is presented in three acts and seven scenes, in which a company of one hundred comedians and singers, as well as beautiful girls, are seen in wonderfully brilliant costumes before background scenes so colorful and costly that they made audiences gasp in wonder. One of the most striking pictures is a panoramic view of an ocean voyage. There is an electric dance on a darkened stage, in which the use of incandescent lights in the costumes of dancing women is seen as never before.

The scene opens with an auction room, in which Chris Wagstaff (Edna Wallace Hopper) is a young man about town in New York who goes to Connecticut to see his sweetheart at her seminary. Chris attends an auction of the curious belongings of a late Yale professor and becomes the owner of the lamp. Miss Hopper polishes the lamp and produces a very modern genie in the person of well-known comedian Jerome Sykes, who undertakes anything and everything, down to imported Washington voters.

An amusing sight in the first act is the dainty boy and the large genie dancing from the auction sale together.

Edna as the boy "Chris Wagstaff" in John Philip Sousa's musical Chris & the Wonderful Lamp in 1900. Cabinet card photo by Gilbert & Brown, Philadelphia Chris wants to be taken to Miss Prism's Academy, where his fiancée (Ethel Irene Stuart) is the star pupil. A quick change transports them to a garden where all the college girls yell, a scene that the amused audiences demanded to be repeated over and over. Another change carried the entire school by ship with the help of a moving background to the land of Aladdin's home, where he and his court had been asleep for 2000 years.

The second act took place in Aladdin's palace, where some cast members did a doll dance, which involved them being wound up to do very clever electrical dancing. There was also an electrical ballet that included fluttering electrified butterflies. The act closes with a spirited troop of soldiers marching on from opposite stage sides and singing "The Men Behind the Guns" while carrying flags of the United States and Great Britain. The audience cheered so loudly as men stood up and hurrahed, and women waved their handkerchiefs with wild enthusiasm.

The show was quoted as "The biggest, brightest, merriest and most tuneful extravaganza seen in Boston" by the Herald before its opening in New York.

The Journal wrote, "Miss Hopper was never more winsome and attractive than as the hero of Mr. MacDonough's book and Mr. Sousa's music."

The Transcript wrote "Miss Edna Wallace Hopper is as dainty and artistic as ever, acting naturally as a boy, and wearing the garb in which olden-time pages used to go about with marvelous grace".

A New York paper wrote, "Edna Wallace Hopper is extremely dainty, vivacious, and a very clever actress, and has a peculiar style that is quite Parisian. She is always like a bit of bisque ware in appearance and is a prime favorite".

The part admirably fitted her, almost continuously before the footlights, wearing a number of "swagger suits" and puffing away at cigarettes in true boyish fashion. When it opened in New York, she went into the role with great spirit. Under the direction of skilled instructors in physical training, she had taken up riding, walking, boxing, bag-punching, and fencing. Edna had long desired to enter into athletics with a serious purpose. She took up boxing in a boxing studio on Broadway under the direction of the famous sparring master, Jack Cooper. She practiced weight lifting with Prof. Atilla, the strong man, rode her horse at the Central Park Riding Academy, and fenced under the instruction of a well-known expert. In two months' time, she transformed her body into a more athletic, more rounded form as opposed to her ever-symmetrical figure.

Boxing instructor Jack Cooper found before him an antagonist with the gloves who could put up four exceedingly fast rounds. In one instance, she actually knocked him out. Edna developed remarkable quickness and precision in her blows in boxing, and could make the bag fairly sing under spirited welts from her gloves.

Edna as "Chris" from Broadway magazine in 1900

Edna created considerable sensation on several occasions by riding horseback astride in Central Park, dressed in a duplicate of the boy's riding costume that she wore in "Chris and the Wonderful Lamp." Equestrian in the park did not know her identity, but wondered who the stylish little fellow could be who sat on his horse with such grace and managed his mount with such skill.

Her interest in fencing continued with lessons that made her develop wonderfully, until she became no mean antagonist with the foil.

Part of her athletic training was a five-mile walk at a rapid pace every day. She used only two-pound dumbbells for weightlifting as they were suitable for her physique. Throwing a six-pound medicine ball for fifteen continuous minutes was part of her regimen.

In two years' time, Edna Wallace Hopper was given the title "The Athletic Girl of 1902".

In January of 1900, Alex is dragged out of bed, cleaned, and dressed in time for the premiere of Chris and the Wonderful Lamp. There in the center box at the Victorian Theater sat Alex, confused as to where he was there, or why he was there, during the performance. Needless to say, he could not recognize Edna either. The interruptions he had caused during the first act had made such a commotion that Edna's new beau, Edward Crowninshield, a young, handsome, well-to-do man from a prominent Newport, RI family, had to remove Alex from the theater during the intermission. While trying to remove Alex as discreetly as possible, Edward turned to Josephine to say, "Don't come with us. It will only attract more attention."

On January 17th, Edna's thirty-fifth birthday, Alex had left his hotel room for the last time and had not since January 1st. He wanted to go to Tiffany's to buy Edna a string of pearls as a birthday gift. There at Tiffany's, he sat in a chair unable to move, requested whiskey, and was sent back by carriage to the Imperial Hotel. He was in a fatal condition. This would be the last outing before his death.

Two weeks later, forty-six-year-old Alexander Dunsmuir had died at the age of forty-six. It was January 31, 1900, just forty days after Josephine became his wife. Josephine was not only suffering from the loss of her husband, but she was also quite ill. Doctor Culbert had examined her and found her to have an advanced case of breast cancer. James Dunsmuir and his wife arrived in New York. Josephine's doctor had told James that she needed immediate surgery and that they must postpone the funeral and trip back to California for his burial until she had prompt surgery. James insisted on having the funeral without delay and having her sent back to New York afterwards. Doctor Culbert said, "I told him that this was a serious condition; that it had already gone too far." Josephine had known of her illness prior to her taking her marriage vows and going to see Edna on their honeymoon. She had waited for their marriage for so long and had no time to tend to her own illness while she stood by her husband's last weeks of illness. "It will be better for her to come out and see her husband buried", James stated to the doctor. "After that, she could come back if she wants to be operated on." Doctor Culbert later said, "She felt it was her duty to go if her husband was to go." Dr. Culbert insisted, "Postpone the funeral. Have the body put in a vault." Dr. Culbert argued angrily with James, who insisted on taking his brother's body to California immediately. It appeared that James was not as concerned with the critical state of Josephine's cancer as one should be. Dr. Culbert told him that the cancer had already gone too far and that Josephine needed to be operated on at once. When the doctor insisted that Josephine not go to the west coast until then, James said, "Oh well, we will see. It will be better for her to come out and see her husband buried. After that she can come back if she wants to and be operated on." This infuriated Doctor Culbert.

Edna's fiancé, Edward Crowninshield, a wealthy and handsome young man from an aristocratic family, assisted Edna, Josephine, James, and James's wife to the train station to transport the deceased Alexander's body back to Oakland for burial. Crowninshield recalled James complaining, "They want $4000 for a casket and box. Go down there and see if you can do better." He ended up negotiating with the undertaker for a charge of $700. Once again, money was an issue for James, even at the expense of his brother's proper burial. Instead of thanking him for making all the arrangements, James was taken aback when he handed him the tickets for the trip. "What's this extra ticket for?" Edward answered, "It's for the body."

"What? You agreed to pay full fare for the body?" James asked with bitterness.

While on the train from New York to California, James explained to Josephine that Alexander wanted her to have $1,000 a month but that he would give her $2000 a month instead. Josephine had seen this as a kind and caring act by James, for she was naïve to the fact that James had convinced Alex to sign the entire contents of his will over to him just prior to their wedding, with the exception of the San Leandro estate.

Josephine had asked James to put this change of $2000 a month in writing. "James, I can trust you, but if anything happened to you, what would happen to me?" she asked.

"My word is as good as an agreement", he replied. After several months, however, she did convince him to put it in writing. The truth of the matter is that James had procrastinated for fear that the contract might appear as Josephine being the heir to Alex's estate instead of himself.

Alexander was buried in the Mountain View Cemetery in East Oakland. Mountain View Cemetery is said to be one of the most beautiful cemeteries in the world. Their dream of being husband and wife at the newly built colonial mansion at Souther stock farm was now shattered. How ironic that Josephine had waited so long, twenty years in fact, for the day of returning to her wedding gift home as a happy newlywed, but returned as a saddened widow, shattered by her dreams, weak, and suffering from cancer. After a few weeks, Edna took the train back to New York while an ill Josephine traveled with James and his wife, Laura, for her first and only trip ever to Victoria. Josephine finally saw the grand Dunsmuir castle from a distance. Her dream of visiting the castle with her husband and being invited by his mother, Joan, never happened. Instead, she stayed at the palatial home of James and Laura along with their children. Original plans of Alex and Josephine were to honeymoon in New York and then go to Victoria to see if Joan would accept their marriage. Whether Joan would have accepted or rejected Josephine would never be known to her.

On February 25th, they arrived in Victoria. The newspaper called the Colonist, Feb. 27, 1900, wrote, "Mrs. Alexander Dunsmuir is 'well-known to the reading public by her pen name of Juliet Wilbur Tompkins, whose charming stories and essays have been a valued feature of the leading American magazines during the years past." This is quite odd, whether the source of this information came from Josephine or from a San Francisco newspaper. I have researched the writer Juliet Wilbur Tompkins and, in a few instances, found it unknown as to when she was born and died, but I did find a profile that shows her as a woman from San Leandro who worked for the San Francisco and the New York newspapers and later on, after 1901, published several books through the 1930s. Is it possible that Josephine had secretly given her stories to Juliet to publish? It is possible that Josephine had confessed to this well-kept secret in Victoria. Now that Alex was dead, and knowing that she would not be living much longer, she felt a need to tell Laura, whom she felt close to. For so many years,

Josephine had been locked away socially from the normal world and had not had a true romantic relationship. This might have been a way for her to act out her desires, her needs, and to hold on to her sanity. She had a need to communicate with other women. Whether or not they knew each other and whether or not Josephine did write in the guise of Juliet remains a mystery. The coincidence of both women being from San Leandro tends to make it quite probable that, at this critical moment of her life, Josephine found a need to reveal a hidden truth of her many years of living with a yearning heart for a solid and stable romantic relationship.

While in Victoria, Laura has a doctor examine Josephine's condition. He tells her and James that it is advanced cancer. He predicts her to live no longer than 18 months. Josephine seemed to have bonded with Laura; she expressed to her staff and to Edna that her stay was pleasant and welcoming. Six weeks later, Josephine traveled back to New York, and Dr. Abbe performed surgery to remove her breast. The cancer had also affected the muscles and glands in the armpit.

A few months after Josephine's surgery, Edna, along with her personal maid Mary Howe, and Josephine took a train back to San Leandro. Edna had arranged for Mary Howe to remain there to act as a nurse for Josephine. Sadly, Edna had to leave her mother to return to New York.

In September 1900, James, Laura, and their five children went to visit Josephine in San Leandro. According to her maid, "She was crazy for them to come down."

FLORODORA & Lady Holyrood November 9, 1900 New Haven, Connecticut

Edna played her first performance as Lady Holyrood, a character specially created to feature Miss Hopper in the American version of the musical comedy Florodora. Florodora was one of the biggest musical hits at the turn of the century.

John C. Fisher, John W. Dunne, and Thomas Ryley produced the Broadway version of Florodora with Edouin repeating his London role in the company of his daughter, May Stuart, as Angela. The creation of a new and special featured character of Lady Holyrood would become Edna's biggest success with over two years and three hundred seventy nine performances at the Casino Theater, transferred to the New York Theater for a further one hundred twenty-two, and reopened the Monday after closing there in another production, with no less than two hundred fifty cast members at the Winter Garden Theater (January 27, 1902) for another Forty-eight nights. Florodora did a grand total of 549 performances on Broadway before it started a world tour that lasted for decades to come. Edna remained in the Broadway cast and had toured as Lady Holyrood for several years.

Florodora was the first show in Broadway history to introduce the chorus line. Theatergoers will forever remember the famous sextet. The sextet all became famous in their own right, as they were the original gold diggers; each one married into wealth. Edna played Lady Holyrood and was not one of the sextet. Evelyn Nesbet, known as the girl on the velvet swing, was notoriously famous when her two boyfriends had an argument that developed into a homicide as one shot the other. The trial was big-time news. A funny story of the time when Edna sent the sextette off to Yonkers Raceway: One day, after a matinee performance of Florodora, Edna decided to treat the Sextette girls to a trip to see her favorite horse in a much-anticipated race at Yonkers. Lady Holyrood Edna made arrangements for carriages to be sent to pick up the girls for a fun day at the Yonkers race track. Edna gave each one of them money to bet along with hot tips on which horses to bet on. Edna was well known for picking winners, as was Diamond Jim Brady. They were instructed to return to the theater in time to do the evening performance. What was about to happen would make headlines in the daily news. The girls had been so overzealous and so excited about the outing that they had been drunk and gone wildly through the streets of New York, onward to Yonkers in a wild cavalcade of horses and carriages. They raced as if they themselves were in the big race, frightening pedestrians who leaped out of the way as the parade of flashy women in their petticoats flashed their large bosoms and frilly undergarments to the passersby. Men whistled and howled like wolves as they caught the flashing glimpses of the flashing circus parade. Not only were the streetcars, carriages, and pedestrians frightened, but the carriage horses became frightened from the frenzy and raced over sidewalks, knocking down pedestrians, causing other carriages to collide and flip over, which now made the girls even more hysterical with laughter. By the time they had arrived at the Yonkers raceway, dozens of policemen were there waiting for their arrest. Edna bailed them out of jail, rushing them back to Broadway for the evening performance audience at the Casino Theater. Meanwhile, the evening audience waited for two hours while wondering why the show was running late.

The six ladies known as the Florodora sextet had made news time and time again. They were very young, although they didn't appear to be so young, with their heavy thighs, high pompadours, and large breasts. Unlike Edna, the sextet learned the ways of the theater from their experience in Florodora, including the kidding of the comedians and how to handle the stage door mashers. The sextet doing the cakewalk dance and singing the wonderful song, Tell Me, Pretty Maiden, was one of the highlights of the show that made it a smashing success.

The dance director and supervisor of the chorus was a crudely comical man named Ben Teel. He was a short guy with a few hairs combed neatly across his bald head. Ben was described by one of the sextet as "a profane man" who made the young ladies afraid of his harsh and foul language towards them. "Wake up, for God's sake! Come on, you lazy bitches!" he would shout. "Get in step. Get the hell in step, you half-witted whores. Jesus! Have you all got lead in your shoes?"

Most of the girls had become immune to his swearing and accepted it as part of his composition, but one sensitive girl decided to take charge of this matter by saying, " I beg your pardon, Mr. Teel, but some of us are respectable ladies."

"Go on, you're a bunch of fancy floozies with two left feet each. Now let's start over again. One, two, three…" he yelled.

A few days later, the girl came to rehearsal with a doctor's certificate stating that she was a virgin. In front of the whole group, she handed it over to Ben Teel, telling the others that she had decided to put this dance director in his place.

"What in hell is this!" he belted out as he gazed back at her.

"That proves that I, for one, am a virtuous girl, and not a… what you've been saying", she responded.

Ben glanced at the certificate and gave a grunt. "Hell!" He shouted, "But this is dated yesterday!"

In another instance, the beautiful black-haired, hazel-eyed Myrtle McKinley and the fair-skinned, blue-eyed porcelain doll beauty Ella Claus were doing a sister act. Ella was kept at the end of the chorus line to show off her radiant beauty; however, she had trouble keeping in step with the others. Ben Teel singled her out to swear at her personally. He grabbed Ella by the arm and stamped his feet alongside hers in time to the music. He tore off his necktie, clutched the few hairs on top of his head, and then tied his necktie to his leg.

"Left… left… left… left… You got it now, keep it. God damn it. Don't lose it. You're left… left… left," he shouted as he marched up and down the stage with her. From her distance, Edna looked on to see this amusing yet pitiful sight.

In the autumn of 1900, something of an experiment was made when the Gramophone Company invited members of the cast of Florodora into its studios to record a few of the songs that they had performed nightly. History was made when Florodora was the first show from which anything approaching an original cast recording was made, in October 1900. The Florodora records were made at four sessions that fall. Commercial recordings began in London by the Gramophone Company in August 1898. Nearly 5000 records, all 7" in diameter, were produced that autumn in London.

The version starring Edna Wallace-Hopper did not begin until November 1900 and ran until the spring of 1902. Unfortunately, Edna was not part of the cast until after the recordings had been made. Owen Hall, the creator, Paul Reubens, lyricist, and Leslie Stuart, music writer, all became quite rich and lived lavishly.

By 1902, both Edna and Cyril Scott were ready to perform in yet another great production by Owen Hall with music by Reubens and Stuart, The Silver Slipper. Cyril Scott and Edna had worked together in her debut of The Girl I Left Behind Me, making this their 3rd show together. Florodora continued on with American touring company performances for some time thereafter.

While performing as Lady Holyrood, Edna Wallace-Hopper had commanded the highest paid wages of any actress on stage. She set the precedent for women of the stage from that moment onward; the door was open for actresses to make comparable, if not more, wages than actors. In fact, Edna Wallace Hopper was the first actress to command more money for her performance than any male actor ever received. A quote from Miss Hopper when asked how she felt about her portrayal of Lady Holyrood, the dashing English widow with her heart set on a second marriage: "She is a great lady." Art did imitate life. A great woman portrayed an even greater woman.

In December of 1900, Josephine and her lawyer Wilson got James to sign an agreement to $25,000 per year plus one-half of the net income from property owned by Alex in California, only after the R. Dunsmuir's Sons Company paid the B.C. Dunsmuir's Company, the present existing indebtedness due from it to the latter corporation. This was a catch-22 situation. In other words, Josephine would receive no profit since the San Francisco office was not free of debt. In return, Josephine agreed "expressly to waive, relinquish, and renounce" any further claim of her husband's estate for herself and her heirs.

Josephine had trusted James; in fact, she said to Edna, "I know I will get my share in two years." Her maid explained, "She thought she was going to get everything at the end of two years, and at the same time, everybody knew that she was not going to live two years." That is, everyone except Josephine.

By the end of December, the cancer had returned, and Josephine went back to New York for a second operation. She had the surgery in January of 1901 and died on June 22, 1901. She was 57 years old.

Edna had played for seven consecutive months in Florodora when she took a leave from the show for two weeks to go to San Francisco for the burial of her mother.

In December of 1901, Miss Hopper returned to San Francisco to settle up her mother's estate. Edna was shocked by what the lawyers had to tell her. Edna had just been informed that her mother believed she had signed a two-year agreement and did not relinquish her right to contest the will. Josephine was led to believe that James Dunsmuir was to provide for her an allowance that she felt was generous to meet her needs of living in luxury. What she did not know was that this agreement gave away all her interests in the estate. Edna then learned for the first time that the Premier of British Columbia, James Dunsmuir, was not only the King's representative. James was now the heir to his brother's fortune. Edna was informed that James had his brother sign this agreement on the day of his marriage to Edna's mother, Josephine. Edna was also informed that since James was the King's representative, a poor, feeble woman such as Josephine could not do anything against such a power. The lawyers tried to make Edna realize that it would be difficult for Edna to go against such a powerful force in court. Although Edna was intelligent enough to understand the odds were not in her favor, she made a decision that she was going to fight this in court. Was this decision to fight in court for her mother's sake, or for her own, or was it possible it was for someone else's sake? One of the first things that Edna did after her meeting with the lawyers was to return to the mansion in San Leandro. She went into Josephine's library.

Witnesses claim that a panic-stricken Edna quickly removed many books, along with some writings of Josephine's, as well.

What did Edna want to keep from being revealed?

What were the secret writings of Josephine in the library? This, too, will be revealed in this book.

1902 The Silver Slipper

Miss Hopper did not aspire to Juliet, Lady Macbeth, or any other of the classical heroines of the theater. She was well satisfied to remain in musical comedy or light opera. She knew this was where her audience loved her. This was a comfort zone now, and her dreams of being a serious drama actress had vanished with the realization that she was successful in what she had become, a musical comedienne. She had offers to star from three prominent managers, Charles Frohman, George W. Lederer, and Florence Ziegfeld. She turned them down to sign for the next season with John G. Fisher's new English musical comedy since Florodora, "The Silver Slipper". Fisher took many of the Florodora players and crew for this next "predestined to be a hit" hit. This was another composition by the great team of Owen Hall and Leslie Stuart. It was a spectacular, grand, laughable, sprightly show whose elegance and beauty dazzled even jaded New York. The subjects of this extravaganza were alien girls from Venus. One of them had broken a law of her world by throwing her slipper to Earth. She was sent with a group of companion maidens to Earth to fetch the slipper. The group of maidens surprisingly drops into the garden of an old astronomer. There, they raised some commotion and were later sent to Paris to be exhibited at a suburban fair. Edna's parts were quite interesting. In one scene, she is a boy in knickers, and in another, she is a dainty lady in a ball gown. In another scene, she is Wrenne, a peirott clown.

The rehearsals of "The Silver Slipper" began on the stage of the Metropolitan Opera House, where, for the first time, all the principals were present and had their parts read to them. The rehearsals for the sextette and the chorus had been going on for several days beforehand, while the general rehearsals had been impossible since Edna and Cyril Scott were not present as they were doing their final performances for "Florodora" in Boston. For two years, they had been playing together continuously. They returned to New York for the rehearsal and then went back to Boston to premiere in "The Silver Slipper".

The first performance of "The Silver Slipper" in Boston was quite exciting to the anxious Bostonians who had waited for a number of years for her return. The show opened at the Broadway Theater in New York and was a huge financial success.

It was sometime in 1902, during this success, that Edna had posed for a painting as a Pierrot clown named Wrenne, a character she had created for the show "The Silver Slipper". She was seated on a small platform stage slightly higher than the artist. Behind her was a deep brownish velvet drape backdrop. She was seated on the floor with her feet planted down and her knees upward. Her elbows rested on her knees, and her head was slightly tilted to one side.

Chapter Five Summary

Before I ever knew the name Edna Wallace Hopper, before I had any plan to investigate her life, something happened to me in Connecticut in 1979 that still feels impossible to explain. After a long day of work, I fell asleep fully dressed and entered a "dream" that did not behave like a dream at all. I could smell the linseed oil, feel the velvet behind me, and hear fragments of conversation as if I were inside a real room. An artist worked quietly, and his subject sat perfectly still, a small, impish figure in a white Pierrot clown suit with blue buttons, a ruffled collar, and a tilted head that held both playfulness and sorrow. Night after night, the scene continued, as though I were witnessing progressive sittings for a portrait. In the final moment, I saw the painting completed, and for the first time, I saw her face clearly. She smiled, and the sight of her laughing directly into my eyes jolted me awake in terror.

By morning, I was shaken and obsessed with one thought: this was real. A sudden car malfunction forced my friend Gary and me off the highway and toward the New Haven Coliseum, where a sign read "Antique Show and Sale." I knew, without logic and without proof, that the painting from my dreams was inside. Gary went in first and came back pale; it was there. When I finally faced it, every detail matched what I had seen in sleep, down to the posture, the color tones, and the haunting expression. The dealers did not know who she was. They said it had been found in an old Chicago Vaudeville area, and they kept it out front because people were drawn to her.

Still trembling, I wandered to a booth stacked with old magazines and, almost without thinking, pulled one from a pile. On the cover, again, was the same image. Only this time, there was a name: Edna Wallace Hopper, dressed as the clown Wrenne from *The Silver Slipper*. In a matter of minutes, the "unknown" woman in the painting had an identity, and my life had been quietly redirected. That single moment became the spark that lit everything that followed.

From there, the story widens into deeper and darker territory. Strange connections to early theatrical history emerge, along with lingering questions about how an early-1900s painting could survive catastrophe, and the shadow of Chicago's Iroquois Theater fire (1903), a disaster that killed hundreds in minutes. A surviving telegram, and later a mysterious note tied to William J. Davis, the theater's co-owner, raise unsettling questions about what Edna may have known, who she may have met, and what secrets were preserved long after the smoke cleared. Even more disturbing is the "full circle" moment that arrives a century later, when an artifact connected to Christmas Eve appears again, exactly one hundred years to the day, as if time itself had been folded.

The chapter then turns to one of the great public storms of Edna's early life: Hopper vs. Dunsmuir (1902–1904), a massive, world-followed legal battle where Edna fought to challenge her stepfather's will and expose what she believed was manipulation, incapacity, and hidden wrongdoing. Testimony, insinuations, and the courtroom's refusal to fully confront certain "irrelevant" details hint at something more personal and more painful beneath the legal arguments. The case becomes not only a contest over fortune, but a corridor of unanswered questions about power, control, exploitation, and the possibility of a child whose existence could reorder everything.

Finally, years later, another door cracks open. A visit to the Dunsmuir estate and the mention of a sealed 1886 letter, not to be opened until the year 2000, are followed by conversations with a guarded informant who suggests that what the family knows will not be easily released. It is here that the chapter reveals its true purpose: to show that what began as one vivid dream and one impossible painting was not an isolated event, but the beginning of a long pursuit in which history, evidence, coincidence, and something that feels like guidance move together in unsettling harmony.

This is what you are about to enter: the moment the painting found me, and the moment the dream became a trail.

Chapter Five

Connecticut 1979

Before I had imagined doing an extensive investigation of
Edna Wallace Hopper, a strange but very true incident happened to
me in 1979. I struggled with the decision whether to include this subject
matter in my book. The fear was that I could possibly lose credibility
among many of the readers. For those of you who find it difficult to believe
what you are about to read, I truly understand how you feel, as I, too, find
it hard to grasp this as reality even still today. What I did know was that I
knew this was the beginning of something that would somehow be a part
of my life. I assure you that this did happen the way I present it to you.

I have wondered so many times how this could have happened. I am
sure many of you have had a similar experience or know someone who
has confided in you. I choose to share this with you as I want you to
experience just what has happened. I have been asked many times why I
decided to write a book and investigate the true story of Edna Wallace
Hopper. Before 1979, I had never heard of her, nor would I ever have
imagined that her life, her legacy, and her secrets would take up so much
of my future hours seeking the whole truth of the events that surrounded
the many lives of this great woman.

After an exhausting day as a computer programmer for Travelers
Insurance in Hartford, I commuted back to my loft apartment in
Wallingford, Connecticut. I put my little kitten in the bathroom and
removed the toilet paper that she loved to unravel while I was asleep. I
would let her sleep with me except for the fact that I would wake to find
her fast asleep on my face as I would wake. Now I find a roll of paper
completely unraveled in the bathroom. I made my way back up the spiral
staircase to my loft bedroom and collapsed on the bed with my white shirt
and necktie, dress pants, socks, and shoes still on.

My intention was to merely relax for a moment, as it was maybe only six or 6:30 pm. Instead, the moment took me into a deep sleep. I went into a dream state, I think, I am not quite sure, as this was like no other dream I had before. I had all my senses as I had never had before in a dream-touch, smell, feel, sight, and sound. In the dream, I could smell the linseed oil paint, feel the velvet behind my back, and see the artist, whom, years later, I found to be Burr McIntosh. I could pick up on some parts of the conversation between the artist and his subject, a small impish woman who was dressed like a clown boy. She was wearing the softest of silks in a Pierrot clown suit of white with blue buttons and a large ruffled blue collar. A pointed hat graced the top of her head, and I could sense her hair to be of reddish auburn color, crimped and cropped very short, as only a young boy would have worn. The conversation was bittersweet. A mix of emotions ran through Edna's face as she was

placed in a deep state of stillness, calmness, and deep breathing technique to clear her mind of her troubles, her sorrows, and thoughts of her success and her independence surfaced to bring a special glow to her face and her eyes.

This was noticed by Burr, who smiled and was mystified by the gleam in her eyes, as so many others were. Each sitting would bring conversation to both of them, of which I had heard in a series of dreams. I cannot recall if they were on consecutive nights or sporadic ones. I remember her asking him, "So how are you, Mr. Photographer?" At this, they both giggled. For the first time, I realized it was a woman, not a boy, not a girl, but a woman. What was the humor that they shared in calling him a photographer? I came to realize later in life that Burr McIntosh was originally an artist, an actor, a writer, and had transitioned from painting to artistic photography. She was teasing him about his Nouveau technique. To be noted as a photographer in 1902 was avant-garde. His magazine, "The Burr McIntosh Monthly," was similar to Vanity Fair. It captured who was "IT", what was in, the rich and famous, exotic travels, luxury advertisements, and the arts.

There were several nights of dreams that followed, in brief moments I could recall upon waking. I wondered if it was a recurring dream or if it was the continuance of progressive sittings, and the artist continued with his subject. On the night I had the final dream, my point of view was turned around the room. I was seeing from his eyes, I had seen the finished painting, and beyond the painting, I had seen, for the first time, the face of Edna Wallace Hopper as she posed for the last time. She smiled so brightly, I noticed a deep space between her two front teeth, and her pupils seemed quite large. She began to laugh, and it frightened me into a state of waking up. I sat up and shrieked. I was soaked in sweat. I had seen a face, but I had no name, no identity, as to who this mysterious woman was.

My friend, who was staying with me, named Gary, had been disrupted from his sleep by my yelling. "What is it?" he asked as he looked at my horror-stricken and confused face. "I saw the clown, it's a woman. She was laughing and looked right into my eyes. I saw the painting, it's all finished." I described the painting and got into the position of her pose. "This is how she was seated, like this. Her hair is wavy and deep reddish brown. The clown suit is satin-like with puff balls on it in pastel blue. I remember pink and pastel yellow detail, too. There is a deep brown velvet background. Gary, I know it's for real, this was not a dream!"

That very morning, we were driving through New Haven, Connecticut. My car had an operational malfunction and began to drift into the left lane as we were going 50 miles per hour. I took an emergency exit, looked around for a place to park, which eventually led us towards the New Haven Coliseum. "That was no accident that we were forced off the highway," I said to Gary. I pointed to the sign "Antique Show and Sale" at the Coliseum. "The painting I've been dreaming of is in there, I know it is. Please go in and see if you notice it in there." Within a few minutes, Gary returned to the car looking somewhat pallid. "Jim, it is in there, as you said. Come on and see it". I had a difficult time getting out, as if I was being pushed towards it, feeling my heart pounding so hard in my chest and neck, and I could hear my heartbeat in my ears. "Is it a boy or a woman?" I asked.

Gary replied, "I think it's a woman." "What's her name?" I then asked him, as I could not get myself to look at it. "There is no name, only a date. "Is it like early 1099s?"

"Yes!"

"Is there an artist name?" "No," I went over to the dealers and asked them who it was. I then got the nerve to glance at it, and yes, it was exactly as I had seen it in my dream. I felt as if it had just finished last night. Who was this, and why did I dream of her?

The dealers told us that it was found in an old Vaudeville section of Chicago that was being torn down. They owned it for many years. It was not for sale. They had tried many times to have it identified unsuccessfully. "We think it is a small woman. We keep it in front of our booths as she brings us a drawer, people seem fascinated with her." I'll wait here," I said with some relief. Gary walked in but quickly returned to the car, looking quite surprised. "It's there, just as you described it. She, I think it's she, is sitting the way you said, with her elbows on her knees, head tilted to one side. "Does she have a small space between her teeth?" I asked as I recalled her image still embedded in my memory.

"Yes, it's kind of haunting, her smile, I mean". Gary had walked ahead of me at my request. I looked down at the floor as we walked down the corridor to the main hall entrance of the coliseum. I remember, as if it were in slow motion, looking up and ahead to see Gary inside the showroom. His eyes were wide open, and he pointed down to a painting that was sitting on the floor upright.

I immediately left the booth, confused and fascinated and determined to know who this was. I randomly walked into a booth where someone had antique books and magazines of every type, thousands of them. Randomly, I picked up a bunch from a stack and crouched down to thumb through them. "What are you doing?" Gary asked. "I want to see her again. I want her name." Just at that moment, I felt Gary tapping me on my shoulder. I turned, and he pointed down to the remainder of the pile on the floor, which I had taken some of. There on top, on the cover, she was again. "That's not her. That's a guy," I said to Gary and turned around to continue thumbing through the rest. "No, it's not, look, it says, Edna Wallace Hopper in the Silver Slipper".

I looked again, confused as she did not quite look the same as the painting. However, the date of the magazine was 1903 as well, and she was wearing the same suit with the same head tilt. I paid for the magazine, ran to the dealer's with the painting, and said, "I know who it is in the painting! Her name is Edna Wallace Hopper!"

This is the cover of the Theater Magazine from 1904, which started the initial passion of the author to find out who Edna Wallace Hopper was. It depicts Edna as the clown Wrenne in the Broadway musical, The Silver Slipper. The antique dealer couple was amazed and shocked as they compared the magazine cover to the oil painting. "Yes, it certainly is!"

"How did you do that?"

"I don't know," I replied. "I don't know why." Gary, in all the excitement, yelled out, "And he dreamt of her last night too!"

I nudged him with my elbow as I did not want to let them know. I found it all too disturbing. Inside the magazine, there was not a word about her or the show. I could only look at her face on the cover of the 1903 Theatre magazine and imagine who this was and wonder why she haunted me.

This was 1979, there was no personal computer, no World Wide Web, and it was difficult for me to find information other than a brief profile about her.

Years later, I found it odd that in "Chris and the Wonderful Lamp," Chris found the magic lamp genie near Yale in New Haven, the place where I had found the painting of Edna playing the male clown Wrenne. I also found that her debut was in New Haven. Another oddity is that I came across a book by David Belasco, "The Return of Peter Grimm".

In it, there is an illustration of a boy dreaming while a ghost of a dead man dressed in a clown suit haunts him. The clown says, "I'm afraid the world will have to wait a little longer for the Big Guesser. The secret you've delved for so long and so loudly was in your hands this evening. And you don't know what to do with it." Another communication with the clown ghost reads, "God's signal light is the surest thing in all the universe. But I'll wait for you, just the same."

The question remained in my mind: Why did I dream of her? How could I have dreamt of a painting, only to find it the next day? How could I identify the subject of the painting after seeing it by finding a magazine with a similar image of her in the same clown suit within minutes? Who is she? Why did these dreams happen, and how can this be real?

The funny thing is, of all the photos and data I had acquired since then, this one made a "full circle" at the end of this investigation, and I believe holds the biggest mystery of all the ones Edna held so closely guarded. I believe this to be the reason why I was led to the painting. At this time in 1979, I had no idea that I would be writing a book and a screenplay for a film on Edna Wallace Hopper and the events that surrounded her life.

I investigated and found out that the fire was in the Iroquois Theater, which was newly built and finished a month before, and was the grandest theater in Chicago. On December 30, 1903, during the first opening performance, a spotlight sparked, igniting a backdrop and spreading through the theater. Some stagehands quickly opened the back doors. The tight vent air system caused a huge fireball that blasted into the audience of 1900 people. Over 600 people instantly perished in less than 20 minutes, making it the largest horrific single building fire in United States history. The doors were made only to swing open from the outside. The combination of errors, such as a stuck fire curtain, sealed vents, blocked exits, and no fire alarm, made the opening performance a horror show. Like the maiden voyage of the Titanic several years later, poor safety planning and fate combined to cause one of the world's worst disasters that could have been prevented.

William J. Davis, the co-owner of the theatre, was accused of manslaughter. Years later, I was given a notecard from Edna to Will J. Davis. Along with this was a note to me that read, "I thought you might be interested in this as well." It was a telegram to William J. Davis, which read Edna Wallace Hopper will arrive near midnight at the train station (Chicago). The date was December 24th, 1904, Christmas Eve.

I researched Mr. Davis, the owner/manager of the Iroquois Theater, the year before. His wife Jessie Bartlett David was an opera star who suddenly died young, due to uremia and nephritis, a probable cause was toxic poisoning to the kidneys, possibly cyanide, cocaine, or heavy metals. I then thought, why would Edna meet a married man at the train tracks at midnight on Christmas Eve? Why did his wife die suddenly the next year, in May 1905? Then months later, Edna sends him a note on December 23rd, arriving Christmas Eve, one year after the telegram? She crossed out the "Mrs.", the "Wallace", and the" Hopper" only to show just Edna. It made me suspicious. It would be another ten years before I would know more about just who Edna Wallace Hopper was, and more than twenty years later to realize why I had dreams of this painting.

Photo by Moffett Studio Chicago, circa 1899. From the private collection
of Jim Alessio

Edna posed for the camera in California in the 1890s. Original photo from
the private collection of Jim Alessio

Photography by Tikelson & Henry, San Francisco, circa 1910. Photo from the collection of Jim Alessio

How did the 1903 painting survive the fire? Did William J. Davis run out with it? Also, why did the telegram of Christmas Eve 1904 survive all this time? Was it a memorable event close to His heart? And the biggest mystery is, how did the Note on Christmas Eve, December 1905, to Will J Davis arrive exactly one hundred years to the day, December 24, 2005, to me? With a note, thinking you might want this! Did Edna keep a dark secret that He was so in love with her that he chose foul play over his marriage?

Hopper VS. Dunsmuir 1902- 1904

One of the most famous legal cases closely studied by newsreaders worldwide of the early twentieth century and the longest trial in British Columbia history, still as of today, was the trial of Edna Wallace Hopper, Plaintiff, and James Dunsmuir, Defendant, representing his family, including his sisters and mother, Joan. James Dunsmuir was now the Premier of British Columbia, appointed by His Majesty, the King of England.

For over a year beforehand, Edna Wallace Hopper had been spending money preparing her case and making arrangements necessary for the securing of expert and other evidence from all parts of the United States, which had been submitted during the course of the trial at Victoria. This was an action brought by Miss Hopper against James Dunsmuir, the executor and legatee of Alexander Dunsmuir, to set aside the will of her deceased stepfather on the grounds of undue influence, incapacity, and insanity. In addition, Edna wanted to set aside a deed made between her mother Josephine, dated December 1st, 1900, whereby in consideration of an annual payment of $20,000, her mother waved and relinquished for herself, her heirs, executors, administrators and assigns all right, claim and interest to all real and personal property left by the testator wherever situate, and all family allowance arising under the laws of British Columbia or California.

On the death of Robert Dunsmuir, the founder of the Dunsmuir millions, most of the property reverted to his widow, Joan. The management of the princely passions entailed large responsibilities. James Dunsmuir, the eldest son, was appointed by Joan to manage the Vancouver Island interests while Edna's stepfather, Alexander, attended to the business of R. Dunsmuir and Sons in San Francisco. It was in San Francisco where Alex met Josephine Wallace, and from that time, she became known as Mrs. Dunsmuir. In order not to offend Joan Dunsmuir, who disapproved of the divorcee, no marriage took place for almost twenty years. Shortly after Joan sold out the business to her two sons, the marriage of Alexander and Josephine was announced on December 1, 1899.

According to the story of the plaintiff, Alexander was for years leading the life of a more or less continuous drinking performance, frequently in a condition bordering on delirium tremens.

On the morning of Thursday, December 3rd, 1903, in the Supreme Court of British Columbia, before the Honorable Mr. Justice Drake, the opening arguments took place. Mr. E.V. Bodwell opened on behalf of Edna. There was no jury in this trial, only the judgment of Justice Drake. There were a total of eighty persons who testified. Among them were Mrs. Helen Stevens, her husband, John Stevens, Dr, Cornelius J. Dumond, William DeWolf Hopper, Edward Crowninshields, Edna's man friend, Mary Ellen Howe, Edna's maid who also served Josephine while ill, Dr. Janeway, Dr. Robert Abbe and many others which included neighbors, friends and work associates of either Alexander, Edna or Josephine.

Entire days were given up to the submission of evidence to show the perpetually drunken condition of Alexander Dunsmuir and the permanent effect this had on his brain. One witness told the court that Alexander was on good behavior if he only drank a bottle and a half of allowance and seemed not to be averse to taking a few punches, wine, or other drinks as well. The hotel boys and porters from San Francisco considered that he was about the finest guest they had ever served, giving a five-dollar gold piece as a tip.

DeWolf Hopper's testimony included mention of having to dodge his father-in-law's invitations to join him in drinking. He described his drinking as "the most awful case of drunk he ever saw." Considering how much DeWolf liked to drink, one can only imagine what that meant.

Edna's testimony as to when they lived on Post Street, San Francisco, in 1885 or 1886 reveals a message to the Judge as to what happened in that little house and may be the driving force that made Edna fight for Alexander's fortune.

Question: And after leaving Oakland, did you go to any other school? Answer: After leaving Oakland, yes, I went to school at the Van Ness

The seminary in San Francisco was on Pine Street.

Question: How long did you remain there? Answer: Several months. I cannot say how long.

Question: How long did your mother continue to live in the Post

Street house?

Answer: She lived there some time, I should say, it might have been two years, I don't know; I couldn't state the time, I know it was a long time.

Question: Now, did you observe anything at all with regard to the habits of Mr. Alexander Dunsmuir before going to the Post Street house, with reference to drinking and so on?

Answer: I did not have a chance to observe anything. I did not see much of him, only on vacations.

Question: Well, did you notice any habits of intoxication at all? Answer: No, I did not.

Question: Nothing, whatever. Now, after you moved into the Post Street house, and during the time you were living in the Post Street house, did you observe anything with regard to his habits?

Answer: Yes, I did.

Question: Well, you might tell us about that, will you? Answer: Well, I noticed then he started—

Question: That would be about 1886, from then on? Answer: About 1886 on.

Question: I understand that you lived there for a year and a half or two years.

Answer: About 1886. Well, I noticed that he was drinking, and I have a distinct recollection of every Saturday and Sunday it being a custom of his to stay in bed and drink.

Question: To stay in bed and drink? Answer: Yes, and other times when he---

Question: Just a moment; did you observe anything else with regard to his drinking habit? For example, what was his habit of coming home at night?

Answer: Well, he would come home at night as a rule—of course, it seems every night, it may not have been—it seemed every night.

Question: You mean, your present impression?

Answer: Yes, my present impression is that it seemed every night, but

I would not want to say that it was every night, but he would come home at night at one o'clock, two, three, or four, as the case might be, and his second, my room was nearer the front door—Question: You might speak of him without any reference to yourself in the meantime.

Answer: Well, he would come into my room and wake me up, whatever mood he would happen to be in. If he was in a playful mood, he would wake me up and bring me into his room to play.

Question: You might leave out incidents of that kind; state what his practice was, about coming in late, and under the influence of liquor or sober.

Answer: Oh, he came in under the influence of liquor, very much so.

Question: Was it a very common thing? Answer: Yes, a very common thing.

During another moment of questioning regarding the time they lived together in a house on Ellis Street, Edna explains about the bathtub incidents: Question: Now, during these times that he was under the influence of liquor, what was his treatment of you? You might just tell us—

Answer: He was always very--- (Interruption)

Question: By the way, I want you to explain and confine yourself to things your mother was aware of.

Answer: My mother was aware of everything. Question: Very well, then proceed.

Answer: What happened when he was under the influence of liquor?

Question: Yes

Answer: Well, various things happened; it depended entirely upon the mood he was in; there were times that he was in a tantalizing mood, and I have known him to come in at night and carry me out of bed in a sound sleep and put me in a bath tub of cold water, and he rather liked that proceeding, and he did it several times, a number of times In fact, in the morning he would still have it in his head to put me in the bath tub of water and would put me in with all my clothes on. And then he would take another turn, and want me to lie alongside him and just pet me; and then he would have another turn, and would have new games and would want to play these games; and various things.

Edna's description of Alex being in a "tantalizing mood" suggests a sexual manner. Keep in mind, this testimony was given in 1903. The bathtub baptism was considered a "proceeding". She explained that he "pet her" and the explanation of having "another turn" at her all seem to suggest sexual acts. He did it several times as she explained. Her explanation that her mother was aware of everything also suggests that Josephine was aware of this but shut it out of her mind. She was at his mercy for her welfare and for her daughter's as well. After all, this was a time when such a woman could not survive without the assistance of a supportive man. Later on in the questioning, Edna stated that Alexander was very kind, affectionate, and gentle when he was not under the influence of liquor.

Other indicators are as follows:

Question: You have said something about your being in very poor health when you went to New York. Was any explanation given of that? Did you consult a physician?

The Court: Really, Mr. Duff, I think you might skip all this until you come down to something bearing on the issues directly; there is no detailing want of health of the witness, which is of no consequence here.

Mr. Duff: I would not think, my Lord, of encumbering the record or taking up your Lordship's time with evidence of this kind if I did not think after a good deal of deliberation that it is necessary to the issues. One argument which we rely on, and very strongly rely upon, is that the very nature of the will itself goes to show that the testator was not himself when he made it.

The Court: That is in 1900.

Mr. Duff: Quite so, my Lord. But our point is, and I desire to address this evidence to that point, that during a long period of years, by reason of the circumstances that have been detailed with regard to Mr. Dunsmuir's connection with Mrs. Wallace and the effect that they had upon her daughter and herself—by reason of these not very lovely things that occurred which he knew of, obligations were heaping up between them, and we shall endeavor to show your Lordship that he realized those obligations; and it is with the hope of showing that it was not a mere question of one or two or three years, but a case of a whole life- time.

The Court: You can take it from the evidence adduced that he acted possibly as an apparent might do towards his child, but as to whether he put her in a tub of water with her clothes on—that has really nothing to do with it. Well, I ask you, the reader of this book, to decide whether you think it has anything to do with it. Do you think that the court was ignoring something that was important to the case?

Mr. Duff later told the Court: I just want to bring out one thing, and that is, the effect, to his knowledge, a certain effect was produced upon Mrs. Hopper by these things, these anxieties, in the first place, on account of the social slights and also on account of the physical treatment she received.

Edna: I was very ill; I had nervous prostration. Question: And went to New York?

Edna: I went to New York for my health in May of 1891.

I told Him [Alex] I could not stand the present circumstances any longer and that as long as they existed and my mother was not acknowledged before the world as his wife, I should have to leave and do something for myself, and earn my own living. He begged me not to do it, offered me anything, said I could have anything under the sun I wanted if I would only stay with him; and I said no, that I felt I ought to go, and I had quite made up my mind to do so; and if he would not help me I would do the best I could. He said he would not help me, he would do everything he could to prevent me from going, he would stop my allowance and not give me any money; he said as long as I stayed in the house, he would keep me, and that he would hold me down.

Question: What did you do then?

Answer: I waited until he left, and then I went to New York and went on the stage. The following February, I think it was in 1892.

A few months into the trial, shocking news was announced one morning. The party of Joan Dunsmuir and her daughters was to join the side of the plaintiff against James Dunsmuir. Something must have happened, perhaps a conversation between Joan or one of her daughters and Edna, which made them want to support her side of the trail. Could it have been that they were informed that a child was born, and Edna intended to get the fortune for this child somehow?

Was the grandchild of Joan Dunsmuir possibly the son or daughter of Edna?

Premier Lieutenant James Dunsmuir Photo courtesy of Craigdarroch Castle Collection, Victoria, British Columbia

Photo from the private collection of Jim Alessio

2001 Reveals 1886:

THE SECRET AND THE INFORMANT

San Francisco, California & Cape Coral, Florida

It was November of 2001. For the first time, I had visited the Dunsmuir Estate outside of San Francisco. A friendly tour guide gave me a private tour before her decorative preparations for the holiday season. In the morning, as I drove up past the sprawling green front lawn that seemed to go on for miles, I was approached by a pleasant woman with a smile and a wave of her hand. It was Theresa, the volunteer tour guide, who had made arrangements to take me through the home on a private tour. I parked at the port-cochere where the coaches once arrived with Josephine and Edna, as well as their guests. The feeling was quite welcoming, yet something was disturbing to me; it's so hard to explain why. The contrast of bright sunlight on the grand veranda and the dark richness of the foyer upon entry can only make one feel as if they are being transported back in time. My eyes were fixed on the library as I stood in the parlor. I asked Theresa about the library, and she mentioned that it is believed that just after Josephine had died, the first thing that Edna had done upon arrival at the home was to remove the books from the library. Theresa went on to say that there was speculation that Josephine had some of her own writings, possibly books or manuscripts, that were removed from there as well.

As we toured the second floor, we went into the bathroom. "Jim, this is the bathtub that Edna would have used", she said as she observed my reaction. I looked at her and could see a bit of puzzlement mixed with despair. We both must have had the same expression. I wondered if she knew of the "bathtub incidents" with Alexander, but I did not want to ask her, at least not at this point. We had only met a few minutes beforehand. As we entered the kitchen area, the conversation somehow turned to where I asked her if she knew of any sexual misbehavior on Alex's part. She turned around briskly and said, "Oh, yes, it was well known by everyone.

It is no secret, Jim". I felt some relief as the ice was broken on visualizing with her the way that things really happened there.

We sat and discussed my book, my research, and my investigation. She mentioned Edna's return to the home, a few years before her death. She had discussed with the current owner just what occurred there in those days gone by. One can only imagine that it was almost like a confession.

"Well, Jim, please feel free to roam the grounds at your own leisure." I thanked her, and we posed for a photo together. Just as I started to leave her, Theresa said, "I know how much Edna means to you, but I must tell you that I am more interested in Josephine. I find her much more of a mystery." "Do you have any photos or paintings of her image?" I had asked. "There are none. She never wanted to pose as she felt unworthy. She had a lot of guilt being a divorcee and living out of wedlock with Alexander.

"I'll bet you I will find an image of her, somehow, someway, someday. I will find you, Josephine. I will also find her secret." At this, we hugged and said goodbye.

There lies in the Dunsmuir Castle, a letter from 1886 that was sealed with wax with instructions that it was not to be opened until the year 2000. I found out about the letter from reading a book, "The Dunsmuir Saga" by Terry Reksten, about the Dunsmuirs, written sometime around 1991. A small footnote by the author had sparked wonder whether this pertained to a child born out of wedlock whose father was Alexander Dunsmuir.

Shortly after my visit to the Dunsmuir mansion, I had a telephone conversation with a man, asking him if he could provide me with some information regarding this letter. The request was almost ignored, with a reply that "The investigation results were found to be inconclusive and that no further information could be available". I then telephoned the person who contacted me and questioned why, and what was considered to be inconclusive. No direct answer was given to me; however, by a series of smart questions, I was able to conclude that this did pertain to a child being born to Alexander.

I then telephone the man, asking for more information. "I am sorry, but that is not available," I explained that I was seeking the truth, and that

I felt that something had happened between Edna and Alexander in 1886. "I understand. I can tell you this much. The letter does not mention Edna." "Well, was the child born in San Francisco?" I then asked. "No, listen to me and listen closely, the child was not born in San Francisco. The child was born in Scotland. And under strict law and order, by the family from Windsor (he expresses with emphasis), I cannot disclose the contents of the letter, do you understand what I am trying to tell you?" "The family from Windsor? I think I do understand you. There is only one family I know of that has the authority to dictate as such. It's my understanding that Craigdarroch Castle was taken into possession by the Queen of England in the 1920s for her son, the Duke of Windsor. But the Dunsmuirs were not any relation to the royal family, or were they?" With a hint of relief in the form of subtle laughter and with a quick breath, he quickly replied, "Jim, you're on the right track". From this point, I felt I could get to find out more, little by little, from my new best friend, my secret informant. Another source who knew of my informant once said, "Jim, he likes to lure you, like a mouse in a maze with a piece of cheese." I do know that Royalty visited Victoria in 1901 in the persons of the Duke and Duchess of Cornwall and York, later known as King George V and Queen Mary, who came primarily to visit James Dunsmuir and family. In addition, James went to the coronation of Edward VII in London and stayed there until 1902. At the same time this was going on, Edna was making plans to obtain some of Alexander's estate, in conjunction with Judge Coyne of New York and San Francisco.

Suddenly, I realized that this was now a game for Mr. X, to see if I was smart enough to crack the code, so to speak. I was ready for my next question about how the mind's eye can do this, simply from the mannerisms and voice control he possessed. After a stretch of pause, he seemed to get the nerve to ask me, "Are you aware of the bathtub incident mentioned during the trial?

"Yes, I am, somewhat. Why? What do you think?" I asked in response. "Well, I think like you, that Edna was sexually abused by Alexander. He drank excessively and was uncontrollable at times. She said that her mother looked the other way." "Well, if the letter refers to a child being born in Scotland, then there is a possibility that two children were born, do you think? "I think you may be on to something, Jim," the informant answered. We both seemed to agree, and at this point, I think we both had mutual respect for each other's needs and grounds. "I don't want to jeopardize you. I understand your high position." I expressed with sincerity.

"It's not that, I don't want to get into any legal problems. You see, there is a man who approached us a year ago. He claims that he is the great-grandson of Alexander Dunsmuir. I then found out he is living somewhere in Victoria, he is somewhere in his sixties, and claims that his grandfather was born in San Francisco in 1886.

"In 1886? 1886! Well, that means he could be the great-grandson of Edna Wallace Hopper!" I said to my informant. "He lost the trial; they found no evidence" is what I was told by the informant.

I spoke with him once again, and this time the discussion showed me that he, too, had much interest in finding out about Edna. Although I could not see my secret informant; I had developed an image of his appearance in my mind's eye, so to speak. His voice was soft and calm, but I could hear an acoustic quality as if his office was in a large room with high ceilings. My mind's eye could see a large antique desk with a leather top and a vision of Mr. X sitting in a large old leather high-back desk chair. My imagination even filled in the room more with floor-to-ceiling books and bronzes here and there. It is funny how the mind's eye works.

"Does he know about Edna?" I asked.

"I'm not sure if he even knows who she is," he replied.

"Look, you must tell him of my research and theory. I think I can help him open a new case."

"No, I cannot go there, Jim, I will not go there, understood?" he said softly but firmly.

"You were asked to help him; you are only doing him harm by not mentioning me and my information." We got into a bit of an argument about who was right, ethically. I felt as if he realized that the truth prevails over all. Knowing the truth is always the right thing to do. Blocking out the truth for the sake of one's reputation or for selfish reasons is not the right thing to do.

I wondered now if it was possible that a woman in the Royal House of Windsor was pregnant by Alexander around the same time that Edna may have been? This would mean that Edna's child would be blood-linked kin to this child by way of Alexander. Suddenly, in the 1920s, Edna became close friends with several people of royalty in Russia and England.

Mentioned in the trial was a visit and stay at the San Leandro mansion by Lady and Lord Hope. This visit turned out to be a disaster. There was a huge argument that developed between the widow Josephine Dunsmuir and her guests, Lady and Lord Hope. It escalated to the point where they were no longer welcome at her estate and were asked to leave immediately.

Conclusion: On February 6th, 1904, judgment in the famed Hopper-Dunsmuir case was delivered. James Dunsmuir won the suit with costs against the plaintiff Edna Wallace Hopper. There was a large crowd in the Assize Court to hear the decision that was in favor of the defendant, with costs against both plaintiff and intervener. It was announced that the judgment was appealed in the Supreme Court of British Columbia. Hopper vs. Dunsmuir; Joan Dunsmuir, intervener.

Judge Drake announced, "I fail to see any right, legal or equitable, which enabled the plaintiff to take such a step. If the testators died intestate, the widow would be entitled to do so, but the plaintiff is no blood relation, and the tables of consanguinity do not recognize a step-daughter, or anyone who is not the blood of the testator."

"With regard to the deed of the 1st of December, 1900, if, as alleged, that deed was obtained by undue influence, as to which I will refer later when I discuss the evidence, admitting for the sake of argument that it was obtained by undue influence, it therefore was a voidable transaction, and is good until disaffirmed. Mrs. Josephine Dunsmuir did not disaffirm it in her lifetime, and the plaintiff cannot disaffirm it now, actio personalis mortuorum cum persona."

"After this action had been partly heard and the plaintiff's case was drawing to a close, Mrs. Joan Dunsmuir, the mother of the testator and of the defendant, applied to be joined as intervener which was allowed, and she, as next of kin, set up, as against her son, the defendant, the same case as the plaintiff, against the will of the testator. This case has taken a preposterous time- 42 days- to try, and although eighty witnesses were examined, many irrelevant testimonies were adduced which had no bearing whatever on the issues: But I allowed considerable latitude owing to the statement of counsel that the line of examination was necessary, which, however, when admitted, did not support their view. Objections were taken to the admission of a great deal of the testimony, but instead of disposing of them as they arose, counsel agreed to argue these objections at the close of the address by either side on these points, and consequently the notes are encumbered with a mass of utterly immaterial and irrelevant matter."

"The testator was about 46 years old when he died. He had been in California since 1877, representing his father, Robert Dunsmuir, until his father's death in 1888. After that date, he continued to manage the business for himself and his brother, the defendant, until 1896, when the business was converted into a joint stock company, of which the testator was president. The business in California was confined to selling coal from Vancouver Island: chartering ships; obtaining employment for the company's own vessels; and arranging all matters of this sort. The testator is spoken of by many businessmen as a man of marked business capacity, very shrewd and keen, but he was rather a silent man, difficult for strangers to get on with; brusque in his speech, and, I should say, rather domineering and arbitrary. He did not go into society, owing perhaps to his social relations with Mrs. Wallace, whom he shortly before his death made his wife."

He continued, "The evidence discloses the fact that he drank to bouts. He had three or four attacks of delirium tremens, but one characteristic of him was that he was never seen by any of his employees under the influence of liquor during his office hours, which generally lasted until about 1 p.m. After that period, he undoubtedly drank more or less. When he was on a spree, as some witnesses describe his actions, he kept away from the office until he had entirely recovered. These sprees lasted from a few days to two or three weeks. This is a character of the man as disclosed in the evidence, and it is on this habit of excessive drinking that the plaintiff's case is founded."

"The evidence runs in two lines. First, the class of evidence relating to his home life, where all the follies of intoxication, the delusions, incoherencies, mutterings, and irrational remarks are all set forth in detail as if they were the ordinary condition of the testator when not suffering from alcoholism. The class from which these witnesses are drawn is bellboys at the hotel, barkeepers, hotelmen, car cleaners, and people of little credit. Others are speaking of a period five to ten years anterior to the will, such as W. D. Hopper, Buzzelo, Geo. Hock, and Mrs. Douglas. This latter evidence is worthless if the medical evidence is correct that the disease, which they alleged he died from, was alcoholic dementia, as that only takes from 18 months to two years to run its course. But here again, the doctors differ. One says he never knew a case of less than two years, and others speak of months."

"The next class of evidence is the medical testimony, and this requires careful consideration. The first witness was Dr. Marshall, who attended from 1886 to September 1897, who says that he had attacks approaching delirium tremens about every six months, and he noticed a gradual breaking down of his health; and he speaks of times when the testator was afraid of being poisoned, and heard voices, and he did not consider him of sound mind. During the time he was attending him, he was called in about twenty times. In all of them, he was always suffering under the influence of liquor, but when sober, he was sensible enough. This evidence refers to the general results of intoxication. All the indications he mentions are clearly due to drinking and not necessarily to insanity, for he says he talked sensibly enough when he was sober." Instead of disposing of them as they arose, counsel agreed that York, who attended the testator in January 1900. He says he was in bed, more or less delirious. The testator had an alcoholic heart, and his speech was incoherent and unintelligible. His mental condition was weak, and he was suffering from alcoholic dementia, which must have been of some years' standing. His examination occurred very shortly before his death, and he certified the cause of death was meningitis, which usually does not last longer than two weeks, and in the case of the testator, it lasted five to seven days; and the symptoms might equally relate to alcoholic monomania, or alcoholic dementia. The latter is a form of insanity from which persons do not recover, and a person suffering from it is incapable of managing business affairs; his judgment is poor and his memory impaired, and he could not comprehend business transactions at all." The judge then commented about a third doctor, Dr. Janeway "Dr. Janeway's standing is, in my opinion, far more important that of Dr. Culbert or Dr. Dumond. He does not diagnose the case as alcoholic dementia, which the other two doctors do in explicit terms, but he says you might call it so, and yet he hoped he might entirely recover. He, therefore, looked upon the recovery as possible if his physical strength kept up. This evidence therefore, is completely at variance with the other medical witnesses. The symptoms, which both doctors speak of, are consistent with other forms of disease arising not only from alcohol but also from other affections of the brain. Dr. Buckley saw him in 1893, said he was semi-idiotic from drink, and had Bright's disease. The latter complaint is denied by all of the medical men who attended him. This statement must arise from lapse of memory or from a mistake in his diagnosis.

Dr MacDonald, an expert was brought into the case to examine all the medical evidence. He came to the conclusion that Alexander Dunsmuir was suffering from alcoholic dementia and mental symptoms do not differ from other forms of dementia. He admitted that a man suffering from alcoholic dementia could not understand the nature and extent of his property, for the disease blunts the capacity of understanding. It might not be noticeable by ordinary laymen, yet in the early stages he could do business. Transact important business, make suggestions, and sign checks, yet be mentally incompetent. This expert testimony is of little value. If a man can transact important business yet be mentally incompetent it is a contradiction in terms which I cannot appreciate."

He then added, "If mental incompetency arising from disease exists it would show itself, more especially when his faculties are engaged in deciding very important matters. If he is capable of deciding important business he is capable of making a will. Men are not all formed with the same mental faculties, and yet if Dr. MacDonald is correct, a man of feeble intellect, yet showing no mental derangement, is still incompetent to manage business matters."

I disagree with the judge's decision based on this. I believe that James Dunsmuir knew of his brother's condition and made sure that his brother was full of liquor before he approached him with the will. The judge is assuming that Alexander was in his sober state, as he usually was at times of important matters. Everyone knows that alcoholics are not always dependable when it comes to times of importance, such as being sober. It may have been true of most occasions of his work, but of matters of the will, I believe that James found his brother's weak spot, booze, and used it to get at his part of the fortune. Edna's witness, former fiancé Edward Crowninshield, presented James' display of selfish greed in the courtroom. Crowninshield spoke of James's disregard for Alexander's remains by requesting a cheap casket and complaining about the cost of transporting his remains on the train. One would think that a reasonable judge could clearly see that James had little concern for the welfare of Josephine and much concern for the cost of his brother's burial.

A kind woman named Drew Waveryn had sent me a photograph of the gravesite of Alexander and Josephine at Mountain View Cemetery. They are buried in what is called "Millionaire's Row" in what is considered to be one of the most beautiful cemeteries in North America. Drew is a member of a cemetery society. Along with the photos she had sent, she wrote a letter that upon her visit to the cemetery, she was particularly interested in seeing the Dunsmuir plot, as Drew is from Victoria, BC, and has a fascination for the Dunsmuir legacy. As she walked past one grand monument more beautiful than the next, it was to her shock and disappointment that she came upon the Dunsmuir plot. A small, inexpensive footstone with the name DUNSMUIR sits on the ground. I expressed to Drew that I am not at all surprised. Drew said that one would think James could have at least given his brother and his wife a decent burial monument, since he took possession of more than ten million dollars of their money. I then wondered why Edna never placed a better stone at her beloved mother's resting place, as I know how much she adored her. Is it possible that something happened to the gravesites of Josephine and Alex Dunsmuir? Could this have happened after Edna's burial there? I am not sure at this point and have not investigated this subject. The more I thought of it, the more I am convinced the reason is that Edna believed in the importance of the test of time. Here lies proof of what she was trying to say in court - James wanted to possess what was her mother's and had no concern for Alexander's wishes either. James was possessed by greed.

My investigation and examination of trial reports and trial transcripts included several thousand pages of testimony. Somehow mysteriously, I would stop the microfilm reader at certain points where Edna was transmitting crucial messages across the courtroom towards the judge. Somehow and for possibly some reason, it appears that the judge either seemed to have disregarded these messages or intentionally wanted to conclude that they were irrelevant to the case at hand. In either fashion, I personally see it more inclined that the judge was favoring the premier justice while keeping the integrity of his diseased brother by masking over the inclinations of sexual abuse and or sexual play between the plaintiff and her "not then" father-in-law. This was done by throwing out unrelated questions either by the defendant's attorney or by the court itself.

The sexual abuse card being played by Edna was something I think she decided upon, outside of any of her legal team's prior knowledge. Perhaps the deep underlying reason to claim his fortune was for payback? I don't think Edna had that type of soul. I think she wanted the fortune to go to the child that came from him. Perhaps the child also came from her womb. This would be a most embarrassing situation for this star of the stage to have her dirty laundry hanging out there for everyone in the world to see. Edna tried, in the shrewdest means, to send messages to the judge with the hope that he could understand the events of her life that she was trying to project into his mind's eye.

All the while, Miss Hopper had in mind that any word of sexual abuse could and most likely would ruin the future of her career. What her adoring fans felt about her was always important to Edna. However, Edna fought for what she felt she had to do, at a risk of losing her career on stage.

The results of the trial in British Columbia did not make Edna give up. She had a trial going in California, and when she lost that one as well, she took the case to the British Privy Court in London. Once again, she lost, and the legal fees cost her well over a million dollars.

Later on in the years ahead, Edna would never forget her mother's loss and disappointment over the Dunsmuir inheritance outcome. She would find another way of gaining richness from what her mother gave her: a secret knowledge of how to remain youthful and how to become more beautiful.

PEERING MYSTERIOUSLY THROUGH THE CHICAGO & ALTON RAILROAD SCHEDULE IN 1904, THE AUTHOR BELIEVES EDNA MAY HAVE HAD AN AFFAIR WITH THE OWNER OF THE ILLIONIS THEATER IN 1904. HIS YOUNG DIVA OPERA STAR WIFE HAD A SUDDEN AND MYSTERIOUS DEATH IN THE FOLLOWING YEAR (1905)

Chapter Six
1906 to 1913

1906

MAD MAX: The Obsessed Attraction of the Trodden Worm

It appeared that one Maxwell W. Hildebrandt, a cello player with the orchestra of several shows starring Edna, was obsessed with the little songstress/ actress to the point where the police broke into his apartment to capture and arrest him.

After four years of being stalked night and day and haunted by the obsessed and crazed fan, she finally had an order of restraint put upon him. Nevertheless, Hildebrandt still sent her about 150 letters, cards, and telegrams per week while camping out in front of her West Side apartment by day and by night. It started while she was performing in Florodora at the Casino, and he was playing in the orchestra.

Upon breaking into his apartment, the short, fat, red-haired, bearded German cellist was in the middle of pleasuring himself while kneeling in front of an altar made to his goddess Edna. On the altar were personal items that he had stolen from time to time from her backstage dressing room, amongst a multitude of lit candles. On the walls, the police noticed 114 photographs of Edna and painted cupids along with arrow-pierced hearts. From this day onward, he was to be known as Mad Max, a name created by the press.

On March 1st, 1906, Mad Max was arraigned in Jefferson Market court and charged with persecuting the little actress.

Wonderful was the love of Max W. Hildebrandt for Edna Wallace-Hopper. All the burning passions of the age of fable rolled into one grand symphony would be a wistful pipe of oboe compared to the thundering of the brass that echoes in the heart of the fat cellist. He was willing to go to a thousand prisons and languish in the profoundest dungeons rather than tear from his breast the shower of Cupid darts that impaled him. The actress came to court accompanied by C. W. Boykin, manager of her current musical company, "The Heart of Maryland". On the other side of her costar was Wallace Ettinger, a tall, blond, and handsome actor.

When the musician saw her, he cried, "Here she comes, I will embrace her." He lunged for her with outstretched arms, tripping over the fat policeman, who involuntarily sat down upon her.

"Oh, Mercy!" cried Miss Hopper as she saw the love-hungry man advancing towards her. "Take him away, what awful eyes he has! And those terrible whiskers! Why doesn't he shave?" Then she half-swooned in the arms of her co-star. Seeing the handsome actor supporting her, the cellist cried out, "Ah, that villain, I will crush him!"

When asked by Magistrate Walsh, who was representing her, she replied, "I am my own attorney, and I will conduct my own case," as she drew herself up. Edna explained to the judge that she was to act as her own attorney against her annoyance in this case, putting him under a $500 bond to keep the peace for three months. The judge smiled, and the crowd in the courtroom craned their necks to get a glimpse of her. Quite a scene was made of this chilly unfolding of events by the obsessed and crazed fan.

An attorney named O'Meara appeared for the passion-smitten man and urged Magistrate Walsh to discharge him, stating that he was harmless.

"I will never consent to it," said Miss Hopper. "Why, he annoys me to death with his letters and telegrams. Some of the letters are such that no lady should read. I left them at home, but have brought with me a few hundred others that are not quite so bad". She opened a sachet and piled up a mound of letters before the court. There were over 20,000 of them that were sent within the past few years.

These are some of the expostulatory love expressions that the magistrate read before holding the cellist under a $500 bond to keep the peace:

My Dear Mrs. Edna Wallace Hildebrandt,

If a wish could stand for a fact, the above would not only be a supposition. After nearly four years' pursuit of you on my part and many acts and writings based wholly on supposition, this would not be an unfamiliar strain. You have threatened me with arrest, but I am not very much afraid, because you are in another State. Besides, I have prepared myself by taking a ride on the college point ferryboat and taking a look at Riker's Island, which I helped to fill in four years ago.

Yours lovingly

MAX WALLACE HILDEBRANDT

Another one read: My Dear Sweetheart-

As I sat and looked at your picture hanging over my writing table, to me an altar where I kneel and pray, I wonder if you have received my last letter. I was riding down to the Brooklyn Bridge yesterday, and a beautiful young lady sat beside me. Her furs brushed me, I opened the book I was reading and put in my card so that she could see who I was, and then she hummed some music (here the cellist has written several bars of "It Was Not Like This In The Olden Days"). Her hat was white and black, and the back of her dress had an open space held together by some netting, through which could be seen also a part of an undergarment that had a blue stripe along the edge. Let me know if it was you. You know, actresses look so different off the stage. In adoration, your trodden worm.

MAXEY P.S. Is it true that you were engaged to marry a society man named Gallatin at the time I asked you to send me a check for $500?

Edna laughed as she presented to the Court a postcard bearing a photograph of a musician standing in a rapturous pose, raising his hat and bowing while he made goo-goo eyes. He had written on the card, "To my Eddie- Eby from Her Trodden Worm, Maxey".

On another card, he expressed that he had shaved. "The Trodden Worm" wrote: "You know how Delilah got the best of Samson. She made him shave. That's what I have done".

Throughout the trial, Edna had expressed that for four years the dumpy musician had sighed and languished. He had turned out love missives with the industry of a duplex press. He had scorched the wires with passion telegrams, used up tons of postcards, bought a dagger with which to slay himself, and madly challenged Wallace Ettinger, who made stage love to Miss Hopper in "The Heart Of Maryland", to a duel.

The climax was reached two days before the trial when Edna received twenty special delivery letters, ten telegrams, and two pounds of postcards from Max. On the same day, Mr. Ettinger got five postcards, all of which were pictured with skulls and crossbones, a letter containing four suggestive bullets, and a challenge to a duel.

Miss Hopper told her story with directness. She said that the defendant had annoyed her with letters and had dogged her footsteps. She wanted the annoyance stopped. On the prior Monday, he had hung about the doorway of her house all day, having come there at noon, again in the afternoon, and a third time at midnight.

O'Meara moved for the discharge of his client on the ground that the complaint was dated February 27th, and that there was no specific offense charged on that day. Miss Hopper arose and dramatically shouted, "He will not be discharged!"

Magistrate Walsh assured the actress-turned-lawyer that the defendant would not be discharged, and she became calm again.

She told the judge that she did not want to subject the man to any unnecessary hardship, but the annoyance must cease.

She won a long trial, having the "poor fat slob" put away for life behind bars. No insanity excuses for this defendant. After she had won the case, she proposed to the defendant's attorney that if he was sent to Bellevue to have his sanity inquired into, she would withdraw the charge of disorderly conduct, but this was refused, and as the defendant was unable to produce the bonds, he was sent to the island for a long period of time in which he could think the matter over.

So many wonderful, odd, and funny stories made their way into the newspapers.

For example, Edna needed to open a show in Seattle in the winter. There was a blizzard that froze up the train tracks and shut down the rail travel in New York. As this was a time when passenger air travel did not exist, Edna woke up a stunt pilot who owned an open two-seater airplane, and begged him to take her to Seattle from New York. "Impossible! Are you out of your mind?" he said. She somehow convinced him to do it. They flew into a snowstorm with all odds against survival on a blustery evening. The stunt pilot recalled how horrific it was to him and yet how Edna was quite amused as the plane dipped, dropped, and did loop deloops. Each time, he could hear her howling with laughter like a child on an amusement park ride. They not only survived the journey, but they broke a world record, taking the highest and longest flight on record. Flying over 4,000 feet above the Sierra Nevada Mountains and covering a distance from New York to Seattle, nonstop! Needless to say, hundreds attended the show just to get a glimpse of the survivor of this feat.

In a London newspaper sometime in the early 1900s, there was an article printed that was not intended to be funny but is historically significant today. Edna had decorated her London flat with furnishings and décor from her travels to the Far East. She wanted the look and feel of being in the Far East to the extent that she included rare birds, porcelain, rugs, and paintings. As she felt something was missing, she had a baby elephant shipped to England, where it resided in her lavish, aristocratic upper-level flat. The article went on to explain that the residents of her building made formal complaints of the plaster falling and chandeliers crashing down as the elephant made his way across the floor, as well as complaints of droppings left on the marble grand stairs and dwellers on the street also complained to police that Edna was not picking up the large droppings left on the walkways of the street after she did her daily walks with the baby elephant.

There was another occasion of Edna purchasing a rectory of a church in New York and wearing clergy like black and white custom-designed fashions that resembled bishops and priests. This was in protest of the injustice of the underpaid actresses on Broadway who were thrown out of their rentals as landlords were unfair to them and disrespected them. Edna actually traded her deluxe brownstone home to the clergy for their rectory.

"The Three Graces" in Chicago. By August, she appeared in "About Town" at the Lew Fields Theater once again in a male role, this time as a Dutch boy named "Little Dutch", then as Winthrop Duxbury in "The Great Divide".

EDNA AS LITTLE DUTCH IN "ABOUT TOWN"

Later in the year 1911, she did a tour in George M. Cohan's "Fifty Miles from Boston" and sang along with Cohan.

By this time, the last appeals of the Hopper VS Dunsmuir case were exhausted. The will of Alexander Dunsmuir was upheld in London. James retained his brother's shares of the fortune while his mother and his sisters received nothing. Edna, however, had possession of the San Leandro estate, but after paying off the debts from some of the repossessions, the taxes and bills due were hardly worth the rent that was being collected from the Hellman family. The wealthy Hellman family, who owned Wells Fargo Bank of San Francisco, had been the tenants for several years and had the highest bid of $50,000 when Edna put up the estate at auction. The sale price of $500,000 was only one-quarter of its value in 1906, worth at least $2,000,000.

Edna's feeling was now to dispose of the whole terrible memory of failure and defeat, to claim what she felt was her mother's right to the Dunsmuir fortune, and Edna's right, as her mother had passed away. The mansion and estate represented a living dream that Josephine never got to live, a fairy tale life that never really existed. Happily ever after never came. Edna had lost Josephine, her dearest and most beloved family member. The blood, sweat, and tears of four years in trial after trial, not to mention the financial loss of well over one million dollars in court costs, was something that she wanted to close as a chapter in her life. At this date of 1906, this was the most expensive court case in British Columbia as well as California. Still today, Hopper VS Dunsmuir is the longest-running trial in the history of British Columbia.

The closure to this saga was padded by Edna's preoccupation with her continuing success on the stage, along with her optimistic outlook on life in general. At this point in her life, she was one of the highest-paid actresses, if not the highest-paid actress, in American theater. In the early 1900s, Edna had made wage demands that no other actress would or could ever dare to. Her demands were met, and then some!

1908

After fifteen years of popularity, the comic opera would die out as the musical comedy hit the stage. Light opera had a distinct European flavor, based solely on romance. In the operetta, the music and the story blend together. In musical comedy, the story and the score may totally ignore each other or send the scenes wildly from one place to another. Comedy in musical comedy was heavier. The musical comedy was born, and its roots were American, unlike the operetta, which was of European origin.

Before 1908, Edna met and fell in love with Albert Oldfield Brown, a Wall Street stockbroker who owned his own brokerage firm. Better known as A.O. Brown, he had come through a disastrous Wall Street failure. His brokerage firm had floundered. Under the guidance and encouragement of Edna, A.O. Brown had stepped out of the stock market world and entered the theatrical business. A.O. became the manager of the William A. Brady Playhouse and secretary of the Playhouse Corporation. It was there he made many friends in the theater business and was made the Shepherd of The Lamb's Club.

Ironically, the same New York actor's club was once organized years beforehand by Edna's ex-husband, DeWolf Hopper.

In November 1908, Edna married A.O. Brown. At the time, Miss Hopper was appearing in a play that was scheduled to go on the road with "Fifty Miles from Boston" by George M. Cohan and co-starring Cohan. Their honeymoon was spent traveling with the show. According to Mrs. Hopper Brown, "A.O. became tired of this mode of living and when they had been on the road for three months, he left the play and returned to his home in New York". Brown had no desire to leave the city, for any reason or anyone, including his new wife, Edna.

1910 Trapped on the River

On June 12th, 1910, the New York Times reported that Edna Wallace Hopper Brown and her husband, A. O. Brown, were trapped for over ten hours on a Friday night on a thirty-three-foot launch, an open racing boat that was stuck on a rock in Little Hell Gate in the East River of New York. It was owned by Mr. Parker, an electrical businessman on Madison Avenue. The Browns were trapped along with Mr. Parker and his wife, Laura Guerite, an actress who had been recently seen in "The Girl Behind the Counter". The fifth person on the launch was John Shriner, who was Mr. Parker's chauffeur and motor boat engineer. Edna, the actress, Laura, and the three men spent the entire night in a downpour while the launch was leaking badly. Signals for help brought no response, and they had to wait for daylight to be rescued.

Everyone on board spent the night pumping the water out of the leaky craft while wondering if they could keep her up until daybreak. According to Mr. Parker, "We expected to be back home for dinner. My wife and I came over in the launch, named the Laura G., from Flushing Bay on Friday afternoon to see the ball game at the Polo Grounds, Shriner attending to the engine of the boat. Leaving Flushing Bay, we ran through Little Hell Gate without any trouble, on up the East River and into the Harlem to the ball grounds."

"There, we picked up Mr. Brown and his wife. The bad luck that fell on the Giants also extended to us. We started back shortly before 6 o'clock with the tide running out. I learned today that the reason we got through Little Hell Gate early, which we happened to pass when the tide was at its flood. The passage is so filled with rocks that it is dangerous to pass there at any time. I know that now, but didn't on Friday." He went to say, "When we started back through the passage, the tide was ebbing. The forward end of the boat slipped over a rope that extends all the way across Little Hell Gate and then ran on a rock a few inches under the water. There we were, with the forward end stuck across the passage, we supposed, by a party of Government dredgers as work at that point."

"The shock of the collision sprang a leak in the bottom of the launch

"

and also put the engine out of commission. We had two pumps, and two of us began pumping the water while the rest tried to attract the attention of the dredgers, who were not more than 300 feet away. They saw us, but made no effort to come out to us. We supposed afterward that the passage at low tide was too dangerous for a rowboat."

Despairing of getting any help from the dredge, they tied the end of the launch to the rope that ran across the gate and prepared to wait until daylight. They all put on life savers and took turns at the two pumps as best as they could. From time to time, they would make noise in the hopes that someone might hear them.

"The first part of the night, we worked in water almost up to our knees. Then shortly after midnight, it began to rain. The launch is an open racing boat. We had no protection whatever from the rain."

The downpour kept up until after daylight. The air was chilly after midnight. "We were chilled to the bone, wet through, and tired out when the time came in at one o'clock. We could have gotten the boat off the rock, but we were afraid to stir the boat until daylight." Both Edna and Miss Guerite took turns at the pumps during the night.

Daylight finally came, in what seemed like a few hundred years to the tired, cold, and helpless five on board. They cut loose the rope between Randall's Island and Ward's Island. They used some pieces of boards as paddles, and paddled their way to Flushing Bay, and from there to the home of J. Parker at Elmhurst. Edna and Laura were put to bed. They were seen by a physician and treated for shock. According to Mr. Parker, they almost recovered the night before, although they remained in bed to rest.

Mr. Parker told the New York Times, "It was a horrible night. I never went through another such ten hours in all my life. Mind you, we never had a bite to eat, not even a drink. Besides that, it was dark and stormy."

1912 to 1917: The Browns

Through the years leading up to 1912, Edna had played in several dramas and musical reviews. Whenever a show demanded her services outside of New York, she was forced to make the trip alone. After four years of this, his attitude culminated in a state of desertion. By 1913, they were separated.

Little is known about the relationship between Albert O. Brown and Edna Brown, and Edna seems to play a role reversal as Albert gains an interest in theater and transitions from the stock market into owning and managing a theatrical company, while Edna takes on an interest in trading with the stock market. Much was learned from each other as both found their new career interest to be successful as well as enjoyable. A scandal was played out in the newspapers regarding a car that was given to Edna while A.O. Brown had declared bankruptcy.

The musical comedy takes a back burner to the revue of vaudeville. Edna does a tour in musical revues and sings medleys from her past performances, and does some new song and dance numbers.

Her marriage to A. O. Brown continued until around 1913, when they seemed to have separated. It had been generally understood that Brown and Miss Hopper had been divorced, and rumors of her respective marriage to a duke, a wealthy man, and others had been published from time to time. Years later, Edna and Brown would declare that they had never been divorced.

Edna's second husband, Albert O. Brown, had an on-again and off-again romantic love affair during their many years of marriage until his death. Many had thought that they were divorced, but in reality, they never did get divorced, only separated several times. Oddly, as Edna's first husband, DeWolf Hopper, was called The Shepherd (of The Lamb's Club), so too was A.O. Brown called The Shepherd.

1914

Fame, Fortune & Beauty Interrupted

Edna had returned to Paris, enjoying the sweet life of fame and fortune. Her plans were to meet with scientists and doctors to concoct beauty aids for herself and her close friends, just as she had done with Josephine on their many trips to France, Germany, and Austria together. Her love of France and her devout interest in the scientific studies being done there for beauty aids had made her decision to take up residence there for a while. Her plan was to temporarily stay to meet with the French doctors and scientists on ways and means of total beauty and care. By 1914, these studies and aids, or "helps" as they were called, were not being much produced in America. By 1914, Edna Wallace Hopper was 54 years old and evermore concerned with fostering and enhancing her beauty and youthful appearance. France was the answer.

In her own words, "French women started years before us (Americans), and forced their ablest scientists to help. Beauty is almost universal with the city girls of France and old-looking women are curiosities. "Lantelme, queen of Parisian beauties, gave me some wondrous helps."

Then came the interruption. The Great War had started. It was only a matter of time until a reason materialized. Each country had built up its military. There are no quick answers as to what started the First World War. The causes are as complex as they are varied.

It all started in the summer of 1914. At this time, no one had any idea of how big this "war" would become. The mere term "war" was considered a quick and decisive action that would take a few months at most to complete. It would not be until 1918 that, in hindsight, the entire series of events would be seen as World War I.

On June 28, 1914, the assassination of the Austrian-Hungarian heir, Archduke Fray Ferdinand, and his wife Sophie took place in Sarajevo. Paranoia among countries ran rampant. This single event of the assassination can be seen as the spark that lit the kindling. A secret society called The Black Hand took credit for the assassination. Later on in this story of Edna's life, you will see a connection between this secret society and one that surrounds Edna's life at a later time.

The military, the political leaders, and the general public all believed that once the war machine was set in motion, it could not be stopped. Mobilization became synonymous with a declaration of war, not a precursor to it.

This was a war of many facets. It basically started as a war of economics. Germany was unified under Bismarck, a revolution was beginning in Russia and Great Britain, and Europe was split by complex diplomatic and military alliances having to do with economics and defense. This had caused a chain reaction.

Germany at that time was the industrial giant. Britain launched the HMS Dreadnought, which was seen as a threat to Germany. This sparked the great arms race. Germany wanted to be on equal footing economically with the British.

No one was safe.

For the next eighteen months, Edna's preoccupation with fame and beauty care would be interrupted. She would become an anonymous face in the crowd, blending in with all the others in the scenes of the Great World War. She put aside her career and high lifestyle and was the first American woman to give herself to France. She volunteered to be a nurse with the British Red Cross, behind the firing lines of France. In her own words, she wrote, "In 1914, when the Great War came, I was the first American woman to offer her services to France. I served her until the war's end. And largely because I owed to France so much." (Edna is referring to owing credit to France for helping her gain beauty and retain her youth.)

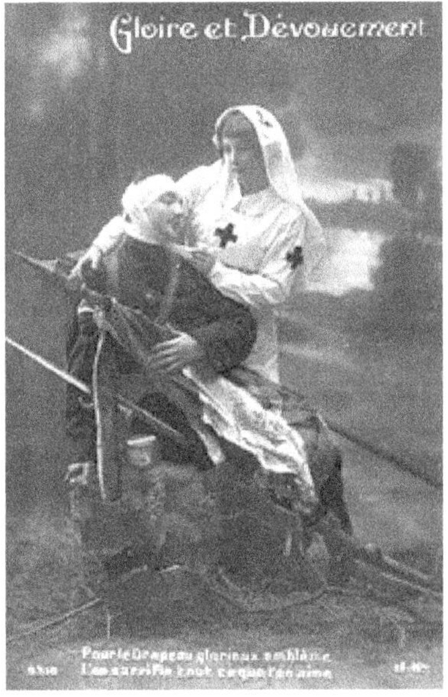

Edna expressed that if it were not for the French doctors and scientists, as well as the French specialists, who showed her and her mother the ways and means of making oneself more beautiful and slowing down the aging process.

During the war, Edna worked tirelessly day and night to heal and comfort the sick, the wounded, and the dying soldiers. Although she had assisted her stepfather's illness for many years, the energy she had exerted now seemed minute compared to the amount she was giving for the multitude of patients she now tended to.

The French motto was "Let the last man on the right brush the channel with his sleeve". Schlieffin's last words were, "Keep the right wing strong". The French plan was based on the notion of élan, the utter spirit to win. "The will to conquer is the first condition of victory". "Offensive to the maximum!" was the French command.

However, the French plan was flawed. The French army was led south, away from where the brunt of the German attack would come. On August 3, 1914, less than a week after Germany declared war on France, the 137th marched out of its garrison at Fontenay-le-Conte in Western France. During its first month in the field, it received the Legion d'Honneur for capturing the commander of the 28th German Infantry Regiment. The 137th regiment was made up of men from the Vendée region of France. They were known for their stubbornness and loyalty. The Vendée was the last to be under the control of the new Republic after King Louis XVI was guillotined during the French Revolution. Some of France's next tenacious fighters were to look to Edna for their care and comfort.

The 137th captured the battle flags of the 68th German Infantry Regiment and successfully pushed the Germans back across the Meuse River. However, Colonel Jules Armand Georges de Marailles was mortally wounded. His last words were, "I shall die in peace, my soldiers have proved their valor…

Praise God… Vive la France."

Germany's plan was called the Schlieffen Plan. This plan, named after Count Alfred Von Schlieffen, was a reaction to the German notion of encirclement. Any war for Germany would be a two-front war. The plan was for a quick 42-day victory over France before its ally, Russia, could complete its mobilization. This would allow Germany's army to concentrate all forces to the east in order to crush its second enemy, Russia.

Germany used four armies, a total of one million men, to form the arc.

The motto was "Let the last man on the right brush the channel with his sleeve".

Schlieffen's last words were, "Keep the right wing strong!"

The French Plan was based on the notion of élan, the utter spirit to win. "The will to conquer is the first condition of victory."

"Offensive to the maximum!"

The French plan was, nevertheless, flawed. The French army was led south, away from where the brunt of the German attack would come. The British Red Cross set up camps just outside the firing lines. The wounded that Edna had treated were the foot soldiers who fought with bayonets, the men known as "bombers", who were trained in throwing grenades, victims of poison gas, those who fell victim to machine gunners, and the victims of the brave patrols who were sent out in NO MAN'S Land, the name of the area between the trenches. The Germans had the best trench system. They even had running water and electricity in the bunkers up to and down to sixty feet below the surface. In the bunkers where the Red Cross Medical was located, Edna could hear the planes shooting down other aircraft and the sound of bombs hitting the earth. This was a sound more dramatic than any operetta she had performed in. Her years of assisting Josephine with Alexander's unending illness seemed to now have paid-off.

Suddenly, all her prior life and past efforts seemed insignificant to the events of the present moment. Her duty to France, Great Britain and America was now all that mattered. One would wonder whether the wounded soldiers had found a release of joy in recognizing the famous star attending to their needs. Perhaps she even sang to some of them. This, I am not certain of, but it would seem most probable.

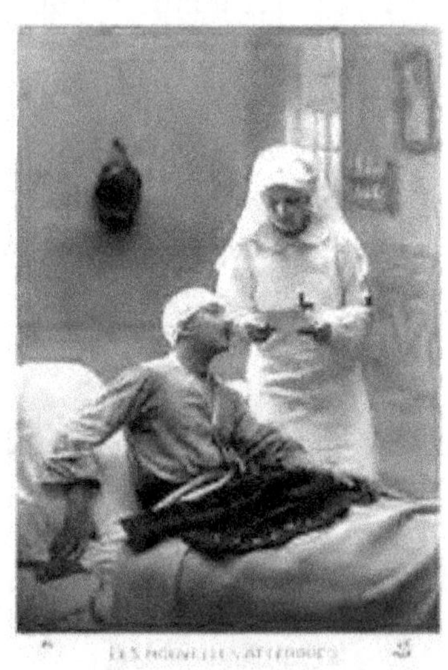

On May 1, 1915, Charles Frohman took his actors and actresses aboard the Lusitania on her 101st voyage from New York to Liverpool, England. That Saturday morning was gloomy and misty as Charles took a cab from his residence at the Knickerbocker Hotel suite and stopped at his office in the Empire Theater, which he had owned since it opened with Edna in The Girl I Left Behind Me. There, he dictated a note to playwright Porter Emerson Browne that read: 'Goodbye. Keep me posted. To his friend, the actor Paul Potter, he had left a note, in case they would miss each other at the pier, at the hotel, which read: 'It's fine of you to come to the steamer with all these dark, sad conditions'. However, Potter was there at Pier 54. As they walked on board, Potter asked, "Aren't you afraid of the U-boats, C.F.?" Appearing much older than he actually was, a forty-eight-year-old Frohman had developed a severe case of painful articular rheumatism and walked slowly with a cane that he called his 'wife'. CF smiled and replied, 'No, my dear Paul, only of the IOU's.' It was as if Frohman had a premonition of the tragedy which was about to happen, yet somehow was at peace in accepting this fate. He was warned, as many others were as well, that he was taking a risk of passing through the dangerous waterway to England. Just before leaving his permanent suite at the Knickerbocker Hotel on Broadway and 42nd Street, he received a telegram from actor and friend John Drew that read, "I'll never forgive you if you get blown up by a submarine." Frohman even had telegrams sent to him while on board, warning him not to continue. He ignored the warnings. That morning, the New York newspaper reporters had spread a rumor that Frohman had secretly married Maude Adams, who was now his leading actress. Their relationship, whatever it was, had been something quite special, for he had groomed her for the stage since she was the age of twenty, and had appeared in Frohman's production of The Little Minister, written by J.M. Barrie. Barrie later had written Peter Pan, and when other producers had thought of it as theatrical madness, Frohman believed it to be otherwise. He cast Maude Adams as Peter Pan, making theatrical history while making a fortune for Barrie, Miss Adams, and himself.

By 1915, Charles Frohman had produced more than 700 shows, had employed over 700 actors paying over $25,000 per week in salaries, and was known as the great importer and exporter of shows between the American and London stages. C.F., as his friends called him, was a private man who encouraged the actors he had managed to live their lives privately as well, staying out of the media's attention off stage. The impresario avoided openings of his shows, fashionable restaurants, and public haunts as much as possible. Whenever one of his new shows would have an opening performance, he would send someone to check it out and then have the person secretly meet him in his office or his hotel room to give him the review. Frohman was managing the top stars of America, such as John Drew, Ethel Barrymore, Edna May, Maude Adams, and Nat Goodwin, as well as the stars of England's stage: Marie Tempest, George du Maurier, Seymour Hicks, and Ellaline Terriss. Charles owned and managed the largest and the finest of theaters on New York's Broadway and five theaters in London, including the Duke of York's repertory theater, which he had founded.

Fortunately, the season of 1914 to 1915 saw the revival of friendship between the impresario/producer Frohman and the great writer/producer David Belasco. Although they had not spoken to each other for twelve years, the kind-hearted Frohman would send wire telegrams of friendly gesture for openings and anniversaries. Together again, they co-produced a vintage melodrama with an all-star cast called The Celebrated Case. It opened on April 7, 1915, at his grand Empire Theater. This reunion of friendship was long-awaited by many who knew the two great men.

Frohman's trip to London on the Lusitania was not part of his regular London and Paris 'play market' trips, usually scheduled in the fall season. This spring, he made a special trip to attend the invitational opening of his friend's new show, James Barrie's Rosy Rapture, the pride of the Beauty chorus, at the St. Martin's Lane Theater in London. From there, it was to open at Frohman's Duke of York Theater on the following Saturday.

Since November 1914, the English Channel had been blocked off. In December, Germany used the submarine U-boat. By the winter of 1915, Germany rationed its food. A war of position was critical. Germany had fewer than 30 U-boats. Tracking where they were was an issue. The area of Ireland was declared a war zone. "Vessels flying the Great Britain flag, beware" was the warning in May of 1915. U-boat 20 was heading toward Liverpool. British code breakers sent a message that U-20 was safely submerged in the waters of the southern coast of Ireland. The U20 then went out into the Atlantic Ocean for five days. The Lusitania had lifeboat drills daily. On May 5th, two wireless messages were received: "Avoid Head Line Stere A Mid-Channel Course." Then, in the morning, the Lusitania entered the German war zone unknowingly. By the night of May 6th, the U20

headed out of the Irish Sea.

The night on May 6th on the Lusitania was festive. Concerts, recitals, and a grand dinner were held in 1st class. A Scottish tenor sang after dinner, and most of the passengers turned in for the evening. Many had talked about the waters they were in, but no one seemed overly concerned. Another telegraph 'Submarine Off Fast Net' was sent to Captain Turner as a warning by the Cunaird office. All men on deck were ordered. The U-boat was thought to be headed away. This was a fatal mistake of assumption.

May 7th was a beautiful day at sea with a blue sky. The midday meal was finished for the first seating in the luxurious gold and white dining saloon. Frohman had come from the luncheon with his usual lively group. He and some of his actor and actress friends had gone to the upper deck promenade. The Lusitania was to be home in Liverpool in just a few hours.

The U-boat had the liner in sight, and the Germans had thought of it as a future transporter of goods from Britain. This war was a war of economics, and so, a torpedo was fired upon the Lusitania at 2:10 PM. The torpedo was noticed by some of the crew as it approached and slammed into the hull. The second seating for lunch was in the dining room at that moment. Charles Frohman was on the upper deck, chatting with George Vernon, brother-in-law of actress Rita Jolivet. Captain Alick Scott, an English officer en route home from India, had joined them just as the torpedo struck. Frohman was calm as usual.

He lit a fresh cigar and, in a soft voice, said, "This is going to be a close call." Captain Scott started to run away, saying, "Stay there! I'll fetch you some life jackets."

Frohman said, "Why not stay here where you are, Captain Scott?" "We shall have more chance by staying here than rushing off to the boats."

Scott ignored his suggestion and rushed off. One of the survivors, actress Rita Jolviet, came up to the deck wearing a life jacket. When she asked Charles why he appeared to have no fear, he asked her calmly, "Why fear death?" "It is the most beautiful adventure in life." Rita later recalled how calm C.F. remained as he talked about the Germans and the war.

Captain Scott had returned with two life jackets, one for Frohman and one for Vernon. Frohman was reluctant, as Scott had fastened the life jacket on him, saying, "Now, Captain, you must get yourself a life jacket." Then Frohman smiled and puffed on his cigar. He leaned over the rail, looked out to the sea, and said ever so softly, "I didn't think they would do it."

Pandemonium struck out as the gigantic liner rolled to starboard. A lifeboat fiasco resulted. As full lifeboats could not take any more passengers, hundreds of desperate survivors flung themselves into the Irish Sea. The cries from those who were trapped in the caged elevators were stifled as the water swept into the B Deck level.

As if isolated from all the turmoil and tragedy, Charles Frohman stood by the sinking starboard rail, smoking his cigar. "Hold on to the rail, you will need your strength", he said to the terrified actress Jolivet. Then, as the great Lusitania lurched, Frohman quoted a line from Barrie's Peter Pan, "To die would be an awfully big adventure." This line came from a scene that Frohman had incorporated during the play's second great run in New York. Rita Jolivet, George Vernon, and Captain Scott stayed close to their friend C. F. It was 2:28 PM as they joined hands. Frohman had begun to speak the line from Peter Pan again, "To die would." when a green wave of water roared and came down the deck, bringing with it debris and dead bodies. The four were swept apart from each other. In less than twenty minutes, the ship was under.

It took two hours for the floating survivors to be rescued and sent to Queenstown Harbour. Two thousand were on board the Lusitania, 1198 had perished, and only 764 survived. One survivor had said that Charles Frohman had saved her life by giving her his life jacket. The Katrina, a Greek steamer, rescued Rita Jolivet. Her brother-in-law, Vernon, Captain Scott, and C.F. had perished.

Charles Frohman was dead, but his name and his legacy remained before the public. His brother, Daniel, wanted to have the impresario's name remembered by forming a company to manage his surviving stars.

Maude Adams, who was rumored to have secretly married Frohman, had decided to end her career with his death. Whatever kind of love was shared between them was now obvious. She made a few appearances later in the 1930s. She never married and died in 1953 at the ripe age of eighty.

Rita Jolivet married a wealthy Venetian count. Two years later, she made a Hollywood film, Lest We Forget, in memory of Charles Frohman. Like most theater actors, her film career was short-lived.

Up until the time of his death, Charles Frohman was the owner of the Empire Theater, the Criterion, the Lyceum, the Garrick, the Savoy, and the Knickerbocker in New York. He also owned and managed five theaters in London which include the Duke of York's, the Globe (where his London office was), the Alelphi, the Globe as well as managing the Vaudeville Theater in London. He also controlled over two hundred theaters throughout America and managed the careers of twenty-eight leading stars, paying out more than $35,000,000 a year in salaries to over ten thousand people on his payroll. He was responsible for the success of many stars, one of his first being a little actress named Edna Wallace Hopper.

He adored his stars. He coached them on how to be on stage and how to live their lives off stage, out of the limelight. Like a father, he showered them with gifts, flowers, and candy, and kind words of wisdom. Charles was a friend, a confidant, and an advisor to many a person.

As fate would have it, Edna would survive the war by being at the right place at the right time. In 1914, she turned down an offer to join Charles Frohman and his acting company in New York. Had she done so, she would have been on that ill-fated ship. Edna had also turned down a request to join the guests of the Titanic. In memory of her good fortune and survival, her friend and fellow actress Lillian Russel would ever after have flowers sent to Edna's ship cabin, with a silver ice pick placed in the bouquet and a card, which read, 'Just in case you need it.'

1916 The Photoplay

From 1895 through 1903, the moving picture was merely a sort of animated magic-lantern show seen in amusement halls called the Nickelodeon. Then, in 1903, the photoplay was born. This was the true beginning of the motion picture film strip. The films were originally sold to exhibitors, but by 1905, they were being rented through exchanges. One such salesman named Aitken would peddle the reels of film out of his suitcase from Nickelodeon to Nickelodeon. Aitken met John Freuler, who owned a picture theater in Milwaukee, and together they formed the Western. The Western, with headquarters in Chicago and branches in other cities, held the Lewis exchange of films and cast its lot with the independents. The General Film Company and the Motion Picture Patents Company took hold of the industry in 1911. Freuler and Aitken organized the Mutual Film Corporation. Aitken went to Wall Street as big money was now in films, and he was the evangelist. While Mutual was making its one-reel dramas and comedies, Aitken, along with Griffith, Sennett, and Ince, got together and formed Mutual Masterpieces, the first American-made multi-reel feature picture. At this time, the audience was unaware of the names of the producer, the director, or any of the actors of the photoplay. They were nameless.

By 1909, David Griffith was making one-reel films from a brownstone front house at 11 East 14th Street in New York City. His business was called Biograph. Mary Pickford was only known as the Biograph Blonde. She and Florence Lawrence, Mack Sennett, David Miles, and Bobby Harron were making $5.00 per day for their acting services. Then, Vitagraph was organized in Flatbush. In 1915, Aitken promoted a newly formed enterprise called the Triangle. The Triangle was owned by the big three: Griffith, Ince, and Sennett. The idea of the Triangle Company was to bring big-name stage stars from the theater to the photoplay media. The company was incorporated for five million dollars, and Aitken was president. He wanted to sign up all the available stars of Broadway, lease the Knickerbocker as a Broadway first-run house, and charge $2.00 ticket in a nationwide chain of theaters. This was at a time when the Nickelodeons were charging only five cents and ten cents. Triangle engaged Billie Birke, Raymond Hitchcock, Sir Herbert Beerbohm Tree, Eddie Foy, Dustin Farnum, Douglas Fairbanks, and DeWolf Hopper to leave the stage as theatrical speaking stars and come to the photoplay as silent actors in motion pictures.

DeWolf Hopper was offered $85,000 a year for a twelve-picture contract. The men and women of the California film colony were only making $25 to $150 per week for their labor as actors. Needless to say, when DeWolf arrived at the Los Angeles train station, he was not showered by a bed of roses by the fellow colony actors.

By this time, Marcus Lowe had opened the Royal Theater in Brooklyn, using $150,000 that he had made from his smaller shows. From there, Mr. Loew profited and ended up owning the most powerful string of picture and vaudeville houses in America. Vaudeville was now taking over the musical comedy market. Later on, Loew became president of Metro-Goldwyn.

In 1911, Cecil DeMille, Goldfish, Lasky, and Friend put up $15,000, and DeMille went westward and found a stable on Vine Street in a Los Angeles suburb called Hollywood, and the first of the Lasky pictures was made there, called "The Squaw Man". Back at the Lambs Club in New York, Lasky and Friend had signed up Dustin Farnum for the lead in "The Squaw Man".

Southern California was ideal for photoplay: Photographs need sunshine, long light hours, and very little rain. The actors would be up at the crack of dawn, on the lot in make-up by nine AM, and would work until sundown.

DeWolf Hopper's first moving picture was "Don Quixote". DeWolf had found his first experience of acting in film to be uncomfortable, hot, sweaty, confusing, and unpleasant. Scenes were not filmed in sequential order. Instead, a set was constructed and all pertinent scenes were done, and then the set was taken down to build another set. The actors had little idea of the storyline. As DeWolf had written, "The actor in the film is the creature of the director. In the pictures, He [director] dwarfs the players. They are puppets dancing at the end of strings to his piping, seldom knowing anything of the sequence of the story they are enacting and little of its sense, theirs not to reason why, theirs but to clown or cry when and as a megaphoned voice instructs them to".

"Don Quixote" took twelve weeks to film and was seven reels of film length. It was not a big success in the USA, but it was a success in Latin America.

From there and onward, DeWolf's film career floundered, as did all the other stage stars with the exception of Douglas Fairbanks and Mary Pickford. They did quite well in photoplay. Pickford had a contract for $150,000 a year with Famous Players. She was the highest-paid actress in films at the time.

Then Charlie Chaplin had arrived. His speech was unacceptable for the stage with his cockney accent, but the silent film was a perfect alternative to display his profound talent for expression. Chaplin broke Pickford's record when he signed a one-year contract for $670,000 to do twelve pictures with Mutual. Among the twelve is the classic silent film "Easy Street".

Mary Pickford was upset with her contract compared to Chaplin's, and the Famous Players offered her shares in the profits of her pictures as a settlement.

Like DeWolf and the many other greats of the stage, Edna Wallace Hopper's career in photoplay was unsuccessful.

In January of 1916, after serving eighteen months in the British Red Cross behind the firing line in France, Edna left France and returned to New York aboard the Lafayette. She began to work two days later at the studio of Equitable Motion Pictures Corporation on 52nd Street, where she had exhaustive tests that proved that her features were well adapted to film work. An especially elaborate film production was in the course of construction, and a cast of special strength was assembled to support the petite actress. Edna would do two films for World Equitable Players. World and Equitable had combined, and the dual releasing plan went into effect. The largest array of stage and screen talent was now under the control of World Film Corporation. While Frank Sheridan was sent off to Miami, Edna Wallace Hopper and Charles Ross were sent off to the mountains of Canada to film "Who Killed Simon Baird?" also named "By Whose Hand?" The first of the Equitable Motion Pictures Corporation's productions introducing three stars was released on the World Film program in April 1916. The three stars, Muriel Ostriche, Edna Wallace Hopper, and Charles J. Ross, were called into play for three difficult and intricate roles for a dramatic story collaborated on by two noted authors and playwrights. Rennold Wolf and Channing Pollock were responsible for five of the biggest hits Broadway had known by 1916. The interiors were shot in the 52nd Street studio, while the location shots were done in Canada.

The second World film Edna starred in was the melodrama "The Perils Of Divorce" along with Frank Sheridan. Miss Hopper played the injured and ever faithful wife who is separated from her rich husband and little daughter by her designing rival, who covets the wealthy John Graham, played by Sheridan. Photoplay Reviews read "Miss Hopper works valiantly in an impossible role through many tribulations to the happy ending. Some good night photography is shown, including a skating carnival with gorgeous fireworks, and Edna palpably ill at ease on her skates". As a melodrama in which the situations govern the characters and not the characters the situations, the five-part picture, directed by Edwin August, made very passable entertainment, although it was scarcely considered the type of photoplay to better the standing of the screen among thoughtful people. The moral tone was not considered objectionable, but instead considered a triumph. However, the story in material and treatment suggested nothing new or elevating. In the film, the husband and wife are an entirely devoted pair, despite a disparity in years, and the young wife's fondness for pleasures that are quite beyond her middle-aged husband, until a designing woman enters the household and deliberately plots trouble. Fortune favors her in the presence of Mason Tegars, a debonair man-about-town, who is in love with Constance, regardless of the barrier of matrimony. Everything works out according to the plans of the adroit schemer. Graham becomes secretly jealous, then openly jealous, and finally, confronted by seemingly undeniable evidence of guilt, he disrupts the happy family, and all the while, there was not the slightest cause for divorce. In the last part of the final reel, the home-wrecker, having taken as much of Graham's money as she needs, runs away with another man, leaving a note that clears Constance and makes possible a fond reunion.

For its variety in locations and the richness of its settings, the picture was highly recommended. The scenes of Edna at an ice-skating carnival at night were especially noteworthy. Constance (Edna) falls through a hole in the ice and is rescued by the man with whom her name is unfavorably linked. Scenes in a restaurant where the divorced wife is employed as a dancer, and those in a Chinatown dive, were also well presented.

February 19, 1916, Moving Picture World magazine read, "Miss Hopper plays Constance with considerable spirit, whereas Frank Sheridan is in danger of becoming too melodramatic".

After doing the two silent films in 1916, Edna's movie career was over. Like all the other great stage stars of the past, the movie business was not kind to their careers. Whether or not it was ended by her own will or if there simply was no place for her in photoplay is uncertain. A new breed of actors and actresses developed and shone on the silver screen. It was a new day in the entertainment world, but not the end of Edna as a celebrity and an entertainer.

Her resilience and perpetual comeback made her reinvent herself again. She was now to embark on a new frontier, the world of vaudeville, with a new image, a new face, a new act, and a new mission- revealing the secrets to the Fountain of Youth.

Equitable Film star Edna Wallace Hopper in 1916

Scene from a 1916 silent movie, THE PERILS OF DIVORCE, starring
Edna Wallace Hopper and Frank Sheridan by World Film Corporation
and William A Brady.

Silent movie "By Whose Hand?" was also named "Who Killed Simon Baird?" and starred Edna Wallace Hopper. Filmed by World Pictures in 1917 for Equitable Motion Pictures Corporation.

1917-1920

Rejuvenation: The Fountain of Youth

In 1917, Edna made a comeback to the performance she was most comfortable with, Broadway, after a long absence. The new and original musical comedy, "Girl O'Mine", had its first presentation on any stage at the Van Curier on Christmas afternoon, and it proved to be a very enjoyable and entertaining production. It is the girl-and-music production, and the girls and the music were pretty. There was a story of sufficient interest to hold attention without taxing the brain, along with some excellent comedy and clever dialogue, enough to make it a success. The scenes are all set in Paris just before the war. In a time when Americans were glad to see the war behind them, it was refreshing to see a show reflecting the gaiety of a time of gaiety in Paris before the war.

The Union Star newspaper reads, "The cast would be notable if for no other reason than it brings back to the stage Edna Wallace Hopper, who had not been in anything in recent years except silent drama." In this new musical comedy, Miss Hopper plays the part of a very chic French model named Lulu, and scores a wonderful success. Lulu is a lively little French girl with a penchant for flirtation and hats. As Edna sang her one song, "Camouflage", she did it delightfully with real French vim. Miss Hopper is just as dainty and artistic and beautiful as ever, and the consensus is that she is even more charming than when she had the world at her feet prior to her temporary retirement from the stage".

The successful show moved to the Bijou and the Times, January 29th, 1918 reads, "Edna Wallace Hopper was greeted by an audience that knew and liked her well, as well at the end as at the beginning of the comedy".

Historically, Elizabeth Marbury demonstrated women's ability in this new, managerial field. It would be years later until women would finally be equal to men as theatrical managers, directors, or producers. It is no wonder that the liberated would have her final show managed by a woman.

Edna may have lost the fortune that her mother had anticipated leaving behind for her. However, Josephine did leave Edna with something more valuable than all the riches of Alex's fortune. Her mother gave Edna the secrets to perpetual youth and beauty.

By 1918, Edna would realize this value and make her own fortune with this gift of knowledge. Since her last show, "Girl O' Mine" in 1918, Edna had decided that she would give up her stage career. This decision was partly due to the fact that she had done it for so long and because the parts for someone of her age were not quite there. She was about to embark on a new enterprise, marketing the Fountain of Youth and teaching America how to be as beautiful and as young as possible.

Photo from the private collection of Jim Alessio

Gorgeous, Glittery, Golden butterfly is Edna Wallace Hopper in her favorite frock of gold embroidered lace and silk. Photographed for Theater Magazine in 1916. Photo provided by Culver Service, East 42nd St., New York

Photo by Hixon Newman, circa 1923, Kansas City, MO. In a pose similar to a Maxfield Parrish art beauty. Edna is in her mid-sixties and looks amazingly like a youthful beauty of 20!

The Eternal Flapper Edna Wallace Hopper looked every bit of 16 years old, yet at the age of 65. Photo by Aveda in 1927.

The Eternal Flapper as advertised for her Ladies' Only Matinee. Here
she is, 63, and looks 19.

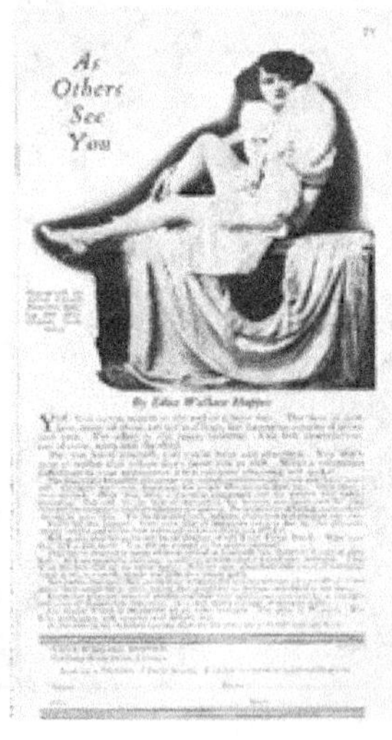

The Roar of the Twenties

At an age of 60, as she was in 1920, most women with fame and beauty would shave off as many years as they could get away with when stating how old they are, instead, Edna became a proud woman who wants to share her secrets of how she kept herself so young. Where it is more commonplace for a woman to conceal her age when she becomes older and in her youth to have the innocent freedom of revealing one's age with pride, the opposite was the circumstance for Edna. Through her youngest days of her twenties and into her thirties, she and her mother hid her true age, pretending that she was about 8 years or so younger. In fact, after the earthquake of 1906, a younger Edna was quoted saying, "No one will ever know (my true age), my birth records were destroyed in the San Francisco earthquake, just in case you have any ideas".

But now, in 1920, after seeing the ravages of war and the many changes of the times, a youthful surviving beauty decides to tell the world her true age- sixty. Most women, especially those of such fame and beauty, would shave off as many years to the true number as they could get away with. This was a proud woman who wanted to share her secrets of how she had kept herself so young and how she had enhanced her beauty in a way that would be most beneficial for other women as well as men. At the same time, she made it a profitable advantage for herself, perhaps a way of healing the wounds of losing her mother's inheritance by gaining fortune from the secrets she had given her. Since she and her mother had done so much research in Europe, Edna felt worthy of its profit, yet she charged the utmost minimum amount for her line of beauty "helps" she offered to share with the public. She was on a mission to help American women.

A quote from the News Bee, Los Angeles, July 21, 1922, reads, "I'm touring the country to impress on American women that they can, by taking care, extend the appearance and spirit of their teens over into their fifties and sixties. I use myself as an example, and my message is chiefly for the flapper to encourage her in her [sonable] vanity".

As to why she and her mother both kept her age a secret in her youth, I will tell you my theory in the last chapter of this book. What I can tell you is that there was a deeper, darker reason underneath it.

The second of her three careers was about to begin, as Edna was about to embark on a new journey, using live vaudeville and motion picture combined, bringing her act to the vaudeville theaters and the movie houses around the country, but before she was ready to go, a few things had to be done to make her show and sale a perfect success. Vaudeville was the biggest form of live entertainment at this time in 1920, and the moving picture show was a hot item as well. Edna would incorporate both in her act. She called it "Matinee For Ladies Only" which was billed "See Her in Bed-Bath-Exercise, in a most elaborate production including $5000 bath furnishings".

The effects of serving during the war had taken their toll on her appearance to a small degree, as she had not taken the care and maintenance that she would have if she had the time. For this, she would undergo an experimental medical procedure, called surgical rejuvenation, or as better known today, plastic surgery. Ironically, the procedure was first introduced during World War I, strictly for changing the physical appearance of some of the disfigured soldiers. And ironically, the stress and hard work of World War I had taken its toll on the face of Edna, who was not eating or sleeping properly during her efforts. In a little cosmetic marketing booklet "My Beauty, How I won it as a girl- How I kept it at my age", Edna explains, "During the four and a half years which I spent in the war, I neglected my beauty helps [aids]. And I worked night and day under strain. After the war, I had sagging muscles of my face corrected by facial surgery". She explained that it made her look older than she would have looked if she had not been under such duress.

While in Los Angeles, Miss Hopper (now her new name), Broadway's "little bottle of energy", wanted to be the same girl she was 20 years before. Having faith in a woman surgeon she had hunted up in California, Miss Hopper had asked the surgeon if she could do something to remove the tired lines and crow's feet on her brow and cheeks. The woman surgeon replied, "Sure enough, come in tomorrow afternoon, and in fifteen minutes of your time for surgery, and allow nature about three weeks to heal, and you will be young again".

Edna agreed to become the subject for an experimental procedure only if the procedure would be filmed with a motion picture camera for documentation, another one of her brainstorming ideas. Once again, using the shock element in her show would regain her popularity.

The next afternoon, the perky little patient climbed into the operating chair and sat perfectly still for the entire fifteen minutes. The female surgeon, assisted by a young nurse, made an incision behind each ear, lifting a slight portion of the cuticle that had no business there. They next sewed together the small operations. The skin was drawn tight where wrinkles had existed around the eyes and the forehead. All the while, the lights were shining while the Edison camera captured the medical moment for preservation. Somehow, the canister of film that Edna carried under her arm from theater to theater has yet to be located by me.

Three weeks after the surgery, Edna decided to surprise the surgeon by having another doctor perform the postoperative procedure of removing the stitches. His name was Doctor John L. Hennemuth, a prominent physician and surgeon in Modesto, California. He was a believer that aesthetic beauty was important to the patient. In arranging his new offices situated in the United Bank and Trust Company building, Dr. Hennemuth had turned the order of things upside down. The somber conventional decorative scheme used in the doctor's office years ago had given way to one of cheer. The suite of rooms was finished in golden oak with hardwood floors throughout. Rugs in pretty oriental motifs lie on the floors. The walls had a Tiffany finish in gold and blue, while the drapes and entire furnishings were the keynote adopted in the same soft colorings, giving an air of comfort. I had spoken with Dr. Hennemuth's daughter, who is living in California. She had explained to me that at the time, her father did not disclose to her or to anyone outside of his office, as a good doctor would do, that the famous actress/singer had visited him for this procedure. It was years after her father had passed away that one of his nurses had told his daughter Margerie of the visit with Edna. I explained to Margerie why I think Edna had her father do the removal of the stitches instead of the female surgeon who did the operation. I found a newspaper article that described Edna giving the female surgeon the element of surprise. It reads, "Three weeks later, a fresh-faced, rosy-cheeked and sparkling blue-eyed wonder danced into the hospital, grabbed the surgeon from behind, smothered her with kisses and then identified herself, as the doctor looked unsure as to who it was." "Look what you've done to me!" she cheered with excitement.

Since 1911, Edna had frequently visited the Grand View Health resort in Waukesha, Wisconsin. This was the first American mud bath spa similar to those of Germany and Austria. The luxurious resort even had a nine-hole golf course. While in Waukesha, she met Otis Glidden, of the famous Glidden brothers, who, since 1916, had one of the hottest products on the market, next to Coca-Cola. They had a product known as Jiffy-Jell, a fruit-flavored gelatin. Since 1916, gelatin was "the rage" as it was originally known to be the last course served to the Royal families of England and Europe. It was now a status symbol, quite affordable for the average American family, who wanted to be recognized as doing the same thing at dinner as the Royals were doing.

Edna had convinced Otis to market her youth and beauty products. Otis formed the Edna Wallace Hopper Cosmetic on Barstow Street in Waukesha. In 1921, the Glidden brothers sold Waukesha Pure Foods to the Genesee Pure Foods Company, which later marketed their product as Jell-O. By 1922, as the millions of dollars rolled in from the success of the Edna Wallace Hopper cosmetic line, the company was moved to 536 Lake Shore Drive in Chicago. Incidentally, the Glidden Brothers Company in Waukesha was the first to create the "coffee break" for the factory workers. It was much photographed, caught the eye of many other American factories and workshops, and eventually became a standard benefit for workers.

Another thing Edna did for the success of her road show was to have herself photographed naked and semi-naked for the press and for her marketing ads and packaging. Alfred Cheney Johnston was a famous nouveau photographer of the Ziegfeld Follies girls. His risqué and nude photos of the flappers and the roaring twenties beauties are considered, still today, to be some of the greatest photography in history. Unlike her avant-garde photo images of the Victorian era done by the finest photographers such as Burr McIntosh, the new Miss Hopper would be even more daring than ever, more sensual and more open. Indeed, she was as daring and as heavenly as any of the young girls who were Johnson's subject models. Here was a woman in her sixties who would astound her audiences through the vision of unending youth and beauty of someone in their twenties. One pose of her semi-nude profile, while draping her breast with a toga-like garment, was chosen to be illustrated and printed on the cosmetic product boxes, as her art logo.

Photography by Alfred Cheney Johnston

Another photo of her depicts a heavenly, almost Christ-like image; instead of a crown of thorns, she adorns a crown of pearls, looking upward to the heavens with one shoulder and breast exposed, wrapped in a cloak of velvet. Around her neck is the long diamond necklace with a small cameo-like photograph of her beloved mother, Josephine. I had noticed that Edna wore the necklace with Josephine's photo in many of her photographs, done to promote her cosmetic line. Edna had once written, "I owe much to my mother. She played a royal part in life because of her wondrous beauty. She died a youthful beauty at age 57, with a child's complexion, girlish contours, and not a gray hair in her head". Photo by Aveda.

A youthful sixty-one-year-old Edna in 1923, Photo by Shauss Peylon

Doctor John L. Hennemuth was a prominent physician and surgeon in Modesto, California. He was a believer that aesthetic beauty was important to the patient. He was the postoperative surgeon who removed Edna's stitches and assisted her healing process after one of the 1st cosmetic surgery operations ever done was performed on her in the early 1920s.

Hopper in a 1928 advertisement, Photo by Alfred Cheney Johnston

The "Matinee for Ladies Only" show was now ready to go on tour. The major theaters such as Grauman's Chinese Theater in Los Angeles, the Roxy and the Apollo in New York, the New Royal Theater in Victoria, British Columbia, and all the other vaudeville theaters and movie houses, both large and small, across North America, were booked to sell out shows. It was an overwhelming success. They called her "the wonderful apostle of perpetual youth".

A new flash is reported
in the press:

"Regained Her Youth Through the New Scientific Surgery."
Starting Saturday, APRIL 22
"Patrons of the New Garrick Theatre will enjoy a distinct innovation next week when Edna Wallace Hopper, the 'flapper grandmother,' will appear in person to tell New Garrick audiences just how she regained her youth and cheated Father Time out of twenty years of life.

Miss Hopper, who was a famous musical comedy star of twenty years ago, recently submitted to a delicate surgical operation which has created a furor of interest throughout the world.

While no one is ungentlemanly enough to suggest a definite age for Miss Hopper, it is safe to say that she was prominent in musical comedy circles when President Harding was a newspaper reporter. Therefore, it follows that she should be a gray-haired grandmother, but instead she is a youthful flapper with face, figure, and features of a debutante.

All the secrets of the operation to which she submitted will be told audiences at the New Garrick Theatre at each de luxe performance, matinee and evening beginning next Saturday."
MISS EDNA WALLACE HOPPER in person
The famed "Florodora" and Belasco Beauty of two decades ago comes to Duluth as a "girl of nineteen".

Through the medium of speech and motion pictures, you will see how this celebrated star regained her youth and beauty - By special permission of Raymond Hitchcock.

Above is a typical scene at one of Miss Hopper's morning matinees for "women only." Photo taken at 10:15 a. m., Century Theatre, Baltimore, Oct. 9, 1925.

The show began with the dark theater showing the film of her gruesome surgery while her voice was heard explaining the procedure and why she had it done. As some of the audience would faint while watching the film, smelling salts were passed around to the audience when the film was over.

Then the next shocker was the live performance. With a background set, painted by Salvador Dali, depicting the decadent interior of the grand baths of ancient Pompeii, and dramatic music from a chorus of girls accompanied by an orchestra that took one back to the times of King Herod, a naked Miss Hopper would be rolled out in a bathtub with elaborate $5000 furnishings by Crane Company. She would rise out of the tub and lecture her audience on how they too could look and feel younger and more beautiful like her with her diet, exercises, and her beauty help. For those who had neglected themselves for too long, the corrective surgery could make them regain their youthful appearance.

166

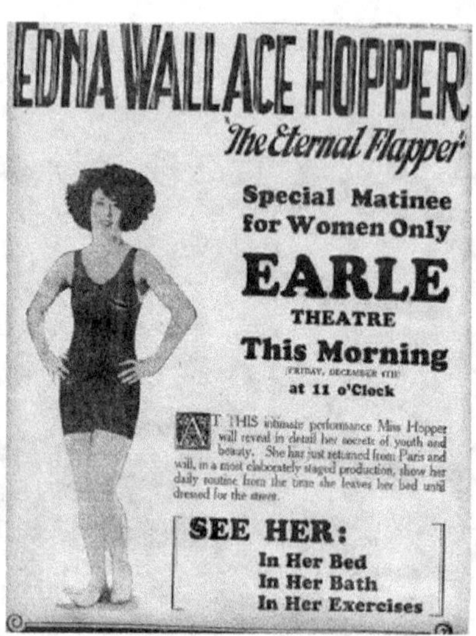

1920s newspaper ads such as this one announced the Eternal Flapper's Vaudeville show "Matinees for Ladies Only" in theaters such as The Roxy, The Apollo, Grauman's Chinese Theater, and LA's Pantages, where Edna performed to sold-out audiences.

Photo from the private collection of Jim Alessio
Publicity photo by Alfred Cheney Johnston, 1926, for Hopper's Cosmetics and for her Vaudeville live performances.

Edna comes out naked on stage in a bathtub with $5,000 luxury bath furnishings by Crane Company. Ironically, the notorious "bathtub incident" mentioned during the Hopper VS Dunsmuir trial years before was a taboo subject matter mentioned by Edna and dismissed by the Judge abruptly. Perhaps being naked on stage in a bathtub was cathartic to a woman who was at last free from her haunting past.

Photo from the private collection of Jim Alessio

Photo by Aveda. The diamond necklace worn frequently by Edna has a cameo photo of her beloved mother, Josephine . This is the only known photo image in existence today of Josephine Wallace Dunsmuir, as discovered late one night by the author.

This photo taken in 1925 was released to newspapers and other publications with credit of Hifou-Newman Studios, K.C, MO. The back of it reads: RETURNING TO PROVE TO LOS ANGELES THAT SHE LOST TEN MORE YEARS BY HER STAY IN OUR BEAUTIFUL CITY. SO SAYS THE FAIR EDNA WALLACE HOPPER WHO WILL BE SEEN AT GRAUMANS (THEATER) AGAIN FOR THE ENTIRE WEEK OF JULY 10TH. Notice

the pendant has the face of her beloved mother, Josephine Wallace Dunsmuir. This could be the only photographic image of Josephine to be found in existence. Photo from private collection of Jim Alessio

My 10-Minute-a-Day
Beauty Program
Works Wonders
By Elsa Wallace Hoppe
Following My Advice
Costs Less than 5c a Day
My Special Invitation
MAIL THIS COUPON TODAY!
Gorgeously Colored Art Panel Box of Seven Beauty Aids—
Quindent
Youth Cream
White and Sheen
White Youth Clay

...at I Do
Watch the new loveliness develop
Your friends will marvel at the change
By Elsa Wallace Hoppe
White Youth Clay
My Facial Youth
A Multiple Cream
My Hair Youth
Your Choice FREE

OVER 60
How to Regain Youth — by the woman who never grew old
Edna Wallace Hopper
LOOKS LIKE 25

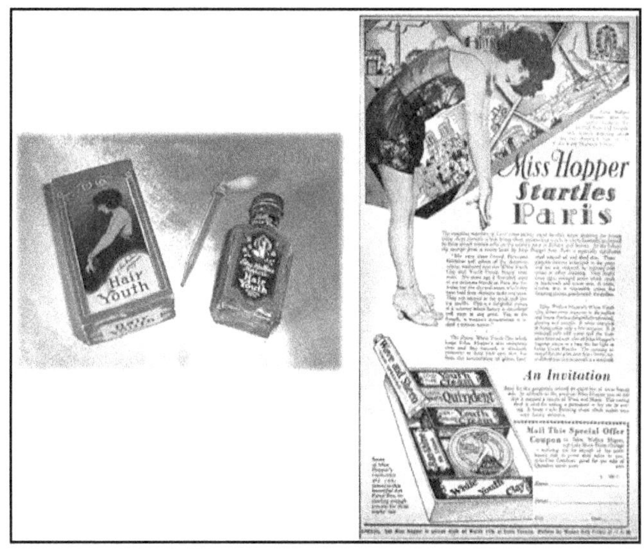

Hair Youth
Miss Hopper
Startles
Paris
An Invitation
Mail This Special Offer
Coupon

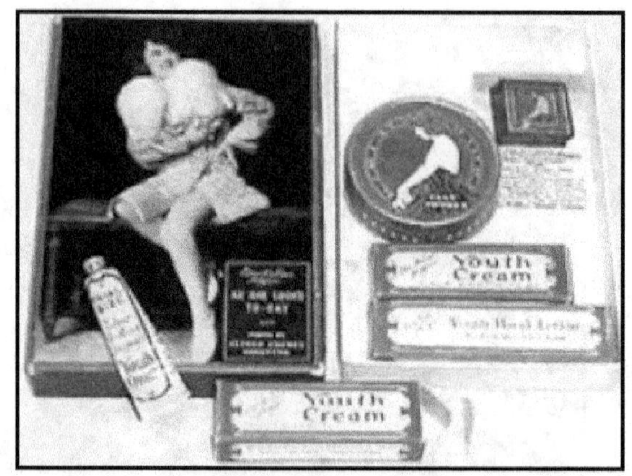

Youth
Cream
Youth Cream

Changing
One's Face
It's Easy
If you follow the method
of Edna Wallace Hopper
Wave
and
Sheen
Facial
Youth

This ad appeared in several magazines, such as Vogue, on November 23rd, 1929. It illustrates the Eternally Youthful Flapper Edna. The ad also depicts the new modern fit woman who is active outdoors in activities such as golf and horseback riding, along with spending time on her beauty with the help of Edna's facial and hair products.

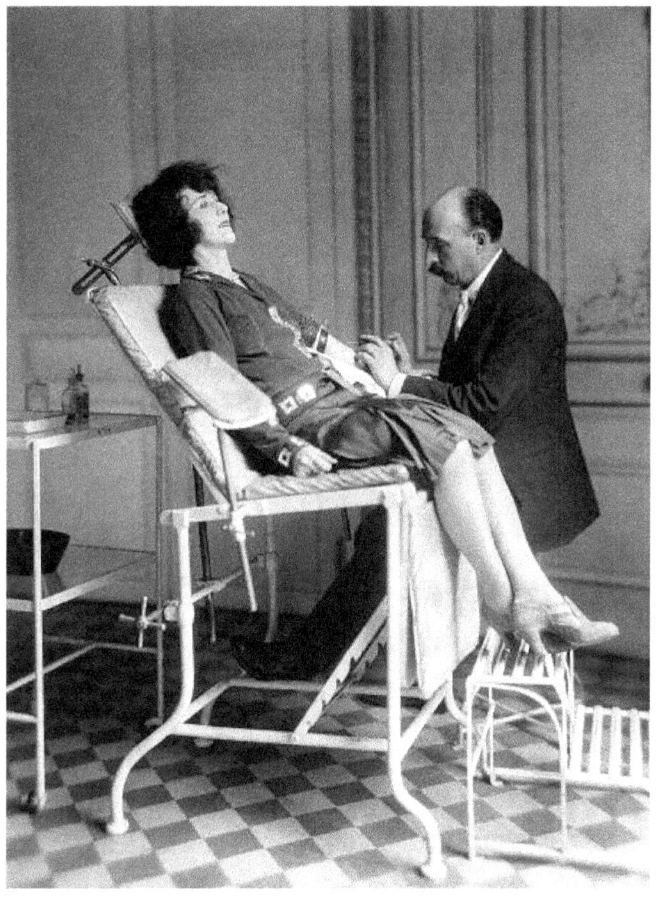

In 1925, Edna had rejuvenation hormone treatments in Paris by Dr. Helene Jaworski.

Photo by Georges Morant, circa 1923-25. Edna is somewhere in her sixties here. She was promoting her acrobatic dancing as performed in her Vaudeville show. Photo from the private collection of Jim Alessio

From Dance Magazine circa 1926, Edna is seen doing her acrobatic dancing along with her longtime dance partner Maurice Grip, whom she met in France. Grip was less than half her age. The magazine declares Edna to be 64 years old. This would make her birth year 1862 as opposed to 1864. Photo by Georges Marant

Edna traveled on ships across the Atlantic frequently. It was part of her lifestyle, and the press seemed to follow her.

The Eternal Flapper posing for a photographer on board a trans-Atlantic ship, September 3, 1925. Notice she is wearing the diamond jeweled cameo with a small photo of her mother, Josephine, as she often wore. Photo by Bains News Service, New York. From J. Alessio's collection.

Sept 24, 1926, The Eternal Beauty on board again, crossing the Atlantic or Pacific. Photo by Bain News Service, New York. From the Collection of Jim Alessio

Sept 13, 1927 National Newsreel reads: THE PERENNIAL FLAPPER RETURNS Edna Wallace Hopper, proud possessor of everlasting youth, waves a big Hello to New York after a four-month trip in Europe. She came back on The Olympic to open in a Vaudeville tour. (photo from Alessio collection)

Photo of A. O. Brown, second husband of Edna Wallace Hopper Brown, as seen in The New York Times on April 13, 1927

In 1923, The Morning Telegraph dated August 31st had an article that said: Edna Hopper to Sue For Divorce. The article reads: "Since there does not seem to be any prospect of reconciliation, Miss Hopper has decided to ask for her freedom. Suit will be filed shortly".

"A.O. Brown, manager of the Playhouse, declared last night that he did not wish to make any comment on the report, as he had no information of the filing of the suit."

The Los Angeles Herald that day read: Former Wife of DeWolf Hopper to Seek Freedom Again, She Says.

Then on April 3rd, 1927, they were reunited. Miss Hopper had not seen Brown since their separation 14 years beforehand. They had met at a party given by "a very dear friend" of both. They were reintroduced, and the result was the reconciliation. It appeared that they still found attraction for one another. Ten days later, they celebrated their reunion with a party at Paul Whiteman's Club, and Edna announced they would leave for Europe on a "second honeymoon" as soon as she finishes the remaining seven weeks of a vaudeville tour.

"We will not resume where we left off", she said, "because we hated each other when we parted. We will begin all over again".

The article went on to mention she had returned to Paris for her rejuvenation, and had been pronounced by her physicians as "mentally and physically but 15 years old". The article also mentioned her rumors of marriage to a duke and that the Browns had never been officially divorced.

This reunion of the Browns was brief and would sadly end with yet another separation.

The on-again and off-again love relationship of Edna and Albert Brown appeared to show that they never really forgot each other. In fact, they never divorced, and Edna kept the name Wallace Hopper Brown for the remainder of her life. Brown may have been the love of her life. It was never reported that Edna had ever fallen in love again with any other man.

The Browns not only shared a passionate love affair, but they also took on reverse roles modeled from each other's careers. Edna spent the remaining years of her life on Wall Street while Albert O. Brown went into the theater business.

Chapter Seven

120 Broadway

The Dark Shadow of Wall Street

On September 10, 2001, I had finished writing the chapter on Edna's life during World War I. Finding only a few references where she had spoken of this time, I wondered what it actually felt like for her to have her life and career interrupted by the surroundings of war. I said to myself, 'Now I must put myself into the frame of mind to write about her years as a trader in the Wall Street market. Since I didn't have any knowledge of or any interest to learn more about the stock market, I worried about what I would or could write about the last thirty years of her life as a trader at L.F. Rothschild & Company, located at the Equitable Building, 120 Broadway in New York. In my wildest dreams, could I ever imagine a connection between this building, its occupants at the time of Edna's career in it, and the occupants of it at the time of this horrific disaster in 2001? Many of the organizations or descendant family members connected to the beginning of the 120 Broadway Building in 1917 were now involved in the events before and after September 11, 2001.

On September 11th, 2001, as the whole world watched the World Trade Center being destroyed in horror, I rushed home and clutched my new pet Chihuahua named Paco, who came to his new home with me the day before. Paco was perched on the top of the sofa and watched the television with eyes wide open and excitement. The little dog gazed quickly back and forth from the television screen and back to my face as if he were wondering what was going on. I only thought of how strange it was that his former owner had moved to New York, only to arrive on this day that no one in New York will ever forget. I grabbed Paco and held him closely in my arms, giving me a feeling of safety and knowing my little Paco was safe with me.

Little was written about those last years of Edna Wallace Hopper Brown's life away from Upper Broadway. What happened in those years? Little did I know that a few days later, I would find that the office where she worked was only a short distance from ground zero. I would find this out only a few days after September 11th, 2001.

The question haunted me as I tried to sleep on the night of the attack on the World Trade towers and the following night as well.

Around 2 AM on the morning of the 14th, I could not sleep, so I walked down the hall to my computer/writing study and typed in a search for a Manhattan map. There on the screen, I could see that 120 Broadway, where Edna spent the last 30 years of her life, was only a block from where the World Trade Center was situated, now ground zero. I then typed in a Google search of 120 Broadway, and to my surprise, a link came up to something called Skull & Bones Society, written by someone who studied Antony Sutton and Craig Hulett's lectures and books during the Gulf War. This person had placed a web page about a super-secret society established in 1832 at Yale, for the elite children of the Anglo-American Wall Street banking establishment. It is, in itself, a sinister outgrowth of the notorious eighteenth-century society, the Illuminati. The Illuminati was organized in 1770 by Mayer Amschel Rothschild. Edna worked for the trading firm owned by Louis Frank Rothschild, a New York man born in 1869. He practiced law from 1891 to 1893, a manufacturing business from 1893 to 1902, and then as a partner of Rothschild & Co. bankers since 1902. He was married to Cora Guggenheim in 1899 and resided at the famous Carlton House in New York. Oddly, he and Edna were born around the same time and died around the same year. I would think that they both being quite old for the stock market business, with all the young studs, would make them fond of each other.

The Rothschild family controls half the wealth of the world. The

Rothschilds rule by proxy. They virtually control the entire planet through their money and power. Their central banks control the money supply of almost every nation except Iran, North Korea, Sudan, Cuba, and Libya. The history of this powerful family coincides with the history of the world wars and shows its power in creating world events.

Just as the Roman Empire, the Egyptians, and the Greeks attempted to create a world power, so have the Rothschilds made an attempt to take control of the world for centuries. In 1770, in Frankfurt, Germany, a man named Mayer Amschel Bauer made a business of trading gold and jewelry. He changed his name to Rothschild, which means Red Shield in German. The red hexagon was a symbol for the world revolution movement. Mayer Rothschild drew up a plan for the creation of the Illuminati. He got together with thirteen members of his secret organization to reach his goal. The goal was to eventually have the power and wealth of all nations. Rothschild entrusts Adam Weishaupt with its organization and development. Adam Weishaupt became a convert to Catholicism and later a Catholic priest. Then, at the request of the Financiers, he defected from the Catholic Church and helped organize the Illuminati, now financed by Rothschild. Every war since then, beginning with the French Revolution, has been promoted by the Illuminati operating under various names and guises. I say under various names and guises because, after the Illuminati was exposed and became too notorious, Weishaupt and his co-conspirators began to operate under various other names. Their primary goal is to form a one-world government to have complete control of the entire world, destroying all religions and governments in the process.

In 1791, through Alexander Hamilton, Rothschild set up a central banking system in the United States called the Bank of the United States. "Let me issue and control a Nation's money and I care not who writes the laws", stated Mayer Amschel Rothschild. His wife Gutle Schnaper declares, "If my sons did not want wars… There would be none." By 1811, the charter for Rothschild's Bank of the U.S. ran out, and Congress voted against its renewal. Mayer Rothschild was not amused and stated, "Either the application for renewal of the charter is granted, or the US will find itself involved in a most disastrous war." Backed up by Rothschild's money and by his orders, Britain declared war on the USA in 1812. He is quoted as saying, "Teach those impudent Americans a lesson. Bring them back to the colonial states." His plan was to get the US into debt so that they would need to surrender to him and renew the charter for his First Bank of the U.S.

In 1815, Rothschild's five sons supplied gold to Napoleon's army. An agent of Rothschild got news of Napoleon's defeat by Lord Wellington and told Nathan Rothschild, the son of Mayer. Nathan spread a rumor to the London stock exchange that Napoleon won the war. This intentional misinformation caused the stocks to crash by 98 percent. Nathan bought up the stock. When the truth about Napoleon's defeat was out, the stocks soared, and Nathan Rothschild ruled England. "I care not what puppet is placed upon the throne of England to rule the Empire on which the sun never sets. The man who controls Britain's money supply controls the British Empire, and I control the British money supply."

"Rothschild is the Lord and Master of the money markets of the world, and of course virtually Lord and Master of everything else", Benjamin Disrach, the British Prime Minister, declared. The Rothschilds had complete control of the British economy after Napoleon's defeat, and by 1818, they had control of the French money supply as well.

By 1816, Rothschild got control of the US money again and formed the 2nd Bank of the United States.

By 1827, Sir Walter Scott wrote a multivolume group of books called The Life of Napoleon. In one of the books he wrote, he claimed that the French Revolution was planned by the Illuminati (Adam Weishaupt) and financed by the Rothschilds.

In the year 1832, President Andrew Jackson wanted control of the American money system for the people and not the wealthy Rothschild family. "Jackson and no Bank!" was his campaign slogan. Rothschild then caused an economic upset, which led to a depression. President Jackson addressed the matter to the Rothschilds, saying, "You are a den of thieves, vipers, and I intend to rout you out and by the Eternal God, I will rout you out!" An assassination attempt on President Jackson's life was made in 1835. Jackson claimed he knew it was Rothschild behind it.

In 1862, an angry President Lincoln printed his own money after being fed up with the high interest rate on the bank (Rothschild) money. He declares, "We gave the people of this republic the greatest blessing they ever had, their own paper money to pay their own debts." This made Rothschild furious, and on April 14th, President Lincoln was assassinated.

Then, President Garfield was assassinated. Are you getting the picture now?

The Rothschilds sell Caspian & Black Sea Petroleum to Royal Dutch and Shell.

By 1913, the Rothschilds set up the Federal Reserve and had a controlling interest. Then, in 1914, they had control of three European news agencies. In that same year, Ferdinand was assassinated by the secret society called The Black Hand. Many believe this is what began the First World War. Many also believe that the Black Hand was part of the Illuminati.

Now you have learned the beginning of the powers of the Rothschild family. The best is yet to come. I will now tell you what I have learned about the 120 Broadway Building and its relation to the Skulls and Bones Society and the Illuminati.

While collecting material for this book, a single location and address in the Wall Street area came to the fore: 120 Broadway, New York City. Conceivably, this book could have been written incorporating only persons, firms, and organizations located at 120 Broadway in the year 1917. Although this research method would have been forced and unnatural, it would have excluded only a relatively small segment of the story.

Never did I think, or even imagine in 2001 days before 9/11/2001, that in the year 2025, I would find the complete truth and possibly, the darkest unspoken secret of Edna Wallace Hopper.

My investigation about her last 25 years as a key trader/investor for L.F. Rothschild and the only woman among the top 30 Bankers in America, and veiled top world bankers, in a building that was for decades known as the biggest office building in the world.

Built in 1915, a twin tower building connected by an elaborate, enormous lobby designed with the most grandiose architecture of centuries, yet a new century look. An almost identical building was built in Nazi Germany in 1914. My research not only opened portholes to the Skull & Bones Society and the New World Order called the Illuminati, but I also found this building to be where the high order members occupied the floors and offices of 120 Broadway.

While profits from wars, violence, and drugs were controlled for the high profits of The Order (members), Edna Wallace Hopper's talent and work became a key element for the secret society that powered everything. Among her key investors were J. P. Morgan, Prescott Bush, Averell Harriman, along with corporate lawyer John Foster and his brother Allen Dulles (look out for my next book to know more about Dulles and Bush). Allen Dulles was a spymaster for the CIA, OSS, and others.

The ORDER was involved in the buildup of Nazi Germany. They supplied the Third Reich with capital and financial arrangements. This was kept quiet. However, there was a small notice that appeared in The New York Times on December 16, 1944. It read "The Union Banking Corporation, 39 Broadway, New York, has received authority to change its principal place of business to 120 Broadway.

In July 1985, the suppressed GAO paper reported that there were "no benefits from the National Narcotics Border Interdiction System, directed by George Bush. In fact, the overall effect was to encourage supply".

Bonesmen have helped create a prohibition where plants and their by-products are sold on the black market for precious metal prices. This market used a corrupted "secret government" for trafficking and propaganda. A cabal existed that used an unconstitutional Drug War for political, economic, and social control.

ORDER members such as Averell Harriman and Sheldon Bush, J.P. Morgan, were behind the creation of the Soviet Union and the Russian manufactured war and the Nazi War as well. The ORDER was behind the control of the World Trade and was the American Order members of the Skull & Bones Society - the American part of the Illuminati.

I have yet to see any proof that L.F. Rothschild, who made fortunes for the members, was from the family that long ago started the Illuminati.

I simply find it too coincidental that his powerful Wall Street firm invested for its members, and his name is Rothschild. He and Edna were quite old and similar in age, and became quite connected. She was his prize major investor and stock trader. The ORDER must have treated her as a Goddess.

I read somewhere that she quadrupled the fortune of J.P. Morgan, whom I researched to be a critical power that made the Soviet Union. A Princess of Russia became one of Edna's closet friends. THESIS was comprised of Marxist Russia, Guaranty Trust Company, The Brown Brothers and Harriman, and Ruskmbank, a joint venture of Guaranty Trust and Soviet operation in 1922.

During 1917, the Bolshevik Revolution was a conflict of World War II and the ANTITHESIS of Nazi Germany. Guaranty Trust Company, along with Union Banking Corp (Harriman and Nazi interests). With ANTITHESIS, Hitler's accession to power happened in 1933 and the construction and subsidy of National Socialism. From both ends (THESIS AND ANTITHESIS), profits turned into SYNTHESIS, post World War II United Nations, as a first step to the New World Order.

The ORDER was neither left-wing nor right-wing. They were artificial devices to bring about change. And the extremes of political left and political right are vital elements in a process of controlled change. This puzzle lies in Hegelian logic. Marx and Hitler, the extreme left and right who appeared as enemies, had both come out of the same philosophical system: HEGELIANISM.

In the Hegelian system, conflict is essential. Hegel and Fichte were in the late 18th and early 19th century in Germany, where the State is absolute. J.P. Morgan used the Hegelian Dialectic Process. The Hegelian Dialectic Process was a means of political control for financial profit.

Edna was Morgan's key investor and stock trader. She must have known that wars and revolutions were created for Profits. Soldiers and victim citizens were used as needed. Was Edna a puppet for the Order?

In summary, the 120 Broadway ORDER was comprised of Edward Harriman, American International Corporation, J.P. Morgan firm, Federal Reserve Bank of New York, The Top floor Bankers Club, Thomas Tracher, Guggenheim Exploration, General Electric, Sinclair Gulf Corp.,

Guaranty Securities. Individual members of the ORDER at 120 Broadway were George Webster Adams (The Order '04), Allen Wallace Ames (The Order '18), and Philip Lyndon Dodge (The Order '07).

I was confronted by an existing family member who expressed his dislike for my exposé of his family's involvement in events and power from the 120 Broadway building's history. Oddly, I started this investigation a few days before the World Trade Center buildings were destroyed. I found out that the power behind the design, insurance, building, and planning of the World Trade Center came from inside the offices of the 120 Broadway building. For decades, this was in the works.

I was confronted in 2009 by a family member of one powerful Order member who stood high in American politics (whose name I dare not mention). In my defense, I told him that Edna Wallace Hopper wanted the truth to be known, and I was assigned to do just that. I now understand why she made it clear to be completed in the 21st Century.

There are many who give reason to think the attack appeared to have created this major quake and shock to shift into the World Order to regain its power. It was not an attack on New York. It was on World Trade. It adjusted the Illuminati back into regaining its strength. Records from the Federal Reserve were removed from the 120 Broadway Building "for Safety" as restoration and remodeling were in place. They were placed in one of the World Trade Towers and were destroyed when the building was taken down for safety reasons. Some think that was a way to wipe away questionable records being investigated. And oddly, it appears to many, including myself, as created on the opposite side of Trinity Church, in the powerful world of the 120 Broadway Building.

In any event, the building at 120 Broadway was known in 1917 as the Equitable Life Building. A large building, although by no means the largest office building in New York City, occupies a one-block area at Broadway and Pine, and has thirty-four floors. The Bankers Club was located on the thirty-fourth floor. The tenant list in 1917 in effect reflected American involvement in the Bolshevik Revolution and its aftermath. For example, the headquarters of the No. 2 District of the Federal Reserve System — the New York area, by far the most important of the Federal

Reserve districts, was located at 120 Broadway. The offices of several individual directors of the Federal Reserve Bank of New York and, most importantly, the American International Corporation were also at 120 Broadway. By way of contrast, Ludwig Martens, appointed by the Soviets as the first Bolshevik "ambassador" to the United States and head of the Soviet Bureau, was in 1917 the vice president of Weinberg & Posner — and also had offices at 120 Broadway.

The original building at 120 Broadway was destroyed by fire before World War I. Subsequently, the site was sold to the Equitable Office Building Corporation, organized by General T. Coleman du Pont, president of du Pont de Nemours Powder Company. A new building was completed in 1915, and the Equitable Life Assurance Company moved back to its old site. In passing, we should note an interesting interlock in Equitable history. In 1916, the cashier of the Berlin Equitable Life office was William Schacht, the father of Hjalmar Horace Greeley Schacht, later to become Hitler's banker and financial genius. William Schacht was an American citizen who worked for thirty years for Equitable in Germany and owned a Berlin house known as "Equitable Villa." Before joining Hitler, young Hjalmar Schacht served as a member of the Workers' and Soldiers '

Council (a soviet) of Zehlendoff; this he left in 1918 to join the board of the National bank fur Deutschland. His Co-director at DONAT was Emil Wittenberg, who, with Max May of Guaranty Trust Company of New York, was a director of the first Soviet international bank, Ruskombank.

In 1934, Rothschild engineered the 2nd World War for profit. Adolph Hitler's father was the illegitimate son Maria Anna Schicklgruber of Vienna. Anna was a servant at the home of Nathan Mayer Rothschild. Oddly, Anna was financially supported quite comfortably during her pregnancy and while raising her son. It is possible that the father was in fact Nathan Rothschild. If this is true, this means that Adolph Hitler was the grandson of Nathan Mayer Rothschild. This also means that Hitler was 25 % Zionist Jew and an offspring of the Illuminati Rothschild. This leaves one to wonder, Who funded the adult Adolph Hitler? How did a man with less than average intelligence get in a position of such power? The answer may be the Thile Society and the Vril Society, the Brown Brothers, Harriman, Shell Oil and NWO Companies.

The Zionist Bolsheviks performed the mass murders of the Russian Revolution as was funded by the Rothschild owned Kuhn, Loch Bank.

According to an article I read, William Huntington Russell's stepbrother Samuel Russell ran "Russell & Co.", the world's largest Opium smuggling operation in the world at the time. George Bush's grandfather as well as George Bush Sr. were and are members of Skull & Bones, as well as William Averall Harriman. His wife, Pamela Harriman was the major backer of the Democratic Party for over 50 years and supplied funds to elect Bill Clinton to office. Major players in Skull & Bones have been linked to the financing of both world wars and the creation of many think tanks and Universities in this country. A member of this was Prescott Sheldon Bush (1917). Bush was a major contributor to the "Hitler Project" as well as the build-up of the Soviet Union. These incidents lead to the World Wars and the eventual set- up of the United Nations in America. Antony Sutton wrote a number of books including "Wall Street and the rise of Hitler", "Wall street and FDR", "Gold vs. Paper", "Energy-The Created Crisis", "National Suicide: Military Aid to the Soviet Union", "Western Technology and Soviet Economic Development 1917-1973", "America's Secret Establishment: An Introduction to the Order of Skull & Bones" in 1984 and then, "The Two Faces of George Bush", another book about Skull & Bones. A focus of many of the books was on the Wall Street Bankers and several organizations they had founded.

Many of the firms with links to Skull & Bones were at 120 Broadway in 1917. Edward Harriman Company, American International Corporation, Federal Reserve Bank of New York, Thomas D. Thacher, Guggenheim Exploration, C.A.K. Martens of Weinberg & Posner (The 1st Soviet "ambassador"), Stone & Webster, General Electric, Sinclair Gulf Corp., Guaranty Trust Company, and then there was L.F. Rothschild

& Company. On the very top floor of the 120 Broadway building was the Banker's Club. According to these authors and researchers, this building housed the creators and the profiteers of the World Wars. They believe the Wars were manufactured, and the gears that turned in the machinery of the monster were mostly located at 120 Broadway.

The destruction of Russia and the creation of the Communist Soviet Union was a special project of the American Illuminati. This was an important first step on their road to killing nations and paving the way for their New World Order.

The co-founder of Skull & Bones, Alphonso Taft, became Secretary of War, Attorney General, and the U.S. Ambassador to Russia in the mid-1880s. Russia was targeted for major brutality via a Communist Revolution.

The headquarters for the operation to make Russia Communist was located at 120 Broadway in downtown New York. It was the address of

E.H. Harriman. George Kennan was the hired hack of H.E. Harriman and the Wall Street Hitler.

The Bankers Club was located on the thirty-fourth floor. The tenant list in 1917 in effect reflected American involvement in the Bolshevik Revolution and its aftermath. For example, the headquarters of the No. 2 District of the Federal Reserve System — the New York area, by far the most important of the Federal Reserve districts- was located at 120 Broadway.

Is this concentration an accident? Does the geographical contiguity have any significance? Before attempting to suggest an answer, we have to switch our frame of reference and abandon the left-right spectrum of political analysis.

With an almost unanimous lack of perception, the academic world has described and analyzed international political relations in the context of an unrelenting conflict between capitalism and communism, and rigid adherence to this Marxian formula has distorted modern history. Tossed out from time to time are odd remarks to the effect that the polarity is indeed spurious, but these are quickly dispatched to limbo. For example, Carroll Quigley, professor of international relations at Georgetown University, made the following comment on the House of Morgan:

More than fifty years ago, the Morgan firm decided to infiltrate the Left-wing political movements in the United States. This was relatively easy to do, since these groups were starved for funds and eager for a voice to reach the people. Wall Street supplied both. The purpose was not to destroy, dominate, or take over...William B. Thompson, who was in Petrograd from July until November last, has made a personal contribution of $1,000,000 to the Bolsheviki for the purpose of spreading their doctrine in Germany and Austria ....

Washington Post, February 2, 1918

Professor Quigley's comment, apparently based on confidential documentation, has all the ingredients of a historical bombshell if it can be supported. We suggest that the Morgan firm infiltrated not only the domestic left, as noted by Quigley, but also the foreign left — that is, the Bolshevik movement and the Third International. Even further, through friends in the U.S. State Department, Morgan and allied financial interests, particularly the Rockefeller family, have exerted a powerful influence on U.S.-Russian relations from World War I to the present. The evidence presented in this chapter will suggest that two of the operational vehicles for infiltrating or influencing foreign revolutionary movements were located at 120 Broadway: the first, the Federal Reserve Bank of New York, heavily laced with Morgan appointees; the second, the Morgan-controlled American International Corporation. Further, there was an important interlock between the Federal Reserve Bank of New York and the American International Corporation — C. A. Stone, the president of American International, was also a director of the Federal Reserve Bank.

Some international agents, for example, Alexander Gumberg, worked for Wall Street and the Bolsheviks. In 1917, Gumberg was the representative of a U.S. firm in Petrograd, worked for Thompson's American Red Cross Mission, became chief Bolshevik agent in Scandinavia until he was deported from Norway, then became confidential assistant to Reeve Schley of Chase Bank in New York and

later to Floyd Odium of Atlas Corporation.

This activity on behalf of the Bolsheviks originated in large part from a single address: 120 Broadway, New York City. The evidence for this observation is outlined, but no conclusive reason is given for the unusual concentration of activity at a single address, except to state that it appears to be the foreign counterpart of Carroll Quigley's claim that J.P. Morgan infiltrated the domestic left. Morgan also infiltrated the international left.

The Federal Reserve Bank of New York (created by Rothschild) was at 120 Broadway. The vehicle for this pro-Bolshevik activity was American International Corporation, at 120 Broadway. AIC's views on the Bolshevik regime were requested by Secretary of State Robert Lansing only a few weeks after the revolution began, and Sands, executive secretary of AIC, could barely restrain his enthusiasm for the Bolshevik cause. Ludwig Martens, the Soviets' first ambassador, had been vice president of Weinberg & Posner, which was also located at 120-Broadway. Guaranty Trust Company was next door at 140 Broadway, but Guaranty Securities Co. was at 120 Broadway. In 1917, Hunt, Hill & Betts was at 120 Broadway, and Charles B. Hill of this firm was the negotiator in the Sun Yat-sen dealings. John MacGregor Grant Co., which was financed by Olof Aschberg in Sweden and Guaranty Trust in the United States, and which was on the Military Intelligence black list, was at 120 Broadway. The Guggenheims and the executive heart of General Electric (also interested in American International) were at 120 Broadway. We find it, therefore, hardly surprising that the Bankers Club was also at 120 Broadway, on the top floor (the thirty-fourth).

It is significant that support for the Bolsheviks did not cease with the consolidation of the revolution; therefore, this support cannot be wholly explained in terms of the war with Germany. The American-Russian syndicate formed in 1918 to obtain concessions in Russia was backed by the White, Guggenheim, and Sinclair interests. Directors of companies controlled by these three financiers included Thomas W. Lamont (Guaranty Trust), William Boyce Thompson (Federal Reserve Bank), and John Reed's employer, Harry Payne Whitney (Guaranty Trust). This strongly suggests that the syndicate was formed to cash in on earlier support for the Bolshevik cause in the revolutionary period. Rothschild ordered the execution by the Bolsheviks they controlled of Tsar Nicolas II and his entire Russian family. And then we found that Guaranty Trust financially backed the Soviet Bureau in New York in 1919.

The first really concrete signal that previous political and financial support was paying off came in 1923 when the Soviets formed their first international bank, Ruskombank. Morgan associate Olof Aschberg became nominal head of this Soviet bank; Max May, a vice president of Guaranty Trust, became a director of Ruskombank, and the Ruskombank promptly appointed Guaranty Trust Company its U.S. agent.

Of all American business leaders, the one who most vigorously patronized the cause of Fascism was Thomas W. Lamont. Head of the powerful J.P. Morgan banking network, Lamont served as something of a business consultant for the government of Fascist Italy.

If this were true, did Edna know of this? Is it possible that this was another deep, dark secret she took to her grave and wanted me to reveal in this book?

Think about this for a moment. Edna had been through many years of caring for and helping to heal the wounded and dying soldiers of World War I in France. Now she was working at 120 Broadway during the tragedy of World War II, and working for L.F. Rothschild.

Since Edna and Mr. Rothschild were both seniors in a sea of young men, these two contemporaries must have been good friends for years. If Rothschild was married to Cora Guggenheim and that name traces to the Skull and Bones Society, did Edna know of it? If so, could she have been a puppet for the war profiteering moguls, or even yet, could she have been part of it? One must think that after seeing the worst side of what war can do, as she had seen by taking part as a Red Cross nurse in France during World War I, it would seem highly unlikely. It was more likely that Edna had found out about the Skull and Bones Society and its part in the war from visiting the Banker's Club, located at the top of the Equitable Building.

The Equitable Building blocked out so much sunlight that the city changed the zoning regulations to require setbacks- creating the so-called wedding cake profile on tall buildings. Just north of Trinity Church and the head of Wall Street, the 1915 Equitable Building rises up 40 stories. The protests of critics who feared that such buildings would make the city a sunless canyon led to zoning laws in 1916 requiring setbacks (in which the upper stories are stepped back to allow more sunlight to reach street level). Though nothing special to look at, the building did New York and the entire country an enormous favor; its towering height and mass led to the nation's first zoning laws in 1916. Hence, I also asked myself, is it sheer coincidence that I found out about the Equitable Building and the Skull & Bones connection on September 11th, 2001? Was this yet another deep, dark secret that Edna took to her grave, and she wanted me to reveal it in this book? Ironically, the first time I had seen the building was after 9/11. The building that was once accused of blocking the sunlight from Wall Street was now glistening in the golden rays of sunlight at the end of the day. I thought that this same building also experienced years of being cast in darkness from the tall towers of the World Trade Center. Since their removal, 120 Broadway now shines once again in sunlight while it casts a shadow on the remaining buildings surrounding its area.

Not much has been documented about Edna's life on Wall Street. What is known for sure is that Edna Wallace Hopper was extremely savvy in stock trading, had an interest in it since the time she was married to A. O. Brown in 1908. In fact, her interest in Wall Street and trading was well before then, back to the time she began on Broadway. Edna was on Broadway in 1878 when telegraphs were installed and Edison's lights were first illuminated at the end of Wall Street and Broadway. Today, the early New York Stock Exchange is known as the "Victorian Internet". Some people were frightened by it all, but not Edna. It fascinated her. Edna was trading in 1896 when the Dow Jones Industrial Average began, the oldest stock market index today. She was there when, in 1899, J.P. Morgan took hold of the market, and the symbol of the Bull and the Bear originated. By 1903, while she was doing "The Silver Slipper", a new space was opened on the great trading floor, and the enunciator board was introduced. She had seen Rockefeller become the richest man in the world in 1906. Edna was there when the American Stock Exchange began in 1928, amongst the great Manhattan Skyline. Edna was also there when a copper speculation caused the 1907 panic and made the banks topple. Edna was back in New York in 1918 when the war had ended, to witness the first ticker tape parade. By this time, New York was full of traffic from automobiles. She had lost her fortune in 1919, and again in the mid-1930s, she had lost most of her money again through stock market speculation.

Edna was working on Wall Street on Black Thursday, October 24th, 1929, the day of the biggest stock market crash. By the 29th, there was an avalanche on Wall Street, and a wild panic was the result. This was the worst economic crisis of the 20th Century. But once again, Edna proved to be resilient and resourceful. She was such a shrewd and steady customer at the brokerage house of L. F. Rothschild that sometime around 1938, she was invited to make her offices with them, having a boardroom desk amongst 35 men.

Did Edna Wallace Hopper have knowledge of the powerful Skull and Bones society members and their positions in the world banking industry? One would think yes, as she was perched on a high seat at a desk positioned in the boardroom of L. F. Rothschild, located in the 120 Broadway Building. She invested for them and quadrupled her fortune for them and for herself as well.

Brotherhood of Death Emblem

In 1963, President Kennedy signed Executive Order 11110, which returned the power to issue currency to the U.S. government, without using the Federal Reserve (which was formed by the Rothschild family). Another attempt to control the Rothschild power is made, and another President is assassinated.

Today, Queen Elizabeth's Grand Visor and Advisor is Lord Evelyn

Rothschild. He is the grandson of Mayer Rothschild. Lord Evelyn Rothschild is the second-wealthiest person on Earth, with a wealth of approximately 500 trillion dollars. He bought the Associated Press. They own the three major television networks, the Royal Mint, control the London gold bullion market, and control the interests of Royal Dutch and Shell Oil.

I read that in 2001, Lord Evelyn married Lynn Forrester. The newlyweds had a honeymoon in Washington, DC, and then moved into their Manhattan high-rise, where they had a bird's-eye view of the World Trade Center Towers as they fell.

By 2009, I did more research, and thanks to a man named Jerry Mazza, an Online Journal Associate Editor, I would like to give you a simplified explanation of his observations on the occupants of 120 Broadway and the events of September 11th, 2001. The information I wish to share with you is what I have found on the internet. I make no claims or declarations to its truth, except I will declare that I believe it to be the truth. As I live in a country of freedom of speech, I wish to share with you my findings in the hope that someday the truth will be declared about what was actually behind the destruction of the World Trade Center Towers.

At the time of 9/11, AIG (occupant of 120 Broadway) was the world's largest insurance company. AIG and ACE were run by the Greenberg family. Maurice "Hank" Greenberg was the kingpin. His son Jeffrey was chairman of Marsh & McLennan in the North Tower of the World Trade Center (WTC) and had occupancy also in the South Tower. Marsh also had ties to the CIA. Son Evan Greenberg was CEO of ACE Unlimited, situated in Building 7 of WTC, which also contained AIG subsidiary Kroll, closely related to the CIA, with a tower also in Building 7. Tower 7 also contained offices of the FBI, Department of Defense, IRS (including Enron's papers), US Secret Service, Securities & Exchange Commission (with more stock fraud records), Citibank's Smith Barney, the mayor's Office of Emergency Management, and other financial institutions.

According to Richard Grove, as a senior manager of software accounts on Marsh and AIG accounts, Kroll also managed the Enron fraud once Ken Lay stepped down. Immediately after 9/11, Marsh established a terrorism team called Marsh Crisis. Consultancy. The Democratic Underground reports that AIG allegedly was laundering drug money and was involved in the Afghanistan oil and gas pipelines. They claim that Greenberg and the Adnan Khasshogi family allegedly benefited from the Afghanistan narcotics trade and had interests in the oil and pipelines as well.

Greenberg Taurig Law firm of Miami represented George Bush in the 2000 Florida election vote recount, partially funded/sponsored a delegation to Israel by House and Senate Armed Services Committee members and government contractors to witness and be briefed on interrogation, resistance procedures, and torture techniques. Taurif Greenberg works with 9/11 victims and their families on planning for them to receive money, as they must sign an agreement never to sue the government for any reason. Today, there is a wife, Ellen Mariani, who is being legally harassed for refusing to sign. I applaud her for her courage and hope to meet her someday soon.

Six weeks before 9/11, Larry Silverstein took control of the lease of all the World Trade Center buildings. Three companies that originally insured the buildings were AIG, ACE, and Marsh. They sold stakes of the original contract to their competition, a technique called reinsuring.

Once the towers came down, the reinsurers got caught holding the bag. Was this merely just lucky timing? On April 26th, 2001, the Port Authority leased the WTC for 99 years to Silverstein Properties and Westfield America Inc.

The mysterious manner in which these massive, well-constructed towers came down in 10 seconds seems unlikely to many who have knowledge of their construction; this is, in all likelihood, the effect of the two jets that collided. The extreme heat caused a meltdown, as the said reason makes absolutely no sense when you can see footage of a woman standing and waving for help in the gaping hole where one of the jets had entered the building. That would be impossible if the extreme heat still existed. Many who witnessed still believe there were simultaneous explosives involved at the same moment, which means well planned out destruction; Could 19 Muslims with box cutters do such a thing alone?

One should carefully think about the event that occurred eight hours after the towers collapsed. Silverstein had Tower 7 "pulled" by controlled internal demolition. How could someone think of doing this so soon after the towers collapsed, and why would he? Building seven did not have any damage from the jets, but it did have many records and files, as mentioned earlier. It was also insured with the same companies, possibly the same policy?

Considering the "luck" of the Greenbergs and Silversteins, who made huge profits from the destruction, it makes one wonder if, in fact, it was merely outside terrorists or was it possibly yet another act in American history with greed behind it, as were the wars mentioned earlier in this chapter. I find it odd that the world wars and the event of 9/11 made riches for the occupants of the 120 Broadway building. I truly believe that Edna Wallace Hopper knew of the schemes that surrounded the World Wars, the greed of the war moguls, and feared that they would continue into the next century with doom to many innocent victims. I fear my own existence to be safe in writing this chapter for you, yet I feel it is my duty to make everyone aware, as I have found many heroic people to enlighten others to be aware of these evil doings, with the hopes that one day soon the people will take a stand and stop this repetition of greed-driven power. For the woman named Edna, who put her own luxuries and comforts aside to help aid the wounded and needy soldiers of war, could not have been happy in finding that she helped gain riches for those who crafted the progression of war for profit. This book is her confession.

Not because of shame, but because of fear of "the people", AIG took its name off the exterior of the 120 Broadway building in 2009, after it became public knowledge of the 160 million dollars of raises AIG gave its members from the taxpayers' funds given to AIG by the government. President Lincoln would be proud to know that the people have finally given fear to these greedy moguls. He predicted he would be killed for finding a way to stop the Federal Reserve (Rothschilds and others) from making slaves of the people. Remember that WE can make it happen, like the wishes of Lincoln, Kennedy, and Obama.

The 120 Broadway building (3rd from left), called The Equitable, as seen in 1917. It is the large building with twin towers built straight upward with an arched portico entryway.

A Chicago Tribune paper dated March 3rd, 1938, reads: Edna Wallace Hopper Brown, who calls herself the eternal flapper, told her age and kept it a secret in federal court yesterday. She wrote it on a piece of paper and handed it to Judge Patrick T. Stone. He didn't tell what she wrote; he merely lifted his eyebrows and handed the note back. So the attorneys and the rest of the world will just have to go on wondering.

Mrs. Brown is suing six cosmetics firms for an aggregate of $250,000 that she says they owe her for advertising their products on the radio".

During the 1930s and the 1940s, Edna Wallace Hopper Brown had a successful profit from her Edna Wallace Hopper Cosmetic Company. It ranked just below Chrysler Corporation in U.S.A. sales and was one of the top fifty successful companies in America. Her position with the company was as vice president. She did numerous NBC and CBS radio advertisements, with her voice now being heard in the homes of millions of women all over the nation. "My strawberry lemon facial cream can also be served as a dessert topping", was a statement that today is still considered to be one of the most absurd and deceptive product claims in the history of advertising. But was it? It was probably made of natural ingredients that were digestible as well as topical. Her innocence, honesty, and natural way of living were difficult to comprehend in a changed world of commodities.

In an interview for Look Magazine in 1938, Edna's frankness is evident as she confesses to wearing two false teeth. "Sometimes I forget to put them in before I leave my home. My maid would ask, "Have you forgotten something?"

There are photos of her having a grand ole time with friends in Havana, Cuba, in the 1930s. She did special performances exhibiting her amazing acrobatic dancing and her still youthful agility, sometimes accompanied by her younger French dance partner.

Edna made special appearances at galas and expositions, including the Chicago and the New York World's Fairs. Now, Edna was a marvel from the past, singing and dancing tunes of yesteryear while being gazed upon by audiences who wanted a glimpse of what life was like "way back then".

Billy Rose included her in his touring extravaganza of beauties, and in 1945, Edna was featured as one of the "Glamour Girls of the Past" while appearing in Billy Rose's Diamond Horseshoe Club in the Hotel Paramount on 46th Street, West of Broadway. George Jessell introduced her at the New York World's Fair's special show of old Broadway song and dance.

Yet, her life was now on Wall Street, and Wall Street was where she remained for the remaining nineteen years of her career.

She conducted daily transactions at her desk in the firm of L. F. Rothschild. Edna made a serious business of handling her own finances, and in fifteen years she had earned four times her initial investment. Each day, Edna would ride the subway to the office, each morning she would be seen, sometimes dressed like a flapper, always wearing a fashionable hat, scrambling up the subway stairs at rush hour, and briskly walking to her office, where she worked a six-hour day. The 1950s were exciting times to be on Wall Street, and the New York Stock Exchange was seeing some of its brightest days.

Edna was in her mid-seventies on a cruise ship in the 1930s.

The Equitable Building at 120 Broadway is in the heart of the Wall Street Exchange in New York City. Built in 1917, it cast the first shadow on Wall Street and was mainly occupied by Skull and Bones society members and associated businesses, including the Federal Reserve.

The front faced Trinity Church and the World Trade Center Towers, which cast a shadow on it until September 11, 2001. September 11th, 1857, was historically the day of the Great Massacre, when the Mormons attacked 120 Arkansas emigrants in Utah.

Edna, as a key stockbroker, exiting the NYC SUBWAY on Wall Street, 1953.

The Toast of Broadway at the turn of the century seems to have a formula for eternal youth- WORK !!! was printed in the worldwide newspapers under this photo of Edna posing at her desk at L. F. Rothschild Trading firm in the Equitable Building at 120 Broadway. March 23, 1953, Mrs. Hopper Brown is approximately ninety-two years old. World Wide Photo from the private collection of Jim Alessio.

In 1943, a reunion performance of Edna with her co-star Cyril Scott at the grand Empire Theater as they sang in The Girl I Left Behind Me by David Belasco. On the left is actress Lillian Gish, and on the far right is Burgess Meredith with his arm around Edna. The young Lillian and Burgess also performed that evening at the Empire Theater.

Chapter Eight

The Final Curtain Call

In 1953, there was one final curtain call for Miss Hopper. At the invitation of the American National Theater and Academy, Edna was asked to appear in a review honoring the Empire Theater, which was to be torn down to make room for a skyscraper.

In the last week of May 1953, the same actress surprised the audience by skipping onto the stage, holding a pail of strawberries, just as she had done sixty years before in the same role in the theater's grand opening show "The Girl I Left Behind Me". The Sunday night performance was a short scene where she wore the same type of straw hat and gingham dress as in 1893, which looked quite similar to Dorothy's in The Wizard of Oz. She recalled the moment when a thorn from the strawberries had pricked the young girl just as she was about to advance onto the stage. The audience was amazed at how she looked and sounded as she did back in 1893. It must have been so bittersweet for Edna, as all of those actors who were once around her were now all gone. Now living in a new world of theatergoers, this was the final farewell to a time that had now passed.

The event was featured in Life Magazine's June 8, 1953 issue. Included in the feature are photos of a ninety-something-year-old Edna taking the subway to and from her New York Stock Exchange world, as well as a pose of her at her L. F. Rothschild office desk while trading over the telephone. These photos were taken by the legendary Swiss-born photographer, Robert Frank. Mr. Frank was a photographer for fashion magazines in the 1940s, and his style of capturing people was a bit ahead of his time. According to my research, Life Magazine was not comfortable with his approach to photography at this time in the 1950s. He later documented the Rolling Stones in a documentary film in 1972, depicting them in wild orgies and taking drugs. The Stones stopped the film from being released to protect their recording careers from having their images shown in this light. In the year of Edna's death, Frank released a book called The Americans, showing hundreds of photographs of the reality of both the touching and the shameful sides of our society. The American book was unacceptable to American marketing at this time, but was well-liked by the French market. Today, it is considered one of the finest documented photography collections of mid-century American life. It was shown on a world tour of museums in 2009, marking its 50th anniversary. I wonder if Edna personally had chosen Robert Frank to capture her last photo layout for a major magazine. I am reminded of how she always seemed to be attracted to talent on the cutting edge, the innovative, the controversial, and those that would stand the test of time. Like a tooth missing from a perfect smile, it is unfortunate to tell you that I was unable to include any photos of Edna taken by Frank, as he refused to have them included in this book. The reason was his overwhelming involvement in the touring exhibit of his 1959 photo collection and book called The Americans, as was regretfully informed to me by a gallery representative.

In the Life Magazine article titled The Sun Never Sets on Edna, Frank captured a mid-ninety-year-old Edna on her daily routine, scrambling up the subway stairs to her Wall Street broker's office at L. F. Rothschild. Also, there is a photo of her posing by a statue of Venus in her rooftop garden of her last home at 330 East 58th Street. Life quotes her as saying, "I have the nerve to stand up beside Venus". The article mentions her final performance a few weeks earlier at the Empire Theater before its demolition to make way for a skyscraper.

1953 became the year that Edna seemed to have started preparation for her future preservation, to be remembered and documented, to remain eternal in the minds of living mankind. Perhaps the realization that the Empire Theater, which opened with the grand beginning of her life on Broadway, was now going to be demolished and forgotten. She, too, must have the abandonment of her life of fame taken away by the hands of time. Edna "set the stage" by doing her final "swan song" at the Empire Theater.

In October of 1953, Edna met with Mike Wallace for a radio program named Star Struck, which aired regularly on CBS to interview stars of radio and film. Edna was to reflect on her longtime career on Broadway, both its beginnings and the Broadway of the current 1950s. This was actually the beginning of Mike Wallace's career, for he tried a career as an actor on Broadway, which was not so much a success. He then went into radio as an interviewer for successful actors, which led him into a career as one of the greatest newsmen in the history of television.

Edna getting on board an American Airlines jet in 1956. This photo may have been taken on her final trip to California to visit San Francisco and the Dunsmuir mansion in San Leandro that she once owned. (photo from the private collection of Jim Alessio)

Edna was seen as Wilbur's Girl in the Girl I Left Behind Me in 1893 (top left & bottom right Sarony Publishing Co., NY) and in her encore farewell performance as Wilbur's Ann in 1953 (top right New York Times). The photo on the bottom right is from her obituary in the New York Times, Dec 1959.

2002

New York City

I wondered if I would ever find a sound bite of Edna's voice. I wondered if one even existed today. One day, while listening to the theme song for NBC's news, as composed by John Williams, I looked over at the photo I had of Edna in front of an NBC radio microphone, and it hit me to search the archives. To my dismay, no sound bites were found at NBC. I then thought of looking into the archives of the Museum of Television and Radio in New York via the Internet. To my sheer excitement, I found a copy of her voice. I telephoned the museum and asked an assistant what exactly was in the archives. He informed me that it was a copy of an October 2, 1953, radio interview program by Mike Wallace on the CBS network called Stage Struck.

In this interview, she is referred to as Mrs. Albert O. Brown, as she is now the widow of her former husband. So far, these are the only sound bites of her voice that I know of today. That is not to say that somewhere else is the possibility of an archive of her voice or a motion picture image with sound unbeknownst to me. I discovered a 1931 silent motion picture newsreel that is located in a vault in Los Angeles, of Edna being formally greeted back to her native city of San Francisco by the mayor. It is my wish that the film be preserved and copied, as presently only the original deteriorating copy exists.

In July of 2002, I made a special trip to New York to hear for the first time the voice of someone I felt I had come to know so personally. As I walked from my hotel to the Museum of Television and Radio, my emotions ran rampant from nervous to sheer anxiety to wonderment, mixed with excitement and ecstasy. Accompanied by my mother, I requested to hear the tape, waited silently until I was instructed to pass through the doors, and then went down the stairs.

Walking down the deep and silent stairway, I felt as if I was walking into the tomb of a great pharaoh as I entered a very dark and somber room, feeling as if I was visiting the dead. The dramatic black room was surrounded by video and audio sound booths, made for two. Sitting there alongside my mother, I felt like I was strapped in a time machine for a ride through time and space. Glancing over at my mother, I wondered if she felt as anxious as I did as I waited to hear her speak for the first time, or if I was possibly the only person in the world today who felt this way about Edna. Fast-forwarding through a good half hour of the program, I finally got to the part about the Empire Theater.

In the program, Mike Wallace introduces her as Edna Wallace Hopper Brown. His first question: When did you first come to New York as an actress?

Answer: In eighteen ninety…(pause) THREE! Question: Who introduced you to Broadway? Answer: Charles Frohman… no less.

Question: What was Broadway and New York like then?

Answer: Oh, Broadway was a lovely street, and so was 42nd. 42nd Street, it was a lovely street, oh, different!

Question: It was different? Answer: Yes, that is true.

Then there was Claude Erlanger, Shubert, Al Woods was 30 years old, and oh yes, David Belasco.

Question: Where did you learn to act? Answer: I never learned to act.

Question: Never?

Answer: Yes. Yes. I never did!

Question: Do you still go to the theater?

Answer: Yes, I always go. I love the theater! It's a different approach- the theater now.

Then Mike Wallace thanks her for joining him in the studio.

Edna's voice exuded sweetness and pleasantry. She carried excitement in her tone yet softness in her volume. Her regal speech was distinctively refined, like most of the early dramatic theater actresses of her time, with a slight influence of a New Yorker accent and a hint of the old western California drawl.

Shirley Booth (Academy Award best actress winner in 1953's "Come Back Little Sheba", also known for television's classic Hazel) had graced the stage in the last running show named "The Time of the Cuckoo", which closed the Empire's doors on Sunday, May 24th. In a very moving interview, Shirley gives a heartfelt tribute to the old theater, comparing it to a dear old friend. Booth comments on the sadness of the great theater's demise. She recalled her first time in the Empire, as a young actress just arriving in New York.

"While rehearsing one afternoon, she paused to look around at the great old theater, feeling such amazement and pride to be in its presence. "None of us had dreamed that the Empire would have a last play. "As I looked around, I noticed all the gilding had tarnished, the worn velvet seats from all the many audiences who sat there. It has flavor, like old wine," She added, "It's a very sad honor… Maybe all the ghosts of the Empire, so rudely disposed of, will feel they have a home whenever someone says, "Curtain going up!" "Wherever there are actors and actresses." She expressed how the Empire was a great landmark not only for New York, but also for the world of theater. She finishes her tribute by introducing a recording of Basil Rathbone, reciting Prospero's "We are such stuff as dreams are made of" speech from "The Tempest". "There are actors who are melted into thin air… faded into a last…"

The Eternal Flapper Edna with Best Actress Academy Award Winner Shirley Booth in 1953. Both aired together on the radio in a tribute to The Empire Theater. Booth was appalled by its demolition, while Edna was saddened by it. Photo from the collection of Jim Alessio

1956

On June 8th, 1956, in the Borough of Manhattan, New York, Edna Wallace Hopper made, published, declared, and signed her last will and testament in front of three witnesses. In it, she left her eyes to the Eye-Bank for Sight Restoration, Inc. in New York. She directed the remains of her body be interred in Mountain View Cemetery at Piedmont, California, beside her mother, Josephine B. Dunsmuir, and her stepfather, Alexander Dunsmuir, in the Dunsmuir family plot, number 27, lot 25. "I request those who shall be responsible for my funeral and interment arrangements to communicate with my good friend, Martin Schwartz, now residing in New York".

The will reads, "I hereby give and bequeath absolutely unto my friend, Jane Sewell, my small evening bag of brocade silk with a gold frame set with sapphires and diamonds, (which was received from my mother and is of high sentimental value to me)".

"I hereby give and bequeath absolutely unto said Martin Shwartz and The Bankers Trust Company, (both of whom are hereinafter named as my executors) or to the survivor of them, all of my clothing and jewelry and other articles of ornamentation, adornment or personal use and all household furniture, furnishings and fixtures, silverware, plate, china and other tableware and all books and pictures and all other personal effects owned by me at the time of my death" This excludes the bag given to Jane Sewell. "I request the said legatees, or their survivor, to sell the same and to include the proceeds thereof in the trust hereinafter in Article Seventh. Article Seventh: All the rest, residue, and remainder of my property, of whatsoever kind and wheresoever situate, I hereby give, devise, and bequeath absolutely unto said Bankers Trust Company. In trust nevertheless, to enter into and upon and to take possession of the same and to hold, securely invest and reinvest the same, retaining the principal thereof in perpetuity, and disposing of the income therefrom as follows: The trust hereby created shall be designated and known in perpetuity as the Edna Wallace Hopper trust. I hereby direct my said trustee to pay over all of the net income from the trust hereby created to HOME OF THE GOOD SHEPHERD, now located at 501 Cambridge Street, San Francisco, California. And now being conducted for the care of delinquent and pre-delinquent girls, or to any similar Catholic institution for the care of delinquent or pre-delinquent girls, by which The Home of the Good Shepherd may hereafter at any time be acquired or with which it may hereafter merge or consolidate, for so long as said Home of the Good Shepherd, or any Catholic successor thereto, shall continue to exist and to be conducted for the care of delinquent girls in a manner sufficiently worthy, in the sole and absolute discretion of my said trustee, to entitle it to public support. The will goes on to read that if The Home of The Good Shepherd ceases to exist, then all such net income would be paid to St Elizabeth's Infant Hospital, also located in San Francisco, or any Catholic successor, which cares for unmarried mothers and their infants in the city of San Francisco. It was clearly stated that any such beneficiary should be conducted for the care of delinquent or pre-delinquent girls or for the purpose of providing care for unmarried mothers and their infants. It appears that Edna's main concern was to provide for a home that was located in San Francisco, a home where it seems possible that she may have given birth sometime around 1886, before she went away to New York to start a new life and a new career, away from Alexander.

I was so nervous to see Edna's will and testament, as I had felt that it would give an answer to a question that seemed to haunt me since I had read the British Columbia trial transcript, and since I had visited the home in San Leandro. Was Edna a victim of sexual abuse by Alexander, and did she bear his child in 1886? This can explain why she went from one private school to another, finally being sent home and having to pretend to be younger, say 14, when in fact she was 22. Having to lie about her age during her youth and later on bragging about it during her middle age expresses two things. One is that she and her mother had a reason to conceal her true age, as there was gossip stirring in New York and San Francisco that Alexander had fathered a child and that the mother was not Josephine. Did they want the public to think that Edna was too young to have been pregnant in 1886?

Where it is more commonplace for a woman to hide her age when she is older, this was just the opposite for the unusual person, Edna. Through her youngest days, while in boarding school in the 1880s, she was a young woman in her teens, while her mother had her in schools with girls much younger than her. It makes one wonder why? Early in her career, she would say regarding her age, "No one will ever know: my birth records were destroyed in the San Francisco earthquake, just in case you have any ideas". But now, in the 1920s, Edna is ready to tell the world just how old she really is, while being in her sixties. This is quite unusual for a woman, especially one in the theater, and especially one who was much younger than she appeared to be. I believe that she and her mother had pretended that she was younger in 1886, as gossip in San Francisco was the place where Alex had fathered a child, and a question lurked about as to who the mother was. Certainly, no one would think a girl of 15 years of age could have been, but if they knew that Edna was 23 or 25 years of age, it might have been noticed. By the 1920s, Edna was finished with her stage career, her mother was dead, and she was free to tell the truth about her age. Not having this sense of freedom since her youth, and then having it was expressed in the loudest way for all to hear, on the radio, and the biggest way for all to see, in Vaudeville. I have found a photo of Edna appearing amongst a hundred orphan children in Los Angeles in 1927. I sense that she never forgot a child born in 1886 who was taken to an orphanage. I believe that child came from Edna.

The strangeness in the fact that the Dunsmuir women switched over to the side of Edna during the Hopper VS Dunsmuir trial makes one wonder what had happened to change their minds? Yes, it is certain that Joan Dunsmuir was at odds with her son James, but she was also appalled by Edna's mother entering the family. What could make the women suddenly sympathetic enough to take sides with the woman who was the daughter of the ever-despised Josephine Wallace? An unplanned child born sharing the bloodlines would be a good reason. There was a reason why Edna was so adamant in getting the fortune of Alexander into her own hands. I never believed for one second, that greed had driven her to three trials for his fortune. I believe that she wanted his fortune to be turned over to the Home of The Good Shepherd someday, just as she did with her own fortune. This was a way to somehow provide for her lost child, and his. To me this will and testimony is a last chance for Edna to provide for someone else who went through the same circumstance as she did. I believe that Edna could never stop thinking about this child, somewhere in the world away from hers. This also explains why Alexander was so distraught when Edna left San Francisco to live in New York. It may also explain why she never bore a child with either DeWolf Hopper or Albert O. Brown. It may be possible that she was forced to abort the child, and had wished carry the baby to full delivery at the Home of The Good Shepherd in San Francisco. Again these are my conclusions and observations that I have researched and hold deep feelings about.

It may just be coincidence.

I must tell you that it took me about six months to request a copy of the will from the time it was found in New York's Surrogate's Court. I feared the truth would be revealed to me in the will, and my fear was that my assumptions on Edna leaving a child behind were false. I was away when it had arrived, I called my friend Dick and asked him to read to me over the telephone, and a feeling of relief, of closure, and of sadness surrounded me. I cried for the first time, for a woman whom I had never met, yet I knew her more than anyone could, or ever did.

They will also state that all purchases and investments for the trust would be made through the New York Stock Exchange firm of L.F. Rothschild and Company. "This firm has shown me the greatest kindness and has been of great assistance to me in advice and service, in appreciation of all of which the foregoing request is made."

In addition to this, the sum of ten thousand dollars was to be given to The Actors Fund of America, located in New York, adding, "Of which I am proud to be a life member". Additionally, $20,000 was to be given to Martin Shwartz, "in recognition and appreciation of his friendship and kindness to me and to aid in the advancement of his career".

I had found out that Edna had made a final return to San Francisco in 1958, the year before she passed on. She visited the Dunsmuir country mansion at San Leandro that she had inherited in 1901. While there, she had met with Mrs. Florence (Hellman) Dinkelspiel, who had inherited the estate from her parents, the Hellmans. The Hellmans had been the tenants for the estate when Edna was renting it, and had the winning bid on it when Edna decided to auction it off. It is known that Edna had discussed with Florence what went on there at the estate back at the turn of the century. It may have been a confession, a means of closure, to the events that had haunted her for the rest of her days. I do not know exactly what was said at this time of writing. I am sure the flashbacks of memory made it an emotional moment for both Edna and Florence. During that same visit in 1958, Edna had returned to the Mountain View Cemetery, where she paid her respects to her beloved mother Josephine and to her stepfather Alexander, both laid to rest. A simple, inexpensive gravestone, which says "Dunsmuir", is at lot # 25. James (Dunsmuir) is the one who arranged for the monument. Here, one can clearly see his stinginess and lack of concern for both Alexander and Josephine, just as James had scolded Edna's man friend for paying full fare to transport Alexander's body on the train, as well as telling him to find an inexpensive coffin. Considering that James had inherited

$6,000,000 from his brother's estate, one would hope that he would have spent a bit more on his burial. It gives one feelings of shame and disgrace and sadness to visit the Millionaire's Row, as it is called, passing by one monument more beautiful than the next, and then to arrive at a lot

25 and see the barren ground with a simple footstone. Edna had made arrangements to have her buried alongside her mother and Alex.

As not to upstage her parents, Edna had a simple upright headstone made, inscribed:

"EDNA WALLACE HOPPER" "DIED DECEMBER 14, 1959"

"THOSE WHOM THE GODS LOVE NEVER GROW OLD"

The New York Times obituary reads Edna Wallace Hopper, Actress with Perpetual Youth, Is Dead.

For now, Edna Wallace Hopper will be laid to rest. I was four years old in 1959.

It would be another half-century until I would help her request for "eternity" and "resurrection" in the 21st century.

The Secret Informant 2001-2006

Just as I had finished writing this chapter, another coincidental occurrence happened. I found an auction catalog from Parket-Bernet Galleries of New York for a public auction held December 7th and 8th in 1960.

The auction featured valuable precious-stone jewelry from private owners including the Estate of Edna Wallace Hopper. Among the pieces from her estate was a pair of diamond and sapphire clips, total weight 7.60 carats that sold for $1200, a diamond ring with an emerald-cut diamond weighing about 9 carats with two baguette diamonds in shank which sold for $11,500, a diamonds (12.80, 4.35, 6.45 carats) and emeralds (2.75 and 4.25 carats) bracelet which sold for $4150, another diamond brooch with over a hundred diamonds in it sold for $975, several strands of cultured pearls, possibly one of them was a birthday gift given to her from Alexander Dunsmuir, who purchased it in Tiffany's three days before his death. And a diamond locket and pearl chain, possibly the one that had a small photo of her beloved mother Josephine, as worn by Edna in many publicity photos for her Fountain of Youth products. No mention in the catalog of the serpentine armband that I had found her wearing so often in her photos. It made me wonder what happened to all the other items from her estate. I was nevertheless pleased to know where some of her treasures went. According to her will, the items from her estate were to be sold off and the proceeds were to go to the Home of the Good Shepherd in San Francisco.

The story still lives on. There is a living, breathing man who lives in Victoria, British Columbia, who may possibly be her grandson and does not know it. I have learned to know of him, from a good source that I cannot disclose, for reasons of privacy and of possible legal action, among other reasons.

A letter exits that was written in 1886 that has something to do with a child who was born out of wedlock. The father of this child is said to be Alexander Dunsmuir. I had done some research, only to find that the mention of the mother was not that of Edna, but was advised, under strict law and order from the "family from Windsor" that its contents could not be disclosed, although I initially had read that the letter was to be opened in the year 2000, which it was in fact. I also learned that the Queen of England had purchased the Craigdarroch Castle around 1920, for her son, the Duke of Windsor who married an American woman and thus declined to take the throne. This son, who supposedly was the firstborn by the Queen, born after 1886. If all this is true, then this child, born in 1886, was indeed the first-born and was secretly raised elsewhere in Scotland. My source of knowledge had informed me that a man, who is in his sixties, had confidentially approached my "mole" for assistance as he was presenting a case in court. The man allegedly believes that Alexander Dunsmuir was his grandfather. This information was given to him by his grandparents, who had said that he (or she) was born in 1886 in San Francisco and somehow ended up in British Columbia. The grandparent was told that Alexander was the father and did not know who the mother was. His investigation led to a woman from Scotland, but it was found inconclusive.

The informant let me know that the letter is in reference to a child born in Scotland, not in San Francisco, in 1886.

Are you confused?

Let me explain what I think - There were two children born in 1886, both were children of Alexander Dunsmuir. The one who was born in San Francisco may have been the child of Edna, who gave the child up for adoption through the Home of the Good Shepherd. As a man who grew up in Scotland, he was informed of his father's identity. He later told his son and his grandson in Victoria that his grandfather was born in San Francisco in 1886, the same year Edna left to start a new life in New York. I was informed that the sealed letter (document) had no reference to a child from San Francisco, but of a child born in England, and under strict law from "the family from Windsor," the reference to the mother cannot be disclosed. I think this child may have been born to a mother of royal blood, possibly the Queen or one of her sisters. If this is all true, which I am not sure of as of this date, and then it would mean that Edna's child and the royal blooded child were siblings. This may be why Edna was so chummy with the royals of Europe, and possibly why Joan Dunsmuir and her daughters took Edna's side closely in the lawsuit. It may also give reason as to why the Royal Family dominated the Dunsmuir Castle in later years.

I told my informant that I wanted to meet this man in Victoria, whose grandparent was one of the Castaways from Society not mentioned earlier in my book. The informant insisted on not doing so, for fear of legal suit as well as for respect for the man. I explained that my intentions were for the good, that this would help his claim, and that I believe that this is what Edna wanted all along, to have a family that would live on and to know about her.

"Does this man even have any idea who Edna Wallace Hopper is?" I asked. "No, and I don't want to go there", the informant said. "Look, it's not incest of any nature. She was closer in age to Alexander, and at the time, her mother was not married to him." She was a wonderful and great woman. If she were his grandmother, he should not be deprived of knowing about her." "No, I can't do that, I am sorry", the informant answered. "Look, you are in the way of the truth, of history. It is wrong for you not to let him know. Don't you want the truth to be known? That is all I want. I didn't spend all this time researching and thinking about what happened for nothing!"

"Jim, I want the truth too, but I don't know how," the informant said with sincerity and understanding. "I may be planning a trip to Florida. Maybe we can talk more about it then. Ok?"

My reply to Mr. X was, "You could merely say to him that there is a man in Florida who believes that Edna may have had a child with Alexander and that he's asking you if you knew anyone who may have known about this or who may possibly be an ancestor. You can then tell him that I approached you and that I wanted to help. Just say that you never mentioned him to me."

"Ok, I will think about it", he said with a sense of relief sounding from his words. It was almost as if he knew I was right and that he was letting plain fear get in the way.

2002 had passed, and in 2003, I was beginning to prepare my book for my agent. I decided to contact my informant friend once again, this time hoping that an update might be available.

I asked if there was any more news regarding the man who may be the great-grandson of Alexander Dunsmuir. What I did find out was this. The information that was presented shows that a child was born in Scotland, which was not of any help to the man. I was also informed that the man is not seeking monetary retribution. He is merely seeking to know the truth of his genealogy. I also learned that even if he was interested in monetary retribution, it would not be possible since the remainder of the Dunsmuir estate has long since been distributed to descendants of one of Alexander's sisters. In simple terms, the money is gone. However, the grandfather told this man that he was born in San Francisco in 1886. This appears to be another child, possibly Edna's. The man does not know of this possibility, but I was informed that if I sent a copy of this book to my informant, he would give it to the alleged great-grandson.

Time had passed, and I did not hear from my informant. I received a call one day in my office on Sanibel Island. The phone rang, and I picked it up and heard the low voice of a whisper. It sounded as if he was saying, "They know about our conversations and have monitored our emails and phone calls." I said in a frightful response, "Oh God. Are you in trouble now? I never wanted this to happen, I'm so sorry". "I'm not really sure about that, but you must agree that the information you have acquired on your own accord, from your own research and not from me." I answered in agreement, "Oh, of course!" I wondered if there was some monitoring going on at this time as well. From the uneasiness of his voice and the tone of his statement, I felt this was the case. The informant then added, "From here on in, Jim, you are on your own. I cannot give you any more advice. These conversations must cease, I'm sorry to tell you." I told Mr. X that I understood. It appeared that the damage was done and that I would no longer be able to communicate with Mr. X again.

Several months had gone by, and one day, another call came into my office. It was late morning. "They have monitored our phone calls and our emails." With a soft whisper, I thought I heard him say, "Jim, they are in Ireland." I questioned him, "They are in Ireland?" There was a short pause, and then I heard Mr. X clearly whisper, "NO, THEY ARE ON YOUR

ISLAND!" At that, there was another short pause, and then a hang-up. The dial tone resonated in my ear as I sat there in shock. I asked myself if "they" meant that the MI5 agents were on Sanibel Island. I panned my vision over to my boss, whose office was next to my desk, with a window separating us. He was sitting with his feet propped up on his desk, wearing the cheap Elvis wig he loved to wear so many times for a cheap laugh. At that time in my life, I was wearing a hairpiece, and John had a warped sense of humor, always clowning with me with endearment. This is what led him to purchase the Elvis wig. John often would come by and tug at my hairpiece and offer to buy it from me. With his back to me, reading and reading the newspaper, I said aloud, "John, I'm taking an early lunch now." It was about 11:30 am. I got in my car and drove on West Gulf Drive to the Sundial Resort. As I made my way down the palm-treed drive, a helicopter came out of nowhere and hovered over the top of my car along the drive. As I pulled into the large and almost empty parking lot of a steamy summer Florida resort off-season, I acted as if I was unaware of the overhead noise of the propellers. The wind from the propellers lifted the back end of my hairpiece up. I must have looked like a rooster. I was not sure which feeling was stronger for me, the fear of the surveillance or the embarrassment of the situation. I made my way to the door into the lobby and pressed myself against the wall once I was inside. I could see the strange glances from the front desk clerks who looked at my messy hairpiece while hearing the noise from the helicopter outside of the main building. I just smiled and attempted to tame down the mess on top of my head while trying to assume back some kind of normalcy by walking past the front desk with a forced dignity. I sat in the dining room with a beautiful panoramic view of the Gulf of Mexico. As it was too early for lunchtime, the Gulf side dining room was empty. My fixed stare was interrupted from time to time by the waitress, who would ask if I was ready to order yet. I held my menu in front of me and found it difficult to concentrate on reading it. My mind was wandering if I was going to get out of there alive. Where are they going to take me, hurt me, or harass me? I eventually ordered my food, hardly ate it, and left. No other attempts were noticed to track them down. I wondered if this would continue at a time I would least expect it.

For the next few days, I watched my back and felt an immense fear. I looked out my windows often and tried to be surrounded by others, not being alone as much as possible. I was now on my own. It was me and "them".

A year or so had passed, and my informant and I connected once again. In either case, I know the feeling was mutual that we both wanted to connect. The fact that he called made me think the call was not planned by him and was monitored.

Mr. X said in a normal tone of voice "I was told by "THE BOSS" that when your book is published, you can place a letter or note to the man inside the book, and I can give it to him. I will present it to him on your behalf", explained Mr. X, who I now consider to be truly a friend." This is the acceptable protocol for her." I was in the process of moving to Connecticut and did not disclose this to him as I thought there was a possibility that our conversation was monitored. I think it was.

Well, all things considered, my afterthoughts took me into a state of shocking realization, that THE BOSS is probably Her Majesty, Queen Elizabeth, and perhaps this man in Victoria, who I believe may be Edna's great-grandson, is someone of considerable affluence and possibly connected within the Royal Circle. Perhaps his great-grandfather was placed into the home of someone close to the House of Windsor. What might have been feelings of satisfaction are overridden by fear, for the words, "If they think nothing of harming their own, they will think nothing of harming you," come back to haunt me since that day I was warned not to disclose my findings regarding the letter in the castle and the dark and secret events that it presents.

Mr. X and I have learned to mutually understand and respect each other's stand in this matter. I've found a friend in my informant, and we plan to meet in person soon. There was a time when I thought Mr. X did not have a good soul. The impression he left in my mind was that he was an arrogant, pompous being who enjoyed the fact that he knew something that I did not and had no concern for Edna's wishes as well as mine. What I realized is that he did care about Edna's wishes and he did care about me as well. He was, in fact, trying to protect me. My informant knew that once I had opened Pandora's Box, I was now stained, or marked as it may, once the knowledge has entered my mind. He also knew that once I knew the hidden truth that I now must tell it in this story. I true story, a long time never been told story. This is the time that Edna wanted the truth to be known. As she had told the Messenger in 1953 that she wanted the true story told in the 21st century. Edna never allowed anyone to write a book on her life during her lifetime, as she knew the missing pieces of the puzzle were of significance to the whole picture puzzle- the one that shows why things happened as they did.

This story is not just a biography, or an investigation story. It is the story of a woman who remained alive for a long time without ever seeing any family members while knowing that somewhere out there was a family of her own. It is my belief that Edna's mission was to connect with her family in the future, so that least they would know who she was, as she never was able to find who they were. I also believe that she was an extremely intelligent yet simple minded person who was not only ahead of her time, but in many ways was ahead of our time.

On December 23rd, 2005 I received in the mail, an envelope containing a telegram I purchased from eBay along with and unexpected gift: a tiny envelope postmarked December 23, 1905, exactly one hundred years to the day. This envelope, card and telegram are what I consider "The Full Circle" of knowledge to this whole story. I always felt there was a missing link, a final mystery that was not yet revealed to me.

This is it. The dream that started this whole reconstruction of her life, the investigation and the writing of this story, was a mystery in itself that was never, and probably never will be explained. But it did happen. I often wondered of all the many facets of her life, why was this painting from in 1903 the element that entered my mind to spark the beginning of this whole recreation, or resurrection, of her life? An answer comes to me in the mail, one hundred years to the day. It was postmarked December 23rd and stamped as arrived on Christmas Eve, December 24th to Mr. William J. Davis, The Illinois

Theater, Chicago, Illinois. It didn't take long for me to recall that the

Silver Slipper was performed at the Illinois Theater, and the only knowledge that the current owners had was that the painting was found in an old theater in Chicago. Now I have a telegram dated December 23rd, 1904, to Will Davis, owner/manager of the Grand Illinois Theater, which reads that Edna is to arrive at the train station on Christmas Eve, 1904. The painting must have been a gift from Edna to Mr. Davis. But who was he? Why did she spend Christmas with him in 1904 and then, for Christmas 1905, send him a simple card that reads "With the seasons Greeting" and inside preprinted with Mrs. Edna Wallace Hopper, where she crossed a line through the "Wallace" and the "Hopper" parts of her name, exposing only the "Edna" reference to him. I did some research on William Davis. He was a grassroots kind of guy, who started as a manager of a foreign touring circus in America and went on successfully to become one of the major owner/managers of theaters in America, being a partners with Charles Frohman, other key owners. He married a diva opera star, Jessie Bartlett Davis, who unexpectedly died in May 1905 of liver failure, as she had not been considered ill. Like Edna, Will Davis loved horses. There must have been closeness between Edna and Will as she chose to spend Christmas with him, yet I have not found any newspaper references to their friendship. One usually plans on spending Christmas Eve with someone very special, someone close to your heart. Why was there no sympathetic mention of his recently lost wife? Was this in itself one of Edna's biggest secrets, and why?

Taking advantage of her last years in good health while understanding that her days were numbered, Edna seemed to have created a runway for her flight to another destiny. The seeds were planted, and her request to have a book done and a film made on her life's true story, with the hopes of having her mission fulfilled of connecting with her family, unknown to her. She revisited the Oakland estate to confess to the well-kept secrets that took place there, she said goodbye to the theater that said hello to her when she arrived in New York, she spoke on the radio to say goodbye and leave her only sound bites that exist today, she had her will drafted for execution and gave her message to someone to help her in the future.

Posing for the painting as Wrenne in The Silver Slipper and giving it to William Davis was the answer to the final wonder I had. If it were not for the dream I had of her posing as a clown in 1904 and then seeing the painting the same day I awoke, this whole investigation would not have happened, and her wish to have this done may have never been fulfilled. I wondered since that day in 1989 as to why this happened. Since then, I wondered about all the images I have since seen of her, why was it this painting that initially entered my awareness? I now think that this was, in fact, her darkest secret of all. Perhaps Mr. Davis was in love with Edna and decided to end the life of his wife in order to have Edna as his true love. Was there foul play involved? I truly believe that Edna had nothing to do with foul play. She may have known of this, however, or at least had a suspicion of it. I think that is why the following Christmas Eve. Mr. Davis merely received a card instead of a visit from her.

Edna Wallace Hopper Brown met the messenger in 1953, asking him to send the message to the writer in 1989. The message was to find the truth and to make a book and musical film on her life. I hoped to fulfill her deepest secret. With the guidance of the informant, I was led to the truth, and I am still on a mission with the same hopes she had, to have her living ancestors know her story one day. You live on through the thoughts and memories of your loved ones. This is the secret to Eternity, as Edna had wisely known.

To protect the identity of my secret informant, I assured him that he would not be identified in my book or in the film for which I am writing a screenplay at this moment. I will tell you this much: the letter of 1886 does, in fact, exist, and someone exists today who claims to be the grandson of Alexander Dunsmuir's illegitimate son. The details of this I cannot share with you, as it could trace back to the identity of my informant. There was a conversation that gave me clear evidence that this man exists today. I have not met him, and I wonder if this book may lead to our meeting someday. Through the telephone conversations and emails in which we communicated in the 21st century, many times my questions were presented in a fearful, almost self-intimidating manner. I felt as if my informant was enjoying this power he had over me and enjoyed the struggle I was to undertake to solve the mystery, just as Hannibal Lecter did to the agent Clarisse in The Silence of the Lambs. I felt all the while that I had become a muse to my informant, who enjoyed the game of sending me out on a wild goose chase. And like the FBI investigative agent Clarisse, there were times I felt a surge of anger, which gave me confidence to stand up to his intimidation. All the while, I never realized that this was not the case. My informant was curious and fascinated by my findings. At the same time, he was hesitant to help me as he was trying to protect me from opening Pandora's Box and being tainted with the knowledge that the Royal Family had kept carefully concealed for so long. In reality, I realized that my informant had questioned me about the investigation more than I had questioned him. It got to the point where I was giving him information that he did not acquire.

I wonder if I will ever have the chance to meet the elderly man who I think may be the great-grandson of both Alexander Dunsmuir and Edna Wallace Hopper. I also wonder if blood or DNA testing would ever be done using a Dunsmuir donor and the man who wishes to find his family lineage. I also wonder if there is anyone living today who knows the truth of Alexander's child, or children, born in 1886.

I also wonder if my investigative work has been done. Have I fulfilled the mission of The Eternal Flapper, or is there more work to be done?

Perhaps the man who is seeking the truth of his lineage will not find the truth. I am hoping that this book and my investigation results will reach him.

I had hoped for a final closure to these wonders before the release of this book.

There still remains a mystery. Perhaps none of us will ever know.

This is the iconic image that was incorporated in the Edna Wallace Hopper Youth and Beauty products sold from the 1920s through the 1950s. The photograph was taken by Alfred Cheney Johnston, who photographed the Zigfield Follies Girls. From the private collection of Jim Alessio

International Newsreel photo, October 15, 1930, Edna with her acrobatic dance partner Monsieur Grip as they arrived on the S. S. Homeric (photo from private collection of Jim Alessio)

Bonus Chapter

Secrets of Youth, Beauty, Diet, and Exercise as told by Edna Wallace Hopper

When once asked about her defiance of time and how she preserved her youthful energy, Edna Wallace Hopper asked, "My secret?"

"It's leading a normal, full life. I keep busy. I take exercise. I've never smoked. I never drink. I eat sensible things, lots of protein, and no fats. I go to bed early during the week, not later than 9:30. Weekends, I entertain or am entertained."

When asked her view on age and ageing, Edna explained, "I do not know age. Do not know, recognize, nor admit it: Age must touch the thoughts before it can touch the face or the body. I have never let myself think of time. This is the principal reason for my appearance (today). Even as a little girl, I never wanted to play at being grown-up. I never wanted to wear long skirts, as so many little girls do. I have too good a time in my short ones.

I have not accomplished the miraculous, but I have done something that few women have had the persistence to do. Therefore, I am looked upon as being unusual. Since my experience adds one more victor to the list of women who have outlived time as it is generally reckoned, I am proof that it can be done. When I began, the world was asleep so far as women were concerned. Now it is awake. Women are letting themselves go." This was said by Edna in the 1920s.

In an interview at her home, which was high up in the Saint Regis Hotel near Fifth Avenue in New York, a young woman named Courtney Marvin was assigned and nervously came to the lovely suite in late November. Courtney was handed her keys and told to let herself in and wait for Edna in her suite. She describes the November sunset in the gilded living room. It burnished the mirrored mantel, the period chairs, and carved curio cabinets. Through a massive window, a modernistic pattern of the New York skyline had turned gray-pink against a flaming heaven. Courtney then compared that to Edna by writing, "That picture was like the woman I had come to see, Edna Wallace Hopper."

On the table before her lay a red beauty case; in the room beyond were her belongings. It was evident that Miss Hopper had learned to avoid small cares. "The door opened and Edna entered briskly. She seated herself directly under an electric light, so that I might see her clearly, I looked critically at the debonair little figure in a beige and lacquer red sports costume. Her abundant brown hair, wound loosely about her head and curling at the ends, showed beneath a brilliant red cloche, such as only youth dares wear. For Edna Wallace Hopper still has a figure that might be eighteen and a face that might be in its twenties. Actually, she laughs happily at sixty-three years and boasts of them."

Courtney added, "The smiling eyes were brown and twinkling." This I find alarming, as Edna had radiant, sparkling blue eyes. I noticed in another article, once in the 1920s, that someone commented on her deep brown eyes. Could she have had her pupils so enlarged that it appeared this way?

Courtney then reports, "I saw no sign of wear nor weariness about the small mouth, no sign of sag in the firm, pointed chin. Even her neck and hands were smooth and unlined. I noticed a light dusting of powder and a touch of rouge." In this early 1920s interview, Edna predicted, "I venture to say that when this generation that is now in their twenties reaches my pleasant age, many will have accomplished relatively what I have". She was right, as this generation was in their sixties in the 1960s. They were the first generation of elders to claim their youthfulness and to look at themselves as still being young in their sixties.

Here is the simplest way to explain what is behind Edna's secrets of total youth and total beauty.

First and foremost is your mental state. Edna explains, "Thought is without doubt the most important factor in retaining youth and beauty. I can safely place all other requisites in a secondary place, because if our thoughts are right, diet, exercise, and a normal life must be considered seriously." "Willpower is the first requisite in my mental beauty kit. Twenty is the proper time to muster a good supply. This should be the stern creed of every woman at this age. I am young now, and life with its glories is before me. I mean to keep this mental viewpoint always. I shall banish every thought of age, which means destructive thinking. I shall accept heartily the lovely things of life, enjoy them, make the most out of them, and live them. With the other things- and they will come to me, of course- I shall linger over them as shortly as possible. Regardless of what art, profession, or business I follow, whether I am a housewife or a worldwide star, my contribution to life is the loveliness that I, myself, put into it. Sensible care of my body and mind will raise a worthy monument to this ideal in my own person."

On Diet

According to Edna, "Diet comes next in importance. Its urgency is better understood, I think, when we realize that this food in turn is what becomes the skin on our faces, the hair on our heads, the slim, graceful ankles we all desire, and so on throughout the entire human anatomy. I am encouraged by the fact that today a large number of women deny themselves temptations of the diet in order to present their better self to the world."

Edna recommended trying this simple diet for one month. "I realize that the food needs of bodies vary. But I can make one hard and fast rule. That is, that vegetables and fruit must predominate in all diets".

"Two beauty requisites are celery and lettuce. These vegetables that are continually on your table are more beneficial than a dozen beauty jars in the bath cabinet. For these greens start beauty from the right point- the inside."

In another interview done at the age of sixty-eight in 1929, she discusses tomatoes. "Ah, tomatoes! Canned tomatoes, stewed tomatoes, raw tomatoes. Any kind of tomatoes. Tomatoes are best. You can eat them in any form, and they are good for you. But all other vegetables I must have fresh... TOMATOES KEEP YOU HEALTHY AND THEY KEEP

YOU YOUNG." "Diet is what does it (keeps one young), and tomatoes are the bulwark of proper eating." "Grapefruit, oranges, lemons, apples, and every fruit, particularly the citrus ones, are priceless in our progress toward beauty." Raw carrots are recommended. "Spinach, a lovely vegetable," Edna says with true admiration.

On eating properly, Edna comments, "Most people don't know how to eat right. They eat as they please and grow old before their time. But a correct diet is second nature to me. I was born with the knowledge of how to eat right. Meat – I eat very little of it. Sweets don't have a large place on the menu. And as for smoking and drinking. Drinking liquor habitually is ruinous to health. Smoking is the same."

In 1925, Edna decided to write and publish a small hardcover book, "My Secrets of Youth and Beauty", published by Reilly and Lee of

Chicago. In the tiny ninety-five-page book, Edna explains that the greatest happiness she has known comes from sharing her beauty secrets with others, especially young girls, as early training brings lasting results.

In her book, Edna gives her commandments of diet. First, never eat more than you need and drink plenty of water daily. Edna would drink 6 to eight glasses per day and preferred room temperature water as opposed to iced water. Second, to avoid sweets and rich, greasy, highly seasoned foods. This will keep the complexion clear and avoid digestive problems.

Edna enjoyed eating hard French bread with meals or dry toast in the morning. If she had an overpowering urge for something sweet, she would give in to a piece of hard candy to satisfy the craving. Edna stayed at 85 pounds her entire life. Keep in mind her tiny stature of only five feet six inches. To maintain her weight, she went on a strict diet once about every six weeks. "I do this because I know it is good for me. It gives my system a complete rest." For breakfast, a cup of black coffee and a slice of dry toast. For dinner, a slice of pineapple and a broiled lamb chop. This diet is repeated for two weeks. "It's nutritious and satisfying, and the results are most satisfactory." I call this the Edna Wallace Hopper diet, and keep in mind her size, as for most people, this would not be sufficient to maintain their ideal weight. Perhaps two slices of pineapple and two lamb chops may be more suitable for your ideal weight control and satisfaction.

On days of a regular diet, a typical breakfast would be one cup of black coffee and a thin slice of crisp brown bread toasted. For luncheon, a dish of fruit, thin crisp toast, and one slice of green vegetable such as carrots or spinach. For dinner, a little fish, perhaps a meat order, a vegetable, toast, and a salad. No exercise after eating. Relaxing or reclining after a meal is a good plan to follow.

"I was taught in my childhood to eat plain, wholesome food. I have always eaten largely of fruits, particularly of cooked fruits. I always eat Hard French bread or toast, never soft breads of any kind. I never eat rich, highly seasoned foods. I never drink water at meals. I never drink ice water at any time. But I do drink a considerable quantity between meals, at least six or eight glasses daily." Avoid Overweight. "Almost everyone knows that the troubles which impair both health and beauty are caused by overeating. It isn't what we eat that counts so much as the quantity. Some people can successfully reduce weight by reducing the quantity of food eaten by one-third. The average person who has been on a reducing diet for a month, consistently following a well-laid-out plan, will have results so satisfying that nothing more is necessary to convince him.

"The whole matter of overweight really simmers down to two points-eating too much and exercising too little."

On Exercise

Miss Hopper asserted that while diet is essential to youthfulness, exercise and the right mental attitude toward life must not be slighted. Walking was a hobby with her, and in her excursions, she had weathered many storms. "While I can be slightly elastic concerning diet, I am definite when it comes to exercise. The unoiled machine will rust. The same happens to our muscles when we don't use them or oil them. Many content themselves with walking. It is not enough, though there is much to be said for it. It takes us into open air and sunshine, it stimulates circulation, and it is impossible to have a depressing thought when walking briskly. But when hips are to be kept slim, calves only gently curved and breasts firm and rounded, something more than walking is required by most of us."

Edna had the flexibility of a young girl at the ages of sixty through her nineties by maintaining it through backbends, shoulder stands, arm movements, etc. "Women (and men) who do considerable walking and dancing need exercises for the muscles of the upper parts of their bodies. Women and men who sit at their desks all day need general exercises, particularly those for the body below the waistline.

For the bust line and breasts, Edna noticed the beautiful bust line of the women in France. No sagging out of line as seen on the women in America. The French jeune fille, from the time she begins to develop, wears a sort of brassiere, or souteneur gauze, day and night. Exercises bringing the deltoid muscles into play will make those muscles strong, firm the bust, and reduce the oversized breasts. Swimming and Indian club exercises are among the best of these.

Edna always exercised in the morning, doing indoor exercises just before her bath. Here are her daily ten-minute recommended exercises:

1.	Standing with feet together, rise on your toes, stretch your arms overhead, bend your body at the trunk, and touch the floor with the palms of your hands, five times. This is similar to a yoga bend.
2.	Standing in position with your feet about six inches apart, knees

straight, body erect, hands at your sides, bring up both arms as high as possible, about five times.

3.   In the same position as in 2, raise both arms even with your shoulders,
five times.

4.   Same position, hold arms out straight from the shoulder, swing each arm in a circular motion, alternating five times with the right, then five times with the left.

5.   Same position but with arms outstretched, twist your body
from side to side, about five times.

6.   End your morning exercises by again repeating the first exercise five times.

I noticed that many of the exercises that Edna practiced appeared similar, even exact, to positions done with Yoga. I have seen photos of her as well, using the medicine ball and boxing. Sports were a favorite thing to do to release stress and keep in shape. Golf, tennis, and swimming, as well as horseback riding, helped her to maintain her youthful appearance.

"How wonderful it would be if everyone could indulge in some form of outdoor exercise! There's a zest and joy about it that never comes when we exercise indoors. Somehow, swimming, tennis, and other outdoor sports seem like play, and we feel young and happy when we are splashing in the water, cavorting around a tennis court, or even chasing a golf ball, although golf seems old and dignified when compared with swimming and tennis. We can hold onto our dignity, if we feel a must, on the gold links, but not when hitting a tennis ball or keeping afloat in the water. And as we play, we forget our troubles and are just happy children, for the time being at least."

Edna went on to note that not everyone is fortunate enough to do such sports, either deprived or limited by time, financial, or physical conditions. Most of us can walk at least two miles every day.

Dancing was a passion for Edna. In her tours in the famous Vaudeville theaters of her "Matinee for Ladies Only" performances, Miss Hopper expressed the importance of aerobic movements, the cardiovascular importance of blood flowing, and strengthening the heart muscles, and the deep breathing that goes along with it. Dancing is the perfect way to do this and is delightful for not only the body but the mind and the spirit as well.

In Bath

As most people think of a bath or shower as merely a cleansing process, that was not the primary reason for Edna to bathe. "I have never taken hot baths. Every morning, I look forward with pleasant anticipation to my cold tub. I enjoy its tonic effect. And I know it hardens my body and increases my resistance against colds. Those who know the whys and wherefores of baths tell me the reason I feel so peppy after I come out of the cold water is because my nerve centers have all been stimulated, and the activity in my circulation has been increased. Before I bathe, I rub my body with cleansing oil".

Years ago, Edna found a wonderful cleansing formula mineral oil in France. She obtained the formula and has included it in her beauty aids, which she sold under her name and called Edna Wallace Hopper's Facial Youth. Before this, she shared this with the stage and society women, but wanted the whole world to experience its effectiveness.

Her line of beauty and youth formulas became a big seller, and her company was ranked just under Chrysler Corporation in highest USA sales by 1925...

Her system for taking a cold bath was recommended as follows: To avoid the shock of the cold water, there is a way of getting into a cold bath that overcomes this shock. This method interested the women who attended her special matinees. They would see a completely nude Edna live on stage, demonstrating this way to enter the bathtub. "They could not understand why my feet go into the water last instead of first," Edna reported.

"This is my system: I grasp the sides of the tub and lower my body into the water so that the base of my spine touches the water first. Then I lower the upper part of my body until the water touches the base of the brain, at the same time splashing my chest and throat. Then I let my feet down, and I am wet all over. And I have no unpleasant shock from the cold water, but instead, a very pleasant sensation. It's really much easier to do than it sounds. I stay in the tub for five minutes, rubbing and splashing all the time. Jumping out, I dry with warm towels if possible. Then a rub of alcohol body youth tonic, which closes my pores, then talcum dusting, and I am ready for the rest of my toilet."

Upon retiring, Edna would cleanse her body with the oil, rubbing it gently and wiping off the remaining amount left on the surface. She would then follow with a splash of the alcohol tonic to feel clean and refreshed before bed.

Her Beauty Products

In addition to Edna's Youth Cream, Edna spent a large fortune on money and time on a whole line of useful products to enhance, maintain, and keep the health of the skin and hair, as well as reducing the signs of aging dramatically. She and her mother consulted specialists in France, Germany, and Austria. They also obtained beauty secrets from famous beauties around the world. Brilliant scientists and able chemists evolved ways to combine dozens of "helps" in a few preparations that were easy to apply. Edna made a total of 34 trips to France to get it right. Ideas had changed, and improvement followed through the years of her beauty and youth line.

"I say these things not boastfully. I am very humble about them, but they exemplify the lessons that I wish to teach. That is, how all girls may foster beauty, as I did. And how women may keep their youth. My skin is like a baby's, my complexion like a debutante's. My hair is abundant, lustrous, and silky. It has never begun to turn gray. I am young in body and in spirit, bubbling with vitality."

Edna expressed that she was not happy about having her name on her products, but knew it was important to gain the attention the products deserved and to have women using them, as she was on a mission to make American women take better care of themselves. Likewise, she always had concerns for womankind in the work force and on the stage as well. She felt that they deserved equality with the working men.

Likewise, Edna made it a point to educate men on the usage of many of the youth and beauty products as well. She expressed, "If you (men) are careless of your personal appearance, as we (women) do not admire you. We (women) demand that you be clean-skinned and youthful-looking. We like to see a masculine head well covered with healthy hair. We do not like the glare of shiny bald heads. Neither do we want you to go back to the styles of wigs. Men should give even more care to their hair and skin than women do to theirs. Why? "Because his closely cropped hair collects dirt and grime more quickly than does the longer, coiffed hair of women."

Edna explained that men need to be aware of overeating and keep a youthful, slim, and well-formed muscular appearance as well. She went on to say that many men do not cleanse their skin properly as well. She said they don't think of cleansing their faces again after eight or ten hours of work. She recommended her hair youth to men as well. Her facial youth was recommended to clean their skin of grease and refuse, as soap could not do. Her talc and eye bath as well were recommended to men. This is a matter of proper care, like brushing your teeth, which is the way she convinced men to make a change in their daily maintenance.

Her line included Fruity Shampoo, which had a luscious fragrance of strawberries and lemons.

No-shine to remove oil from the foreheads and the nose area. Youth hand lotion to protect from weather elements and keep a soft, smooth feel to your hands and feet. Hair remover, eye bath wave, and sheen hair dress to keep curls and give sheen lip stick, which was the first waterproof lipstick ever invented, it came in two shades: natural and brilliant White youth clay which contained two mineral laden clays to purge the skin of all that clogs the pores, to remove grime, dirt hardened oil and dead skin cells. It also brings the blood circulation back to the skin; it acts as an astringent as well and decreases enlarged pores, retaining smoothness and softness to the skin surface. It corrects the signs of aging and improves its clear appearance. Powder: Four different ones available, containing 52 ingredients. It came in white, flesh, brunette, and peach.

Hair Youth, as her hair was her greatest glory, this product seemed to be the biggest seller. Edna claimed it restored hair, cleansed the scalp, thickened the density of hair, made hair flourish, and increased pigment, which reduced and eliminated gray hairs.

On Eyes

Care of eyes by relaxing them a few times a day by closing lids and resting for a minute. Reducing eye strain is important to keep bright-looking, clear eyes. Edna sold an eye bath that she used morning and night. She moisturized the lids and used the same ointment on the lashes to keep them protected. She recommended tweezing the eyebrows when needed to shape them, as well as removing long nose hairs. Edna recommended darkening the brow or lashes be done by a professional if needed, or use mascara to enhance the look and thickness.

On Teeth

Edna had recommended Quident, which contained five things in one-cleaners and polishers, four antacids, four antiseptics, iodine, and breath deodorants. This was in the year 1925. Since then many types of dental cleaners had advanced, but in 1925, Edna recommended this new era of combined ingredients and technological advances in dentistry.

On Feet and Hands

Edna recommended giving the feet as much attention as your hands. Rubbing them with cleansing oil, wiping the remaining amount off, and following with alcohol rub, the same as for the body. Then, talcum dusting on the feet. A proper manicure and pedicure keep nails looking well-shaped and clean. The foot treatment is restful for the feet after hours at the end of the day.

On makeup application, "Makeup is an art which should be carefully studied. The woman who plasters a lot of rouge on her face, covers it with a thick layer of powder, regardless of whether the shade blends with the tint of her skin or not, and who, as a crowning touch, paints a pair of bright red lips over her own, without regard to line, makes a caricature of herself. But the woman who has experimented knows just the shade of rouge and hue of powder best harmonizing with her coloring."

Edna recommended applying your makeup so cleverly that it gives a natural appearance, pleasing to the eye of the beholder.

Apply the foundation or base cream over the face and neck. Remove surplus with a soft, clean cloth. Don't use powder with a base cream first.

(Since this was printed in 1925, concealer has come into play and has been added to proper makeup application, and eye concealer should be done first before foundation application.)

Next, rouge or shading to contour and enhance, define, or slenderize. Orange shades can be worn by certain blondes or brunettes only. A brighter shade can be worn in the evenings. "Every woman should study her face under different lights to learn which shades seem the most natural. A little experimenting will show just where the rouge should be applied. The round face should be rouged with an up and down stroke, heavier to the cheekbones. The thin face with a circular stroke, heavier in the hollows of the cheeks. If neither full nor thin, the rouge should be applied in a sort of triangle. Never should there be a sharp line of contrast. It can be toned down with powder if needed.

The correct tone of the powder is important, and sometimes, combined powder tones may be best for your skin tone. Peach is good for the outdoor girl with sun-tanned skin.

Lipstick and Lips

Keep lips smooth and moisturize at night. Apply lipstick following the lines of the lips. For thin lips, carry the color a bit outside of the lip if carefully blended. For thick lips, the reverse is not quite to the line of the lip. For a small mouth, one can go a trifle beyond the corners, and the reverse for a large mouth, not quite to the edge. Relax the lips when applying and do not pucker. Edna personally preferred a bright red for herself and stayed away from natural tones. She liked the brilliant hue on her lips.

Correct Posture

Of utmost importance to defy the signs of aging is correct posture at any age. This will prevent and reverse rounding of shoulders, a hump back or camel back, a curved neck, and a shallow chest.

Edna never ever slept with a pillow from the time she was born. She was taught to sleep lying on her back so that her face would not be creased. This may be difficult for many people, but it definitely will reduce the slumped neck and wrinkles in the face from becoming deep creases from the nose to the mouth and in between the brows.

When seated, do not slouch and keep your shoulders back as much as possible, keeping the head from bending downward as well.

On her beauty "Helps"

In the beginning chapter of her book, Edna speaks of her ageless beauty, her mother, Josephine. She attributes her knowledge and training to her mother on how to make oneself ageless and how to improve one's beauty. As an infant, Josephine would smear Edna with a cold cream from France and never let water touch her skin. The cream acted as a barrier between the harsh water and her gentle skin. Edna kept this in practice for the rest of her life, as you will read about her bath technique later on in this chapter.

On her mother, Edna, once said, "I owe much to my mother. She played a royal part in life because of her wondrous beauty. She died a youthful beauty at the age of 57 with a child's complexion. Girlish contours and not a grey hair in her head." She urged me from my youngest years to foster and enhance my beauty as she did. She taught me her methods and gave me her formulas. Twell-being, they traveled the world in search of better methods.

In general, Edna Wallace Hopper's rules are similar to many we have heard throughout our lives, some even from our parents. Her foundations for wellbeing are: Cleanliness within and without. Within, the elimination of waste properly is achieved by eating plenty of green vegetables and fruits. A well-balanced diet and six to eight glasses of water daily between meals. Without cleaning the body, hair, face, teeth, and nails. Sleep, fresh air in your sleeping room, good ventilation, exercise outdoors or Indoors, breathe deeply, persistence, and regularity. Irregular habits do not bring good health results.

My favorite of all Edna's advice is "Don't lose your sense of enjoyment. Joy ensures a youthful heart. A good laugh is a wonderful tonic. Keep smiling.

Of all the advice that Edna gave to others, she believed this to be the most important of all: My message to the world - Keep the Spirit Young.

Edna posing in bathing suits of the early 1900s and in the suit of the late 1920s off the boardwalk at Crystal Beach, California. She is in her sixties. International Examiner, Los Angeles publicity photo from the private collection of Jim Alessio

Chicago, IL – Photographer & camera artist Paul Stone is posed and, at the same time, amazed by how Edna's appearance made time stand still. As a young boy in 1900, he went to see her performance in Florodora. Edna sent him an autographed photo, and he would gaze at her beauty for long hours. He later went to New York and joined the show's famous Sextette. Miss Hopper visited him in Chicago and posed for this photo. Stone expressed, "Because I wish to point out that, though she confesses to being seventies of age. She is beautiful and hasn't even a suggestion of a double chin." Credit 25754 International Chicago 6-27-38 STAGEOGRAPHY OF EDNA WALLACE HOPPER Broadway and Touring Theaters

The Club Friend, Sept. 1891, Boston Museum. Produced and played by Roland Reed, Star Theater, New York City, for six weeks Lend Me Your Wife With Roland Reed Nov. 9, 1891 While performing this show, Edna meets Charles Frohman, who becomes her manager and joins his company.

Jane Charles Frohman Stock Company Edna plays a soubrette named Lucy Morton, Dec 1891-? Chums Charles Frohman Stock Company Edna plays Mrs. Patterby 1892-? Men and Women Charles Frohman Stock Company Edna plays Margery Knox 1892-? The Girl I Let Behind Me (musical melodrama) Jan. 25, 1893 grand opening Empire Theater's Premier opening New York City Edna plays Wilbur's Ann in the first musical Western Written by David Belasco (The Bishop of Broadway) Edna meets DeWolf Hopper who watched her performance on opening night Panjandrum New York Broadway Theater Aug 1893-Dec 1893 DeWolf Hopper Opera Company Edna takes on the role as Paquita as Della Fox became ill. Written by J. Cheever Goodwin, composed by Woolson Morse Poor Girls London 1896-1897 Sept 28, 1896, inaugural performance at the opening of the New Academy of Music in Baltimore, MD Written by John Phillip Sousa, A comedic operetta Performed in New York City and toured Poor Girls American Theater in New York Jan 22, 1894 Edna plays Betsy Doctor Syntax Sept 3, 1894 Broadway Theater, New York, DeWolf Hopper Opera Company Edna plays Merope Mallow, the "girl with the auburn hair".

Wang 1894 Road tour performances as Mataya, along with husband DeWolf Hopper as Dr. Wang. Performances included a run Oct-Nov 1895 in San Francisco. Photo from the private collection of Jim Alessio

El Capitan, April 13, 1896, premiered at the Broadway Theater, NYC, April 20, 1896 100th performance at Broadway Theater, July 1896, toured nationwide, and performed in nationwide

Edna plays Estrelda while husband DeWolf plays Don Medigua (El Capitan)

El Capitan is an operetta in three acts by John Philip Sousa and has a libretto by Charles Klein (with lyrics by Charles Klein and Tom Frost). The piece was Sousa's first successful operetta and his most successful stage work. El Capitan was first produced at the Tremont Theatre in Boston, beginning on April 13, 1896. After this tryout, it transferred to The Broadway Theatre in New York on April 20, 1896, where it ran for 112 performances, starring DeWolf Hopper, Edna Wallace Hopper, John Parr, and Alfred Klein. It was then toured almost continuously for four years in the United States and Canada. It was produced at the Lyric Theatre in London beginning on July 10, 1899, where it ran for 140 performances. Thereafter, the operetta was produced numerous times internationally and remained popular for some time. Synopsis: Don Enrico Medigua, the viceroy of Spain-occupied Peru, fears assassination by rebels. After he secretly has the rebel leader El Captain killed, he disguises himself as El Captain. Estrelda, the former viceroy's daughter, impressed by tales of El Captain's daring, falls in love with the disguised Medigua, who is already married. Meanwhile, Medigua's wife and daughter search for him, and the rebels capture the Lord Chamberlain, mistaking him for the viceroy. Medigua leads the hapless rebels against the Spaniards, taking them in circles until they are too tired to fight. The Spaniards win, the mistaken identities are revealed, the love stories are untangled, and the story ends happily.

Yankee Doodle Dandy, July 4th, 1898, opening at Casino Theater, New York City. Tour included Philadelphia, November 1898, by George Lederer, Gus.

Kerker and Hugh Morton: A musical comedy. Edna plays a boy named Teddy Twoshoes (and Willie Wildwave) La Belle Hellene opened April 1899 Casino Theatre, (1/12/1899 - 2/25/1899) Harlem Opera House, (4/3/1899 - circa. 4/1899) Grand Opera House, (5/29/1899 - circa. 6/1899) The musical opera revival about Helen of Troy (played by friend Lillian Russell) and Edna plays the controversial role of Greek boy named Orestes A comedic operetta by Offenbach 68 Performances Description: An opera in three acts Setting: Jupiter's Temple, Queen Helene's Royal Palace, and a seaside resort near Sparta Produced by George W. Lederer Music by Jacques Offenbach; Musical Director: Ludwig Englander; Featuring songs with lyrics by Louis Harrison; Featuring songs by Ludwig Englander and Julius Einodshofer.

Cabinet card photo from the private collection of Jim Alessio,

Chris, and the Wonderful Lamp [Original, Musical, Extravaganza] Performer: Edna Wallace Hopper [Chris Wagstaff] The Colorful Musical by John Phillip Sousa, based on the story Aladdin and the Lamp from the Arabian Nights book, and the book Chris and the Wonderful Lamp by Glen MacDonough, Jan 1, 1900 - Feb 24, 1900. Edna plays a boy named Chris Wagstaff, while Jerome Sykes plays the magical Genie of the Lamp.

Florodora [Original, Musical, Comedy]

Nov 10, 1900 - Jan 25, 1902

Performer: Edna Wallace Hopper [Lady Hollyrood] By John C. Fisher Produced by Fisher, Dunne, and Riley.

This is the American version, which was the most successful show of its Time. A total of 549 performances. 379 performances at the Casino theater in New York City, then 122 performances at The New York Theater.

The show was reopened at The Winter Garden Theater in New York for another 49 performances.

In addition to this, the show was performed on tour in the U.S. The American version was the first show to introduce the chorus line and was Broadway's longest-running show of its time.

The Silver Slipper [Original, Musical]

Performer: Edna Wallace Hopper Music by Owen Hall and Leslie Stuart

First performed in Boston, October 27, 27,1902-March 14.1903, then at The Broadway Theater in New York

About Town [Original, Musical, Revue] AUG 30,1906-DEC 1906

Star Performer: Edna Wallace Hopper as Duchess of Ehwattington 53 Performances Herald Square Theater NYC

New version of the same piece with interpolated numbers by Victor Herbert, A. Baldwin Sloane, and Gustave Kerker

Produced by Lew M. Fields

Music by M. Ellis and Raymond Hubble Lyrics by Joseph Herbert

A Country Mouse (comedy) by Arthur Carr, Hyperion Theater, New Haven, Connecticut

Edna's return to legitimate comedy in a new play after years of musical comedy.

She plays a demure country girl placed suddenly among the guests of a London society leader.

Dec 10, 1904 Fifty Miles from Boston by George M. Cohan [Original musical melodrama]

Starring Edna Wallace Hopper Brown as Sadie Woodis, a village postmistress in love with the hero of the Harvard baseball club, played by George Parsons.

Synopsis: This show salutes Edward Harrigan of Harrigan and Hart. Cohan names a central character after him, composes a hit song, "H-A-Double-R-I-G-A-N," and invites him to the opening. In the show, Harrigan, played by George Parson, is smitten with Sadie, played by Edna Wallace Hopper, but she loves a baseball star. Cohan's play runs only four weeks.

Feb 3, 1908-Mar 8, 1908, Garrick Theater, Broadway, New York. Toured Feb 1909, starting in New Orleans

Jumping Jupiter [Original, Musical] Mar 6, 1911 - Mar 1911 Performer: Edna Wallace Hopper as a model named Connie Curtiss 24 Performances Produced by H. H. Frazee and George W. Lederer Music by Karl Hoschna; Book by Richard Carle and Sydney Rosenfeld; Lyrics by Richard Carle and Sydney Rosenfeld; Musical Director: Hans S. Linne; Featuring songs by Grace Le Boy, Harry Auracher, Irving Berlin and Albert VonTilzer; Featuring songs with lyrics by Junie McCree, Gus Kahn, Francis DeWitt and Ted Snyder Staged by Richard Carle New York Theater 1514-16 Broadway In 1895, Oscar Hammerstein opened an entertainment complex for which one fifty-cent ticket admitted you to two main auditoriums (Lyric, Music Hall), two small theatres (Concert Hall, Roof Garden), an Oriental cafe, bowling, and billiards. On June 29, 1898, the debt-laden Olympia was auctioned. The Music Hall reopened as the New York Theatre. In 1912, it was the Moulin Rouge for the run of "A Winsome Widow," starring Mae West. In 1915, it became part of the Loew's movie/vaudeville chain.

Edna as a model named Connie Curtiss in Jumpin Jupiter in 1911,
by Moffett Studio, Chicago (photo from private Jim Alessio collection)

Edna as Baby Edna for the Children's Theater performance of
Racketty-Packetty House

Racketty-Packetty House [Original, Play] Children's Theater NYC Dec 23, 1912 - Mar 1913 Based on a children's book. This is part of a new Broadway series played for children.

Performer: Edna Wallace Hopper as "Baby Edna"

81 Performances Written by Frances Hodgson Burnett

The Things That Count [Original, Play] 224 performances Performer: Edna Wallace Hopper Dec 8, 1913 – [unknown] Produced by William Brady

Maxine Elliott's Theatre, (12/8/1913 – circa 6/1914) Playhouse Theatre, (12/22/1913 - Closing date unknown) Total Performances: 224

The Elder Son [Original, Play] Sept 15, 1914 – Oct 1914 Performer: Edna Wallace Hopper

Original Play written by Lucien Nepoty, based on the book by Frederick Fenn. Playhouse Theater, 137 West 48th St, NYC 23 Performances.

Girl o' Mine [Original, Musical, Comedy] 1918

Performer: Edna Wallace Hopper as Lulu Bijou Theater, NYC, 48 performances in 1918. Music by Frank E. Tours; Lyrics by

Philip Bartholomae Produced by Elisabeth Marbury Book by Philip Bartholomae;

Music by Frank E. Tours; Musical Director: Frank E. Tours

Directed by Clifford Brooke and Edward P. Temple, Choreographed by Edward Hutchinson and Allan K. Foster

Category: Musical, Comedy, Original, Broadway Description: A Musical in Two Acts and 3 Scenes Setting: A railway station and a hotel in Paris

The Matinee Girl [Original, Musical, Comedy] Feb 1, 1926 - Feb 20, 1926 Performer: Edna Wallace Hopper [Miss Sparklin Wyne] Forrest Theater, NYC music by Frank H. Grey; lyrics by Bide Dudley and McElbert Moore Musical, Comedy Description: A musical in two acts

Setting: A New York Theatre, aboard a yacht, and Cuba

Book by Bide Dudley, McElbert Moore; Lyrics by Bide Dudley, McElbert Moore; Music by Frank H. Grey.

Vaudeville

Ziegfeld Follies of 1927 [Original, Musical, Revue] Aug 16, 1927 - Jan 7, 1928

Performer: Edna Wallace Hopper, among many other stars.

New Amsterdam Theater, 214 W. 42nd St., NYC

Built by Klaw & Erlanger. With its elaborate architecture and decor, it brought Art Nouveau to Broadway. Beginning in 1913, Ziegfeld brought his "Follies" to the New Amsterdam.

Music and Lyrics by Irving Berlin, along with songs by other composers. Total 167 performances. A musical review, original Broadway

The Eternal Flapper as she appeared at The Earl Theater during the national tour of "Matinee for Ladies Only" from 1918 through the late 1920s.

"Matinee for Ladies Only" starring Edna Wallace Hopper, 1918 through the 1920s

A touring show of Bed, Bath, Beauty and Youth Secrets, Diet and Exercise of the sixty-something naked beauty Edna Wallace Hopper was shared with women all over America. Gruaman's Chinese Theater in Los Angeles, the Roxy and the Apollo in New York, the New Royal Theater in Victoria, BC, were just some of the theaters where this showed to sold-out audiences.

ENCORE PERFORMANCE BY EDNA WALLACE HOPPER FROM "THE GIRL I LEFT BEHIND ME"

JUNE 1953 TRIBUTE TO THE EMPIRE THEATER (BEFORE THE DEMOLITION OF THE THEATER)

Edna does a final command performance as Wilbur's Girl in The Girl I

Left Behind Me as she did when the theater opened in 1893. EMPIRE THEATER NEW YORK CITY

The Empire Theater is said to be the grandest theater ever built in the 19th Century.

Filmography

By "Whose Hand?" also billed as Who Killed Simon Baird? by Channing Pollock and Rennold Wolf, Equitable Motion Pictures Corporation released in April 1916. Filmed in New York City and Canada, Starring Muriel Ostriche, Edna Wallace Hopper, and Charles J. Ross. "A star Triple Alliance in the Greatest Mystery Drama of the age"

Perils of Divorce by William A. Brady, in association with World Film Corporation, was released in February 1916. Filmed in studios in New York and in Chinatown, New York. Starring Edna Wallace Hopper and Frank Sheridan. "One of the most interesting treatments of this powerful subject ever shown on the screen." In this melodrama, Edna plays the injured wife, Constance, whose rich husband, John Graham, is having an affair with another woman.

Sources, Acknowledgments, and Suggested Readings

Newspapers

The New York Times The San Francisco Examiner, The San Francisco Chronicle, New York Daily News, Victoria Daily Colonist

New York Public Library: Robinson Locke Collection archives, including newspaper articles, photos, and magazine articles from the Billy Rose Collection at the Metropolitan Museum Archives, Lincoln Center, NYC.

Magazines

Look Magazine, Jan 3, 1939, Life Magazine, June 1953 Nixon's Apollo Theater Program, The Dance Magazine, July 1928 The Burr McIntosh Monthly 1900-1907 Screenland Oct 10, 1922 Theater Magazine 1903, 1904 Theater Arts Feb 1943 Time Magazine Feb 8, 1943 Physical Culture January 1929 Vogue Nov 23, 1939 Parke-Bernet Galleries Public Auction Catalog 1960

Documents and Manuscripts

Hopper VS Dunsmuir Trial Transcript, British Columbia Archives and Records Service

Craigdarroch Castle Collection in British Columbia

Last Will and Testament of Edna Wallace Hopper (Brown) 1432/54 State of New York Surrogate's Court, County of New York, June 8, 1956

Sound Bites from The Museum of Radio and Television, New York City, Recording of Stage Struck with Mike Wallace, CBS Radio Interview with Edna Wallace Hopper and Shirley Booth, Oct 3, 1953

Books Referenced and Suggested To Read

Alex Dunsmuir's Dilemma by James Audain Copyright Canada 1964 Printed by Mitchell Press Limited, Vancouver, BC The Bishop Of Broadway by David Belasco, The Dunsmuirs: A Promise Kept A play written by Rod Langley, copyright 1992 by Rod Langley Published by Talon Books, Vancouver, BC

The Dunsmuir Saga by Terry Reksten, Published by Douglas & McIntyre, Vancouver/Toronto, 1991 Craigdarroch The Story of Dunsmuir Castle by Terry Reksten 1987 Orca Book Publishers Victoria, BC Captain January by Laura E. Richards Published Dana Estes & Co. Boston 1902 & L.C. Page & Co Boston 1927.

Chris and The Wonderful Lamp by Albert Stearns Published by the Century Co. New York 1984. 1895.

The Things That Count by Lawrence Eyre Published by Little, Brown & Co Boston 1914

Mother Wore Tights (The story of Myrtle McKinley, one of the Florodora Girls)

By Miriam Young Published by Whittlesey House McGraw-Hill Book Co. Inc.

London New York 1944 Once a Clown Always A Clown The Reminiscences of DeWolf Hopper by DeWolf Hopper Written in Collaboration with Wesley Winans Stout copyright 1925, 1926,1927 by Dewolf Hopper Published by Garden City Publishing Company - Garden City, New York.

Yankee Doodle Dandy The Life and Times of Tod Sloan by John Dizikes copyright 2002 Published by Yale University Press New Haven and London

My Secrets of Youth and Beauty by Edna Wallace Hopper Copyright 1925 by Reilly and Lee Company Chicago Secrets of the Tomb by Alexandra Robbins

Skull and Bones, The Ivy League, And The Hidden Paths Of Power Copyright 2002 Printed by Back Bay Books - Little Brown and Company Boston New York London

A Special Thanks to :

Bruce Davies and The Craigdarroch Castle Museum Victoria, British Columbia Canada for your assistance and providing images for use in this book. Thanks so very much.

Thanks to the New York Public Library , The Lincoln Center Museum Archives and The Metropolitan Opera House Archives for your assistance in finding information and images for this book.

Thanks to the Royal BC Museum in British Columbia.

Very special thanks to the Messenger, the man who met Edna in 1953 and waited so patiently to meet me in 1989 at The Met Lincoln Center. I thank you for assigning me to this wonderful project which surrounded the best years of my life.

Thank you, Larry Johnson, former production manager of the Today's show on NBC, for guiding me to the Messenger and advising me to do this book and a screenplay for a film. Thank you for your help, your former friendship and hopes to reunite with you someday.

Curator Theresa and The Dunsmuir Historic Estate and the Dunsmuir Historic Society Oakland, California, thanks for your help, the private tour and conversations were so moving to me.

My dear friends John and Ann Gee, Clo Whitney, Dick Frawley and Dave Putzel, I thank you for their encouragement and advice. Thanks to Dick and Sherry for listening to me for years, that's what friends are for. I love you all. Joe, Jacque and Sandy – Wish you could have lived to see this completed.

I dedicate this book to you my dear friends Thanks Cindy Donaldson for helping.

I thank photographer/ writer, film director Cindy Sherman for her professional critique. I hope to connect with you .

Thanks to Time Life for their cooperative permission to use quotes from Life Magazine.

Richard J. Maturi, author of a book on life of singer/actor Will Rogers and of a biography of actress Beverly Benson by McFarland Publisher. Thanks for your unending help and assistance with news clippings and images of Edna Wallace Hopper.

Thanks to eBay and the sellers for helping to acquire my extensive collection of original photographs and archives of Edna Wallace Hopper and her performances.

Margerie, the Daughter of Plastic Surgeon Dr. John L. Hennemuth. Many thanks for your wonderful story of Edna's post operative procedure in California and for providing me with Dr. Hennimuth's images and permission of usage in this book.

Thanks to Sue, owner of Yesterday's Whisper Largo. FL for her help finding photos of Edna

Thank you to the many great photographers who once captured the beautiful images of Edna Wallace Hopper and the other characters to enhance this book and help the readers to enjoy a bird's eye view of her life story.

To Mr. X, I keep my promise to protect your privacy and thank you for understanding the importance of my mission, to find the truth and to tell the true story of this great legendary woman. You helped guide me to finding the truth on my own. Thank you for understanding the importance of this book. I leave it up to you now to fulfill her mission of bringing her story to her living ancestors.

The Photography of Edna Wallace Hopper and The Photographers

All images appearing herein are either in the public domain (that is, they predate 1923), or were issued by theatrical agents or performers as publicity that conventionally waived copyright to encourage wide dissemination. Only images created for exclusive publication in a single periodical (either as 'exclusive' images or under work-for-hire conditions) or images bearing a copyright symbol or stamp claimed copyright protection during the 1910s and 1920s. No such images post-dating 1923 are employed as illustrations here. All images derive from vintage prints distributed as part of publicity campaigns. That is, no images here were recently printed from photographer negatives whose imagery has never been heretofore published.

I have included the following biographical information about the outstanding and legendary photographers whose works have captured Edna Wallace Hopper and other images in this book about her life. It is for informative purposes to the readers and as a tribute to their historic significance in changing and contributing to the art of Photography.

Textual material regarding the following photographers is copyrighted in the name of David S. Shields. This information was designed for educational purposes, consequently permission to make use of the information contained herein will be granted gratis provided that its source will be properly credited to Dr. David S. Shields, that the information not be sold to profit a private citizen, corporation, or public institution, and that its findings will not be misrepresented. I herein give credit and thanks to Dr. David Shields for his permission to use his written text. I also give special thanks Jay Parrino's The Mint for a selection of images I have purchased to include in my private collection of Photographs of Edna Wallace Hopper.

Sarony Studio

Founded by the lithographer and bon vivant Napoleon Sarony (1821-1896), continued by his son Otto Sarony (1859-1903), and other owners well into the 20th century as an agency employ staff photographers, Sarony Studio dominated the theatrical portraiture market during the last half of the 19th century, remained a power in theater publicity circles until the mid 1920s, and a viable brand as a portrait studio until late in the 20th century. Sarony proved to be the most enterprising celebrity photographer of the post-Civil War era. His studio on Fifth Avenue, a famously extravagant temple of odd props, old art, and stuffed exotic wildlife, hosted sittings with the important personages of the era. Napoleon's task was to pose the sitter. Specialists exposed the plates and processed the prints. He mass marketed images–first carte de visites, then cabinet cards–of actors and actresses, pioneered the business of securing exclusive rights to produce celebrity images, and realized that projecting an extravagant persona helped in establishing brand identity. He dressed in exotic costume, injected himself in every high toned social scene he could manage, and with Barnumesque élan, cultivated publicity. He was a clubman, art collector, drama critic, gourmand, and philanthropist. In March 1896 sold the bric a brac from his studio in a grand auction: 'arms and armor, antiquities, curious, and rare stuff of various sorts.' His important collection of American paintings was auctioned as well, failing to fetch the prices it deserve because the art market had gone mad for French painting. The great irony of this history was that none of the images bearing the name Otto Sarony were ever taken by Otto. His own work had all been released under his father's signature. During the seven years of the Otto Sarony brand's activity, Marceau installed several unaccredited photographers at the studio: Margaret Ewing, during the brief period between the time she worked for Bushnell on the west Coast and before partnering with George Harris to form the famous Washington, D.C., portrait studio, Harris- Ewing, was the most important. Burrow's Sarony studio retained Benjamin J. Richardson, who had worked with Napoleon and Otto, as photographer. The names of subsequent staff photographers were not credited. One of these craftsmen, during the later 1910s was an exceptional portrait artist whose images are very collectable. The name remained a brand until the mid 20th century, but ceased to be important in theatrical photography by 1930. Sarony developed the genre of the artfully posed celebrity portraits that he inherited from Brady and Gurney. Napoleon Sarony was the first to specialize in stage portraiture. Periodically he indulged in allegorical photographs, and hybrid graphic works that mixed drawing and the depicted image. His forte was making a sitter seem relaxed despite being clamped into a head or torso brace. He would stand by, arrange, and chat with the sitter while the cameraman (B. J. Richardson) would open the shutter. He loved surrounding sitters with props and emblems of elegance. An ornate swag curtain often appeared as a backdrop, and became a photographic cliché in the 19th century it was so widely emulated. The 20th-century portraiture, bearing the posthumous name of Otto Sarony, accorded to the modern ideal of visual glamour, with few props, flattering lighting, and a diplomatic erasure of blemishes and vagrant hair.

BURR MCINTOSH (1862-1942)

Time Period: 1895-1910

Location: W. 33rd Street, Manhattan

Actor, film studio executive, radio personality, professional caliber pool player, magazine publisher, lecturer, and photographer, William Burr McIntosh was born in Wellsville, Ohio, educated in Lafayette College and Princeton (where he was the U.S. sprint champion and star catcher on the varsity nine), and worked briefly as a reporter for THE PHILADELPHIA NEWS. His theatrical career began in 1885, premiering in Bartley Campbell's 'Pacquita' in New York City. He quickly became an international star, spending part of each season in London. On Broadway he made a specialty of western and frontier roles in plays by Augustus Thomas. His most memorable creation as an actor was Taffy in the hit, 'Trilby. In the 1890s, he became fascinated with photography. He convinced the editors at FRANK LESLIE'S WEEKLY to let him go to Cuba and cover the siege of Santiago in 1898 as a camera-wielding journalist. He became a popular public lecturer in the wake of the Cuban adventure, stirring controversy by deriding the valor of Col. Theodore Roosevelt and the Rough Riders. As part of his lectures, he projected photographs he took during the expedition. Their popularity stimulated McIntosh's second career as a photographer. In 1900, he displayed a set of portraits of actresses at Veerhoff Galleries in Washington, D. C. To great praise. He left the Broadway stage in 1901 and founded in late 1902, BURR MCINTOSH MONTHLY magazine, a lavishly illustrated periodical in the arts & crafts mold. His photographic career lasted twelve years, ending when he closed his New York Studio on W. 33rd Street, suspended publication of his magazine in 1910, shortly after the financial backer, William Annis, was gunned down by a jealous husband, and went to California to open a film studio/artists colony. His career as a film mogul was short-lived, but he became a significant character actor in the silent cinema. During WW1 and during the 1920s, he lectured and broadcast optimistic pep talks, characterizing himself as 'The Cheerful Philosopher,' until he went bankrupt from 'altruism' in August 1923. During the 1930s, he devoted himself to charitable causes, particularly collecting toys for poor families. His photographs, including many portraits of theatrical colleagues, are in the collection of the New York Historical Society.

The first theatrical portraitist to manifest the modernist sensibility, actor-photographer Burr McIntosh showed performers in naturalistic poses off stage, without the aura of a studio, or engaged in their art on stage, portrayed from the viewpoint of a fellow player, attentive to the point of the moment's action. He may have been the inventor of the close-up. His non-theatrical photography was photojournalistic, driven by an aesthetic that dramatized the distinctiveness of events rather than the representativeness of typical persons and activities. Along with the important portrait photographers of the first decade of the 20th century, he was indifferent to the print as an art object, conceiving of the image as a reproducible entity. Confronting the difficulties of making legible photographs in a mass printed medium, he became sensitive to the sorts of lighting and pictorial arrangement that would communicate best on the magazine page. David S. Shields

Copyright 1904 by Burr McIntosh Titled OUT IN THE COLD WORLD

270

Alfred Cheney Johnston

Time Period: 1917-1939

Location: Hotel de Artistes, Manhattan, 1 W. 67th Street

ALFRED CHENEY JOHNSTON(1884-1971) was born into a New York banking family. Educated as a painter and illustrator at the National Academy of Design in New York City, he attracted the notice of Charles Dana Gibson. Shortly after graduating, he married in 1909 and, for this reason, did not serve in World War I. Johnston was cavalier about the information he dispensed about his beginnings. One myth, captured in a feature story about him in the BRIDGEPORT SUNDAY POST of March 4, 1951, had him training at the Art Students League, photographing a student, and being hired by Ziegfeld when the sitter's family showed the image to the producer. According to legend, Ziegfeld invited him to the Midnight Frolic, looked over the portfolio, contracted with him, and said, " Let's go back and meet the girls. In truth, shortly after his graduation from the Academy in 1908, Johnston attempted to become a portrait painter and failed. He took up the camera, which he had used as an aid in his painting setups, and made it the instrument of his art. He supported his wife by working as an unaccredited retoucher and later camera artist for Sarony Studio. By 1915, he had become one of the two chief photographers working for the most famous theatrical photography company in New York. Florenz Ziegfeld, taken with Johnston's portraits of Showgirls in the 1915 and 1916 Follies and at two portrait sessions of Billie Burke, his wife, that were published in VANITY FAIR, hired Johnston to photograph his theatrical enterprises. There was no long-term contract--rather, Johnston was paid by the job, a fact he revealed to newspaper columnist Charles B. Driscoll in 1938 on the verge of retirement. Driscoll asked Johnston whether he ever had difficulty getting paid by Ziegfeld (an endemic problem for talent contracted for the Follies). 'Yes, always. I know he often failed to pay bills, but in my case, there was no difficulty. I was employed at the job. He would ask me to take on the work for a forthcoming production. We would agree on a price. So much work for so much money. He never quibbled over cost, and I was paid promptly.' Johnston's name appeared next to images for the first time in 1917. His portraits of showgirls in that year's edition of the 'Follies' were featured conspicuously in the summer issues of VANITY FAIR. They created a sensation.

Thereafter, his images appeared in many of the important magazines: PHOTOPLAY, MOTION PICTURE CLASSIC, SHADOWLAND, and THE

THEATRE. Shooting primarily in his studio, Johnston became famous as the foremost chronicler of feminine beauty of the period. Movie stars, Broadway headliners, and society women come to be 'glorified' by Johnston's camera. In 1918, Johnston developed a second career as an advertising photographer and became an important figure in the history of male fashion photography with his ad campaign for Dobbs Hats. In 1920, shortly after James Abbe had contracted to work for Mack Sennett in Hollywood, Johnston allowed himself to be persuaded by director Allan Dwan to go west. Dwan, who was raiding the Follies for Jacqueline Logan, promised Johnston work as a still photographer, lighting designer, and wardrobe consultant. Johnston arrived in Los Angeles in November 1920, shot stills and publicity on "A Perfect Crime" and "The Forbidden Thing," and shot a number of portraits before the factory mentality of the studio drove him back east. Throughout the 1920s, he would be contracted for special production images for motion pictures, most frequently on movies designed by his friend and colleague at the Follies, Joseph Urban. With the exception of four images, these stills did not bear his name in print. At the same time, he privately experimented with color processes. His professional colleagues, out of respect for his artistry and technical prowess, made Johnston a trustee of the New York Camera Club in 1926. When Ziegfeld died in 1932, Johnston's fame as a camera artist and commercial photographer was such that he weathered the Depression with little difficulty. In 1930, he became associated with Broadway producer-director Alexander Leftwich, serving on his production team as art director for the musicals "Dollars Up" and "Daisies Won't Tell," which ACJ co-produced with Leftwich. It died during its out-of-town try in Philadelphia in January 1931, but would eventually transmute into the 1937 musical "Orchids Preferred". Johnston incorporated himself on December 3, 1931, and began the direct sales of his nudes to the public, broadened his commercial work, and provided lighting design credited ["Sea Legs"] and unaccredited for several Broadway productions. In October of 1934, the Smithsonian Institution exhibited a selection of his portraits, which garnered extravagant praise in the press. In 1937, Swan Publishing Co. of New York City issued a collection of Johnston nudes, ENCHANTING BEAUTY. It sold for 75 cents. He retired in 1939 to Connecticut. In 1941, he revisited Hollywood, pondering the possibility of studio work. The studio system of publicity production still did not appeal to him, so he again returned east and "became an amateur." He died thirty-two years later in 1971. Shortly thereafter, in January of 1973, the Library of Congress mounted a memorial exhibition of his portraits.

Photo by Alfred Cheney Johnston, the official photographer for the Ziegfeld Follies Girls. His ten years of art studies are reflected in his beautiful photographs, which appear as paintings.

Moffett Studio

Time Period: 1895-present

Location: 57 East Congress Street, Chicago Biography: MOFFETT

STUDIO

Chicago's premier venue for visually recording civic culture, Moffett Studio, was founded by photographer George Moffett circa 1895 and is still in operation in 2005. George Moffett was a versatile camera artist with a talent for architectural photography as well as portraiture. His Michigan Avenue Studio became the favored place for public figures to sit for portraits at the turn of the 20th century. Moffett, after establishing the studio as the premier gallery for celebrity portraiture in the city, cashed out, selling the business to photographer and real estate entrepreneur Evan Evans. Under Evans's guidance, the studio became nationally famous for political portraiture and theatrical publicity. Following the corporate studio model, Evans published all images under the Moffett name, denying credit to his staff of photographers and himself. Evans excelled at elegant portraits in fashionable settings: seated actresses as windows (gesturing at the 'home photography' fashionable in Society portraiture), dancers on stone benches, standing vaudevillians amid statuary. Moffett Studio developed its interest in theatrical portraits in 1908. Evans's images were widely published in magazines and newspapers and hugely admired. Evans appears to have turned over the direction of the studio to a management team appointed by Underwood and Underwood in the late 1920s. In the 1940s, Moffett Studio was sold to the partnership of Robert T. McKearnan and Jack Russell. McKearnan took over complete control in the late 1950s. In the 1980s, it was purchased by Arthur Cournoyer. At that time, the stock of negatives in possession of McKearnan was deposited in the collections of the Chicago Historical Society.

Specialty:

Evan Evans of Moffett Studio had a penchant for shooting whole figure or half-length portraits done in relatively sharp focus, often in elaborate studio settings. When he produced head shots for theatrical publicity, they were often strong profiles. Images he produced personally were signed in bold red characters. Photographs by Evan Evans and other Moffett photographers were signed in the negative with a copyright symbol and MOFFETT STUDIO in sans serif unicals.

Edna as Connie Curtiss in Jumping Jupiter in 1910 in a dress adorned with pearls. Copyright formerly Moffett Studio, Chicago, IL

Apeda Studio

Time Period: 1906-1990

Location: 33 W. 34th street, 102-104 W. 38th St; 212-216 W. 48th St; 525 W. 52nd NYC Biography: APEDA
ALEXANDER W. DREYFOOS (1877-1952)

Apeda was a diversified corporate studio located in New York City and organized in 1906 by partners Alexander W. Dreyfoos and Henry Obstfield. From its organization, it pursued two business strategies: shooting original portraiture and reproducing uncopyrighted images by other photographers of newsworthy scenes or celebrities under its own trade name. Dreyfoos was the head photographer and to him goes credit for developing sports portraiture as a field analogous to theatrical portraiture in its treatment and promotion. The studio became the primary metropolitan photographer of boxers and baseball players, as well as a publicity manufacturer for Broadway performers. Apeda's great advantage among the New York metropolitan studios was its possession of industrial photograph developers and postcard printers. Whenever a New York photographer took a shot that they could not reproduce and market themselves, or took a photograph that could not be copyright because there was no contract between photographer and sitter (the situation of flashlight stills of Broadway plays for instance), Apeda would secure a print, eradicate whatever name or trademark appeared on the print and affixed their own Apeda signature. In 1912, they began selling copies of White Studio's production stills for 'The Chorus Lady,' 'A Gentleman of Leisure,' 'Gentleman from Mississippi,' and 'Thais' under the Apeda name, provoking a lawsuit, White Studio v. Dreyfoos, that Luther S. White would eventually lose. Like Underwood & Underwood, Apeda would buy up the entire production archive of photographers who had business difficulties or were moving to other parts of the country. Apeda, for instance, bought up the negatives of the Geisler-Andrews firm after the partners split. In the 1920s, the business was managed by Harold Danziger, whose background was in theater management. During the 1930s and 1940s, Apeda turned away from theatrical work to develop High School and Armed Services photography on a large scale. In the late 20th century, it was reorganized as Apco Apeda and operated until the 1990s, when its New York headquarters had difficulties with the Environmental Protection Agency for chemical pollution. David S. Shields.

Specialty:

The several photographers who contracted for work with Apeda over the years were conversant in every contemporary portrait style, often imitating the signature features of the leading photographers of the day. If there was any discernible ability characteristic of the company's photography, it was the ability to portray the whole body of the subject. While whole body portraiture was normal in sports and dance photography, it grew infrequent in 1920s theatrical portraiture, whole body shots being associated with production stills. Apeda photographers bucked the trend, producing whole body non-production portraiture after it went out of fashion in Manhattan.

Photo by Apeda circa 1925

Edwin Bower Hesser

Time Period: 1913-1947

Location: 34 West 58th Street, Lab at 146 West 56th St., NYC
Biography: EDWIN BOWER HESSER (1893-1962)

Hesser belonged to the generation of photographers who saw the marriage of image and performance as the future of the art. Born in New Jersey and apprenticed in photography in New York City, Hesser became smitten with the potential of the art form. Prior to World War I, he toured Northeastern theaters with J. Townsend Russell in a series of 'picture readings' illustrating Longfellow's 'Tales of a Wayside Inn. Townsend recited the poem, accompanied by a string orchestra, while illustrative photographs were projected on the screen. In 1913, Hesser introduced Roald Amundsen, the first man to reach the South Pole, to New York audiences, presenting motion pictures to illustrate the trek. Using family money, he incorporated on February 3, 1915, the Hesser Motion Picture Corporation with a capitalization of $50K. Later in the year, he was in Atlanta opening the Hesser School for Motion Picture Acting. With America's entry into World War I, Hesser joined the

U. S. Army Signal Corps with the rank of Captain, and oversaw land photography. While in the service, a scenario composed by Hesser, "The Freedom of the World," was made in 1918 into a semi-documentary feature film by Goldwyn. After the armistice, Hesser decommissioned, set up a photographic Studio in Manhattan employing as his assistant a talented Italian, Nino Vayana, to oversee production. He was drawn to the world of movies and worked as a contract photographer for a number of silent stars based in New York, particularly Norma Talmadge, Irene Castle, and Marion Davies. A fire in 1922 destroyed his production facilities and his stock of early negatives. He began to make regular trips to the West Coast for photographic sessions with Hollywood stars, and finally moved his operations to the West Coast. By 1923, he realized that the real money in photography lay in periodical publication, not in the service of film publicity offices or stage PR men. He saw a particular opportunity in the subject which the 1920s stage explored with great daring, but the screen, even in pre-code days, could not pursue: female undress. Throughout the late In the 1920s, he published EDWIN BOWER HESSER'S ARTS MONTHLY, and other titles, exploiting the association between art and nudity, and sold it to an anonymous readership of 'art students.' The magazine published work by Alfred Cheney Johnston, John De Mirjian, George DeBarron, and Strand Studio. Hesser's exploration of the netherworld of publishing brought him in contact with the Hollywood underworld. In 1928, he was arrested for suspicion of narcotics peddling, battery, and impersonating a police officer in connection with the death of starlet Helen St. Clair Evans, who was murdered by her husband, Arthur. He was released, but the Depression shut down Hesser's successful exercise in niche publishing. Fortunately for Hesser, he experimented with color photographic processes, and his experience with mass reproduction of imagery made him attractive in the eyes of the NEW YORK TIMES, which hired him as a technician. Later in the decade, he returned to California. Hesser continued to practice photography until the late 1940s, placing occasional pieces with magazines. His photographic archive is stored in the special collections department of the UCLA library.

Specialty:

A versatile artist whose air nudes of Showgirls in natural light became the academic standard for art photographers in the 1920s and whose portraits of movie actresses and stage stars were greatly influential images of glamour from 1925 to 1930. He was one of the few portraitists who regularly depicted sitters' heads on. His penchant for back-lighting so that hair seemed lined with light gave certain of his 1920s sitters a halo or aura. Expert at landscape photography, he often shot nudes in parks and glades. Possessed of an inquiring and entrepreneurial mind, he developed and patented a color process, "Hessecolor," that intrigued mass circulation publishers during the 1930s, but did not prevail in the marketplace. David S. Shields.

Photo by Edwin Bower Hesser, 1924

Ralph Frank took the last magazine photographs of Edna Wallace Hopper ever taken, which were printed in Life magazine in 1953. The article was titled, "The Sun Never Sets on Edna". It may have been possible that Edna had selected Frank to capture her last images for the world to remember her. 2009 marks the 50th anniversary of Edna's death and of Frank's book, The Americans. Oddly, Mr. Frank declined to have his photos of Edna included in this book.

Photograph by Apeda 1920s from the collection of Jim Alessio